WOMEN
AND AGING

COVER ART
"Her Strength is in Her Convictions"
by Elizabeth Layton.
Reproduced by permission
of the artist.

Suggested Library
of Congress cataloguing
in Publication Data Main entry
under title: Women and aging: an anthology.
Includes bibliography. 1. Aged women—United States.
2. Aging—Collected works. 3. Old age—Collected
works. 4. Women—United States—Collected
works. 5. Aged women—Illustrations.
I. CALYX. II. Alexander, Jo [et al.]
HQ1061 W61 1986
ISBN 0-934971-00-5

WOMEN
AND AGING

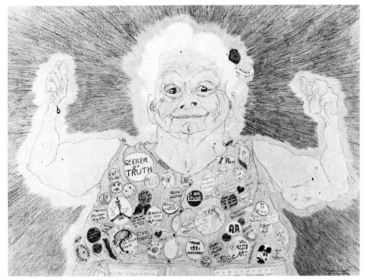

an anthology by women

Edited by

Jo Alexander
Debi Berrow
Lisa Domitrovich
Margarita Donnelly
Cheryl McLean

CALYX BOOKS
Corvallis, OR

WOMEN AND AGING ANTHOLOGY

CONTENTS

FICTION

JOURNALS

POETRY

PROFILES

ART

The problems that confront all of us who are working for social change and a better world form an inextricable network of interrelated issues. In my bleaker moments I allow myself to be overwhelmed by the enormity of the task we face if we are to disentangle this skein. When I feel more optimistic I recognize that everyone who is fighting injustice and hatred and discrimination, in any of their myriad forms, is in actuality fighting the same battle and, with so many allies, we must ultimately prevail.

By working on this special issue of CALYX I have learned a lot about society's ageism and my own, and realized that this is yet another strand in the skein. And that fighting ageism—in myself and in others—is another way in which I can fight for a better life for us all. My thanks to all those women who submitted work for this issue, whether or not it was ultimately published. I have learned a great deal from you all.

JO ALEXANDER

Initially, as the youngest person on the editorial board of this anthology, I struggled with fears of not being able to adequately empathize with issues of aging and questioned the validity of my input. But as patterns of ageism grow more visible around us through the expressions of Old Women, I am aware that my energy is needed to reflect and create new social symbols and transform misinformation that debilitates all women who grow old.

I am grateful to the women in this anthology and to my OLD friends for this insight, and for radically exposing this part of ourselves that we can no longer ignore.

DEBI BERROW

As a young woman existing in a culture of youth, I found that *WOMEN AND AGING* forced me to travel unexplored territory. A year ago, I had never questioned the stereotypes and myths of the "old lady" (although I did know old women who did not fit those stereotypes), had never considered the rights of old women as a political issue, and certainly never realized the deep connection between the life-denying patriarchal attitudes and the "invisibility" of old women.

Working on *WOMEN AND AGING* was like taking a trip to the South Pole. Preparations such as reading Macdonald and Rich's *Look Me in the Eye*, attending the 1985 National Women's Studies Association Conference, and the tortuous consciousness-raising/editorial meetings with my colleagues warmed me to the task, but the ageist glare off the snow of patriarchal indoctrination is blinding. A letter from Baba Copper simultaneously congratulating and warning us summed up perfectly the situation: *"You must be very brave. Otherwise you would have never attempted such a difficult task. It is a little like putting out an issue on being a woman in 1955."*

Aging and ageism is a vast continent to discover. The tracks left by this anthology leave a record of illumination and omission. *WOMEN AND AGING* provides some analysis of ageism and attempts to give voice to the real experience of the aging woman. It's a start, but there are huge areas yet to be explored more fully, including the experience of minority women, of women internationally, issues of sexuality, menopause, age-passing, drug and alcohol problems, elder abuse, and age-encompassing issues surrounding disability, euthanasia, and death. I hope that *WOMEN AND AGING* becomes a part of a more detailed map as feminists make visible the existence of yet another critical frontier.

LISA DOMITROVICH

Working on this anthology I was forced to confront my own ageism. At first I wasn't excited by the topic, but once the decision to do this anthology was made I began to examine the topic and was appalled and stunned by what I found. In my early forties with my child "out of the nest" I looked forward to single life again. As an activist since the sixties I had put in time, fought some battles, and survived. I looked forward to time for myself instead of "others" but discovered there are new battles to fight as we get older. As I studied and identified the issues I began to experience that old "click" (Remember it? From the sixties?). Invisibility . . . yes, it's already been happening to me but I didn't identify its source . . . being mistaken for the grandmother of a younger friend's baby . . . feeling a little strange when younger people find out my age and I hear, "You don't look that old!" . . . remembering the job I wanted and didn't get that went to a less experienced "younger" woman . . . I began to read again in the same way I read when I first became a feminist. I looked for images of older women, began to analyze the literature I have read (and published) and the pattern was very clear. Older women, aging women, women who are past a certain age (which seems to be about 55) are not reflected in our society or are depicted in negative stereotypes. They are also absent from the feminist media and literature, and I have been a part of that erasure.

"Ageism" is insidious and real and functions in different ways toward women and men, working to keep women more powerless and invisible. We hope this anthology is a beginning and helps uncover older women's realities.

As we selected manuscripts and art for this anthology we were lucky to have the guidance of Barbara Macdonald's book (*Look Me in the Eye*) and her speech at National Women's Studies in Seattle. I also benefited from a lucky meeting with Baba Copper at the 1985 Women in Print conference. We discussed her manuscript and letter and she gave me an invaluable short course on "ageism." Macdonald and Copper's theories helped guide this anthology through difficult, uncharted territory. I thank them and all the women who submitted work. Sally Corliss and Gloria Layden, who worked with us as consultants to the editorial collective, also deserve recognition and special thanks.

MARGARITA DONNELLY

When we began the monumental task of editing a special issue on women and aging, I had no idea how much of my soul would go into this work, nor did I anticipate how the experience would alter my perceptions of aging, of old women, of myself.

That it has been a consciousness-raising is an understatement. It has been an awakening, and it has caused a wide rippling among my family, my friends, even casual acquaintances who use ageist clichés or definitions. I have to admit that I am a bit "born-again," now so suddenly attuned to "ageism" that I find it everywhere. It is everywhere. And that led to one of the most difficult aspects of editing this issue: publishing an anthology that was free from ageist stereotypes of women or ageist sentiments about women and aging.

As young and midlife women, we in the editorial collective had to spend a lot of time raising our awareness of aging and ageism. Several women who submitted work taught us a great deal. And we benefited from the insight of two consultants, older women sensitive to the issues of aging and ageism. With their help we tried to select works that see women as individuals — as *who they are now* — and not as superficial images or stereotypes. We've made no attempt to gloss over the images of women by presenting only vibrant, healthy, active old women. We wanted to present strong, powerful images of women, yet we did not want to fall into the trap of treating as invisible those old women who are, by reason of health or choice or depression or whatever, not active or healthy or vibrant.

I hope that the voices in this anthology will create a wave of awareness and discussion and consciousness-raising that will send its ripples through the feminist community and beyond. I hope that these women will force us to confront our own ageism and examine our beliefs about aging and the images our minds relate to the words "old woman."

CHERYL MCLEAN

Meridel Le Sueur Reading, Albuquerque   *Photograph by Margaret Randall*

MERIDEL LE SUEUR   *Remarks from 1983 poetry reading,*
                          Blue Heron Center for the Arts, Vashon Island, Washington
                                          Transcribed by RAYNA HOLTZ

Introduction to her poem, "Rites of Ancient Ripening"

I would like to read my litany to age and death. The title of this comes of the fact that I'm doing away with the word "age." Aging? You've heard of that? Aging or age or death? Aging? You never hear of anything in nature aging, or a sunflower saying, "Well, I'm growing old," and leaning over and vomiting. You know, it *ripens*, it drops its seed and the cycle goes on. So I'm ripening. For "Age" you can say "ripening."

It's a terrible thing in women's culture that you're supposed to be dead after menopause in our culture. You're not beautiful any more, nothing. Since I was 60 I've written more and had better energy and more energy than I ever had in my life. I went to a doctor when I was about 70 and he said, "Oh, just take these tranquilizers." I said, "Are you kidding?" I said, "I'm going to do my best work before I'm 70, between 70 and 80." "Oh," he said, "that's ridiculous!" And he gave me the most brilliant description of decay you ever heard. He described sclerosis, and cutting off your wind, and total decay, stroke, and on. "Just take these tranquilizers." I said, "No, I'm not going to do that. I'm really going to do my best writing before I'm 80." In three years *he* was dead!

That's really a terrible thing. In American Indian culture after you give your children to the world, serve socially your nation, and contribute *then* you can become a shaman, women too, or a medicine man, or a holy person. And you're considered an asset to the nation as an elder, because of your history.

I was broke in New York, and they had an agency. You could rent yourself out as a grandmother, at minimum wage an hour, $3.40 or something. The children never saw an old person! They wanted to touch you, take out your teeth. They really wanted to know what age was. They never saw older people! I must say the younger persons weren't so great to look at.

So this is the title, "Rites of Ancient Ripening."

RITES OF ANCIENT RIPENING

I am luminous with age
In my lap I hold the valley.
I see on the horizon what has been taken
What is gone lies prone fleshless.
In my breast I hold the middle valley
The corn kernels cry to me in the fields
                    Take us home.
Like corn I cry in the last sunset
Gleam like plums.
                    My bones shine in fever
Smoked with the fires of age.
Herbal, I contain the final juice,
Shadow, I crouch in the ash
                    never breaking to fire.
Winter iron bough
                    unseen my buds,
Hanging close I live in the beloved bone
Speaking in the marrow
                    alive in green memory.

The light was brighter then.
Now spiders creep at my eyes' edge.
I peek between my fingers
                    at my fathers' dust.
The old stones have been taken away
                    there is no path.
The fathering fields are gone.
The wind is stronger than it used to be.
My stone feet far below me grip the dust.
I run and crouch in corners with thin dogs.
I tie myself to the children like a kite.
I fall and burst beneath the sacred human tree.
Release my seed and let me fall.
Toward the shadow of the great earth
                    let me fall.
Without child or man
                    I turn I fall.
Into shadows,
            the dancers are gone.
My salted pelt stirs at the final warmth
Pound me death
            stretch and tan me death
Hang me up, ancestral shield
                    against the dark.
Burn and bright and take me quick.
Pod and light me into dark.

Are those flies or bats or mother eagles?
I shrink   I cringe
Trees tilt upon me like young men.
The bowl I made I cannot lift.
All is running past me.
The earth tilts and turns over me.
I am shrinking
    and lean against the warm walls of old summers.
With knees and chin I grip the dark
Swim out the shores of night in old meadows.
Remember buffalo hunts

Great hunters returning
Councils of the fathers to be fed
Round sacred fires.
The faces of profound deer who
                    gave themselves for food.
We faced the east the golden pollened
                    sacrifice of brothers.
The little seeds of my children
                    with faces of mothers and fathers
Fold in my flesh
                    in future summers.
My body a canoe turning to stone
Moves among the bursting flowers of memory
Through the meadows of flowers and food,
I float and wave to my grandchildren in the
Tipis of many fires
                    In the winter of the many slain
I hear the moaning.
I ground my corn daily
In my pestle many children
Summer grasses in my daughters
Strength and fathers in my sons
All was ground in the bodies bowl
                corn died to bread
                    woman to child
                        deer to the hunters.
Sires of our people
Wombs of mothering night
Guardian mothers of the corn
Hill borne torrents of the plains
Sing all grinding songs
    of healing herbs
Many tasselled summers
                    Flower in my old bones
                    Now.
Ceremonials of water and fire
Lodge me in the deep earth
    grind my harvested seed.

The rites of ancient ripening
Make my flesh plume
And summer winds stir in my smoked bowl.
Do not look for me till I return
                        rot of greater summers
Struck from fire and dark,
Mother struck to future child.
Unbud me now
Unfurl me now
Flesh and fire
            burn
                  requicken
                        Death.

MERIDEL LE SUEUR

                        * * *

Care to estimate how many miles you walk on two legs in 83 years? Including fleeing from the FBI and the picket lines.

I feel it's always a ceremonial moment like this, when we come together in space, and also in time. I don't think we have enough continuity in our history, of time, and of generations. It's there, but it disappears in the water.

But one of the great things about growing older, I think, is the cyclical return of time. You can see the same idiots in office, the same wars ... When I was standing on the steps of the St. Paul, Minnesota, capitol at the beginning of the year, with my grandson, great-grandson, against the draft.... I suddenly saw myself being arrested on those same steps in 1916. This might seem to be very depressing to you, but I don't think so. It's a short time, really, and in the continuity of the cyclical movement I feel we're not turning on the same spiral, on the same level: consciousness is much higher now than it was then. In the first world war, a few people objected to the war, more than you think. The prisons were full of people in the first world war. But there was not the global con- sciousness, the consciousness of the third world. We hadn't had any of those experiences.

It's interesting, in my lifetime everything that was taught before the first world war is no longer true. Just about everything, including the physical world, science, the concept of matter. I mean then, I was studying mechanical Dar-

Poem reprinted by permission of the author from *Selected Work 1927-1980* by Meridel Le Sueur, edited by Elaine Hedges, published by the Feminist Press, 1982.

winism. You know, we all came from an ape or you had the controversy with religious people. It was a darkness, a lack of consciousness, or a conflict of consciousness.

It seems to me that now everything is entirely on a different key. Being this old and seeing this continuity I feel it's important to convey it, that this kind of change is very organic. Science now says all nature moves toward a blooming. The impulse of matter is to manifest itself, is to rise to a higher transformation. It's an urge, an energy in all of life.

All of these concepts, I've tried to embody them in my poetry, because it shows a change of consciousness, . . . the radicals in my time were all Ingersollian atheists. People had Ingersoll on their tombs in North Dakota. Ingersoll was a great folk hero, a great orator, a great drinker . . . on the frontier.

The change of consciousness is so enormous that I think we live on a marvelous edge of ecstasy and despair, a turbulence—that's what it is—and turbulence means transformation, or growth. So I think it's very important that we have and manifest this image. There's such a downpull in our culture, that has a deliberate teaching of despair, melancholia, cynicism, Sartre, existentialism, T.S. Eliot, Ezra Pound, those sick ah . . . and we don't realize how this has affected us. T.S. Eliot wrote "The Waste Land" and it was published in 1923 and it was a death knell to my generation. I knew that . . . "The Waste Land", "The Hollow Men" . . . just recently the letters of William Carlos Williams have been published, in which he wrote—I never saw this before—he wrote to T.S. Eliot in 1930 and said "The Waste Land" is a great disservice to our culture, and to our young people. And he said a strange thing, "*it leads to the bomb.*" We were trying to split the atom, but no one talked too much about the bomb. He said, "'The Waste Land' leads to the bomb, it leads to destruction." And it certainly led to despair, which has become part of several decades of people.

I believe that it's very important for all of us, everyone, all the time, to bring forth the image of the new world. I mean the image of the old world is stinking, dead, a corpse for two centuries, and we've had great descriptions of it, and we all bear the image of it, of the skeleton of death. We all bear it very faithfully, but we don't have to think any of those thoughts, or have any of those images. And I think it's up to people who have the images of the birth in the corpse, they have a responsibility to bring that image into the despair and the annihilation and the cynicism and the existentialism and all. Do you know that we had Tate and Robert Penn Warren in Minnesota, both at the same time? A disaster in itself, and do you know that they had a school of writing called *Ambiguity*? They wrote a book called Seven somethings of Ambiguity. It sounded like a striptease or something. It taught how to write so nobody would know what you meant . . . I think it was just like being bitten by a widow spider to go to their classes every morning, . . . I know young, good prairie people were destroyed by that kind of cynicism. It's very important to me to look even now. The seduction of individuals' philosophy is so enormous. . . .

I hope we have some time for some kind of discourse, with an old root.

We're on the verge of an extension of consciousness. Most of our poetry, English poetry, is all about despair—you can read Shelley, and Walt Whitman is marvelous—but so much of our poetry, especially so much of modern poetry, is "why live?" So what are these symbols? I have various ones here. Like the pipe symbol is the pipe of communality, for example. All of the ceremonies of the Indians are how to raise the magnetic field, how to raise everybody into the highest magnetic field.

As I say, you don't have too much of a chance to question an old root, not every night. It's very important. You all were born so late. You'll have to talk a little loud. I've heard too many lies with this ear, I don't hear too well.

QUESTION: *What are you working on now?*

LE SUEUR: What am I working on now? Well, you shouldn't ask a person this old that question, because I'm working on all my unfinished work. I call it getting in my crop before frost, and I was interfered with several times, like the McCarthy period, and several major wars, so I didn't get to write. So now I have three—I'll call them books—books that could be like symphonies that I want to—I won't say "finish," because you don't finish a circle—but at least get turning in the ellipse before I am cut down by these dire things that come with age. Well, you don't want to live forever. But I'm really having the best time in my life writing. In the first place, I don't have to feed anybody. Do you realize how much time that takes? I don't feed anybody, or earn anybody's living. It's amazing. You know the terrible story of Tillie Olsen. She had a life kind of like mine, but she raised *four* girls. I only had two. But she worked, and she was active in the labor movement, and she didn't have time to write. So finally, when her children were gone and she had gotten a great deal of recognition for her great story, *Tell Me a Riddle,* and got the Guggenheim, *Money* she had for the first time, and . . . she said it was too long ago, the well was dried up. And she had a complete nervous breakdown. Now she writes critical articles and historical articles. She can't go back and try to get into that place that was abandoned. Well, you couldn't have a pianist—they practice every day, and I think writers do too. I think I kept myself alive during all those periods by keeping notebooks. Not diaries, but just writing every day, no matter what. Thomas Wolfe describes meeting Sinclair Lewis after he got the Nobel Prize, dead drunk in London, doing his morning writing! He couldn't see the type-writer, he couldn't see what he was doing, but he was practicing, for the game. . . . I wrote in these notebooks, which also are probably my letter to the world, probably my best writing. In 2002 someone will find them in a jar—but I wrote every day. It's like being a runner or anything, you know, you do it every day. I don't take any credit for that, because I had to do it. I couldn't live without doing it. It was just a natural thing for me to try to express what I experienced or saw that day.

But that's the problem with women writers, . . . their time is broken up. . . . I wrote all the time when I had children, and I also earned a living all that time. But my children had to feel this . . . If I was working, they would say "Be quiet"—we often lived in one room, in the Depression—they'd say, "well you have to be quiet. Momma's writing us a pair of shoes." So I gave them a stake in the corporation.
QUESTION: How do you see our country 80 years from now?
LE SUEUR: Huh! That's an athletic exercise. But I believe that all the old world, all the old concepts that capitalism is trying to make alive . . . [don't] *work!* I mean the beautiful thing about our time is that those concepts, like scarcity—capitalism is based on scarcity—and scarcity doesn't work any more. It doesn't exist. You can have plenty. Still we're trying to cut out the planting of corn in the Middle West. In the Depression they killed a million little pigs, in order to keep the price of meat up, which nobody could afford anyway. . . . It was like the Wizard of Oz. That would be a good thing, if Reagan would become an Oz. It won't work.

I see the possibility of tremendous plenty and some kind of golden distribu-tion of energy. Now all this brings up, as Buckminster Fuller says, that energy cannot be depleted, that you cannot spend energy, you can only misuse it.

I went to a very rich school in St. Paul, and I thought the children would be very out of hand, as they often are. Well, I spoke to a whole series, between the ages of 8 and 14, and I've never heard such marvelous knowledge and conversa-tion. I figured out it was because they take nothing but science. I mean their people have never heard of Darwin, or mechanical evolution, or the mechanism of the object. They've just never heard of it. One little boy said to me, he was about 14, and he talked so *boldly*, he said, "I have one criticism of your speech." He said, "You call our system imperialism, and it is really an advanced state of monopoly capital." I said, "My God, have you been reading Lenin?" He said, "Yes."

They learned relativity. My grandson, 14, explained to me about relativity, and I understood it. And they never heard of that 19th century world, that Victorian [time], they don't even count the same way. Everything that was, even in *their* father's time, they're not repeating what he learned in physics. It's really fantastic, wonderful.

I stopped at a tavern on the Mississippi River and an old man, an old river man—there's a few of them left—was sitting there. He explained to me why—talking about DNA and the spiral, he picked up a little snail shell—and he explained to me that the little spiral was the strongest form in the world, and he tried to smash it between two rocks, and it was fine. He gave me a whole Einsteinian thing on relativity. He hadn't read anything, he took it out of the river. A description of the fourth dimension.

So I think, it's either not going to be at all, or it's going to be fantastic. Eighty years is really going to be working on that energy that they're talking about now, that doesn't have any wires, energy in plants. God, if it grows as fast as it has in the past ten years, it's going to be a whole new consciousness.

QUESTION: I hear you speaking about predators and capitalists as if not only are they embodying the forces of evil, but as if you see them doing that deliberately, in full consciousness. Is that really what you mean to imply?

LE SUEUR: Well, I don't mean to say they're evil in the Christian sense of good and evil. I think they represent forces that I consider destructive. I've come through two major wars, and my youth was almost ruined by the first world war. Every young man that I knew never came back. Not one, that I knew when I was 18 years old. I tried to kill myself.

It's that kind of consciousness . . . I believe in dialectics. Like yin and yang, when things become this bad, the opposite is also true. To change the world, you really have to have the destructive force and the creative force. It's like death and birth perhaps. Engel said in 1870 there were only two philosophies and two images for the modern person. One was the corpse of the dying society, which was already rotten, and the other was the birth of the new society, the new form, out of the corpse.

But I think I had to study how it's going to be, how I can be on the side of the birth, and not the corpse. It's like attending a birth. I think it's very important for everybody to have that consciousness. Capitalism isn't evil, it's a polarity of force that has come to a dead end. It doesn't work any more, it's dangerous, and so people should be able to say, "We don't need this any more. We don't need this danger, this blind force that is world market, or getting a profit off of labor and off of production." We don't need it any more, I don't think. We've got enough things right now to produce plenty for everybody in the world with just the machines we have right now, to produce the clothes and shoes . . . we could have a remarkable world, I think.

No, I don't mean to say that capitalism is evil. Only in the sense that they lower the vibratory rate of our lives quite a bit: depression every four years, and on. I won't even name them all, I won't even get through them.

No questions about being a woman writer? I'm a specialist on being a woman, so you can ask me anything about it.

The editor of *The Girl* sent it back to me in '39 and said I didn't know anything about women, which I thought was really surprising . . . his arrogance. Then he also told me—and I don't think he'd ever say this to a young male writer, I bet you he wouldn't—he told me I'd better just stop writing, that *The Girl* showed I didn't have any talent, and I'd better just get a good job and support my children. Of course people were always telling me that. There was a great thing about women having children alone, much more than now.

I just realized recently how much it was to have a male editor. I never had a woman editor until the Feminist Press. And as I say, they [male editors] were always telling me what to do like that. Or they'd say, the editor of Harper's or Scribner's—I guess it was Scribner's, I had a couple of stories in Scribner's—and I sent in my story about the birth of a child, called "Annunciation," which later became quite a famous reprinted story, and he wrote back, this young man, and said, "You have such a lyrical and beautiful style," which to me was an insult. It was like saying, "You're a pretty girl," you know, "You're . . ."[chuckles] "But," he said, "you write about such funny subjects. *Birth?* [chuckles] Scribner's? Writing a story about *birth?*" Then he said, "Well I think you should write more like Hemingway." Here I was, holed up with two little babies in a Kansas roominghouse. So I wrote back and said, "You know I really can't consider writing like Hemingway. I don't exactly have the same experience. Fishing, fucking, and fighting are not my major interests."

I wrote True Confessions during the McCarthy period, all kinds of things under other names, and so on, but how much you're confined in subject matter, like birth, for example. Or like, who'd write a story like Faulkner, about how an old man saved his self esteem by shooting an old bear? Now that hardly would occur to me as subject matter for a story. If you just look at the subject matter you can really get a laugh out of it, because it's so funny, the subject matter that men write about. I think that was my first envy of men. Not what Freud says it's supposed to be, but because I couldn't go where they went. In my youth I couldn't go into a bar. In a village, a nice girl didn't walk on the street after 6, or you went clear across the street to pass a bar, to pass the bar door. I couldn't go anywhere. A lot of women writers, you can see how their writing is curtailed because they can't know half of what happens on the street. I wanted to be part of that. I just discovered through the women's movement that I wrote two short novels from the viewpoint of a young man. I didn't know it, I didn't even remember it, like Willa Cather who wrote her first two novels as a young man.

Well, I got a young man that just got back from going up to Alaska on a freighter, a fishing boat or something, and I always wanted to do that. So I locked him in a room and made him tell me the whole story. I stole the material and I wrote a short novel about it. Then he wanted some of the money, so we divided up two bottles of whiskey.

When you did write like a woman . . . I don't think Virginia Woolf would ever have been published if she hadn't had money. She had her own money. She wrote a letter to Katherine Mansfield and said, "I envy you that you can walk on the street. I always wanted to talk to a prostitute and I've never been able to." She couldn't walk on the street as a lady, belonging to the Bloomsbury bunch . . . what are they? Those awful men? They smashed her down. She had no following. Sometimes I'm talking to a women's group, in women's studies, and I see 30 or 40 young women sitting there, and I just feel like weeping! If she could have sat with *five* women, you know, any kind of sympathy, she wouldn't have killed herself. But she didn't have any *readers* even then. Lots of women didn't like her things. She really didn't have any critiques about her work. She wrote, in '23 and '24 she began to get published, and the women's market was very conventional. You couldn't write hardly about anything but women and virtue and . . . That's why I wrote low fiction. Women have always written and hidden their stuff.

QUESTION: When were you first published? Was it in the '30's when you first began writing?

LE SUEUR: No, I wrote when I was ten years old. My family were socialists, and I wrote the report on Ludlow in 1914, when I was 14. I wrote for the IWW and labor press, and I was on a strike on the range. I considered myself a person to write for people who didn't have a voice. I think that's how I began to write. And especially about women. I didn't read anything about women. I never read a book by a woman. No, I didn't remember any women writers. I hid everything I wrote from my grandmother. She hated it.

[end of tape]

Transcribed by RAYNA HOLTZ

OUTSIDE THE SISTERHOOD:
AGEISM IN WOMEN'S STUDIES   *BARBARA MACDONALD*

Speech presented to the National Women's Studies Association, Plenary Session on Common Causes: Uncommon Coalitions, Seattle, June 22, 1985.

I have not come here out of NWSA's spontaneous commitment and concern about ageism. I am here after a four-year fight, after other old women along with me wrote to the NWSA planning committee and demanded that ageism be addressed at a plenary session. We insisted that NWSA confront the question of how it is possible that the last thirty years of women's lives have been ignored in Women's Studies. This morning I have twenty minutes to speak to that topic.

I am not going to talk to you today about organizing. Old women do organize. That organizing ranges from a lobby watch of 132 women in a Detroit housing project to protect themselves from male violence, to the Older Women's League of 12,000 women throughout the United States who work to make legislative changes that affect the economic oppression of old women. But today I want to talk about what is *not* there, because until we see how invisible the lives of old women are, and why, we cannot even begin the kind of radical change that the challenge of feminism demands.

From the beginning of this wave of the women's movement, from the beginning of Women's Studies, the message has gone out to those of us over 60 that your "Sisterhood" does not include us, that those of you who are younger see us as men see us—that is, as women who used to be women but aren't any more. You do not see us in our present lives, you do not identify with our issues, you exploit us, you patronize us, you stereotype us. Mainly you ignore us.

Has it never occurred to younger women activists as you organized around "women's" issues, that old women are raped, that old women are battered, that old women are poor, that old women perform unpaid work in the home and out of the home, that old women are exploited by male medical practitioners, that old women are in jail, are political prisoners, that old women have to deal with racism, classism, homophobia, anti-semitism? I open your feminist publications and not once have I read of any group of younger women enraged or marching or organizing legal support because of anything that happened to an old woman. I have to read the *L.A. Times* or *Ageing International* to find out what's happening to the women of my generation, and the news is not good. I have to read these papers to find out that worldwide old women are the largest adult poverty group, or that 44 percent of old Black women are poor, or about the battering of old women, about the conditions in public housing for the elderly in which almost all of the residents are women, or that old women in nursing homes are serving as guinea pigs for experimental drugs—a practice forbidden years ago for prison inmates.

But activists are not alone in their ageism. Has it never occurred to those of you in Women's Studies, as you ignore the meaning and the politics of the lives of women beyond our reproductive years, that this is male thinking? Has it never occurred to you as you build feminist theory that ageism is a central feminist issue?

I look at the indexes of your recent texts—on women and economics, women and unpaid work, women and psychology, images of women in literature, on Black women, on working-class women, on women and violence—and I find nothing under "old" or "aging."

Read those books used in Women's Studies as an old woman reads them. They discuss the socialization of little girls from the moment of birth, the struggles of women through adulthood—and it turns out that "adulthood" ends with menopause, or with some attention to the woman in her 50's who is a displaced homemaker. Well, just try being an 85-year-old Black woman in a shanty-town in L.A., just trying to cross the street, when her life is valued at only $265 in the courts—try that for a displaced homemaker. But we are not women to you; we are not adults. We are as invisible and as irrelevant in your classrooms as we are in the hostile male world—a world where we fight not only the same oppressions younger women do, but the oppression of ageism as well, and all without the support of the women's movement.

Meanwhile, as the numbers of old women rapidly increase, the young women you taught five years ago are now in the helping professions as geriatricians and social workers because the jobs are there. They still call themselves feminists but, lacking any kind of feminist analysis of women's aging from your classrooms, they are defining old women as needy, simple-minded, and helpless— definitions that correlate conveniently with the services and salaries they have in mind. All this week on this campus, workshops on aging have been going on, under the auspices of the Institute on Aging. Because ageism is not addressed, these workshops will do nothing to end the oppression of old women and will do much that contributes to that oppression, and Women's Studies has not done its homework sufficiently on its own ageism so that it can begin to effect change in the academic community to stop it.

But it is worse than that. For you yourselves—activists and academicians—do not hesitate to exploit us. We take in the fact that you come to us for "oral histories"—for your own agendas, to learn *your* feminist or lesbian or working-class or ethnic histories—with not the slightest interest in our present struggles as old women. You come to fill in some much-needed data for a thesis, or to justify a grant for some "service" for old women that imitates the mainstream and which you plan to direct, or you come to get material for a biography of our friends and lovers. But you come not as equals, not with any knowledge of who we are, what our issues may be. You come to old women who have been serving young women for a lifetime and ask to be served one more time, and then you cover up your embarrassment as you depart by saying that you felt as though we were your grandmother or your mother or your aunt. And no one in the sisterhood criticizes you for such acts.

But let me say it to you clearly: We are not your mothers, your grandmothers, or your aunts. And we will never build a true women's movement until we can organize together as equals, woman to woman, without the burden of these family roles.

Mother. Grandmother. Aunt. It should come as no surprise to us that ageism has its roots in patriarchal family. But here I encounter a problem. In the four years it took to get NWSA to address ageism, feminism has moved from a position in which we recognized that family is a building block of patriarchy, the place where sexist hierarchical roles are learned, where the socialization of girls takes place, the unit by which women are colonized, manipulated, controlled, and punished for infraction—from that basic tenet of feminist theory, both mainstream and radical feminists have moved back to reaffirming family. Mainstream feminists are buying the notion that as long as a woman has a "career," family is a safe and wholesome place to be. Radical feminists have affirmed family as the source of our cultures—as a way of understanding our strengths and our oppression as Black, Jewish, Hispanic, Asian-American, Native American, working-class women. This return to family is reflected in our writings, where less and less is father seen as oppressor, but more as another family member, oppressed by white male imperialism. (*And, believe me, he is.*)

It will be for future feminist historians to explain how it was that in our return to family we never questioned its contradictions to our earlier feminist theory. Not that we can't contradict our own feminist beliefs—they aren't written in concrete—just that we never acknowledged the contradiction.

Nor can history fail to note that our return to family coincides with a reactionary administration's push back to family values, any more than it can ignore that our lesbian baby boom coincides with Reagan's baby boom to save the Gross National Product.

But if we are to understand ageism, we have no choice but to bring family again under the lens of a feminist politic. In the past, we examined the father as oppressor, we examined his oppression of the mother and the daughters, in great detail we examined the mother as oppressor of the daughters, but what has never come under the feminist lens is the daughters' oppression of the mother – that woman who by definition is older than we are.

The source of your ageism, the reason why you see older women as there to serve you, comes from family. It was in patriarchal family that you learned that mother is there to serve you, her child, that serving you is her purpose in life. This is not woman's definition of motherhood. This is man's definition of motherhood, a male myth enforced in family and which you still believe – to your peril and mine. It infantilizes you and it erases me.

This myth of motherhood is not a white American phenomenon. Barbara Christian in her book *Black Feminist Criticism* points out how this myth is uncovered in the fiction of Alice Walker writing about Afro-American life and by Buchi Emecheta writing about Ibuza life. And nowhere, I believe, is it as bad as in white imperialist culture. This myth is summed up by the Ibuza saying: *The joy of being a mother is the joy of giving all to your children.* It is internalized by the young mother, but then internalized and perpetuated by her daughters. So that even when – as in Emecheta's *The Joys of Motherhood* – the mother has come to some insight, her daughter continues to see her as existing only for self-sacrifice.

The old woman is at the other end of that motherhood myth. She has no personhood, no desires or value of her own. She must not fight for her own issues – if she fights at all, it must be for "future generations." Her greatest joy is seen as giving all to her grandchildren. And to the extent that she no longer directly serves a man – can no longer produce his children, is no longer sexually desirable to men – she is erased more completely as grandmother than she was as mother.

It is for these reasons – because of everything you learned in family – that you, as feminists, can continue to see the older woman as a non-person. It is for these reasons that you believe our lives as old women are not important and that we exist only to serve you.

We have all been so infantilized in family we have never made ourselves, as daughters, accountable as oppressors of the mothers – and we should know only too well that the failure to acknowledge the oppressor in ourselves results in confused thinking and a contradictory image of those we oppress. Thus you who are younger see us as either submissive and childlike or as possessing some unidentified vague wisdom. As having more "soul" than you or as being over-emotional and slightly crazy. As weak and helpless or as a pillar of strength. As "cute" and funny or as boring. As sicky sweet or dominating and difficult. You pity us, or you ignore us—until you are made aware of your ageism, and then you want to honor us. I don't know which is worse. None of these images has anything to do with who we are—they are the projections of the oppressor.

I want to close by giving three very recent examples of ageism in some of our best writing as feminists. These are writers whose work I admire. But the ageism in their writing will be passed on through Women's Studies to other young women if it is left on the shelves unexamined, and I am not willing any longer to leave it there. *These writers are no more ageist than the entire women's community.* They have not personally failed me—they, like all the rest of us, have been failed by the women's movement.

In the novel *Triangles*, by Ruth Geller, we use our living grandmother as a character, and we make her the comic relief. We show her photograph on the back cover, with a blurb making her the subject of laughter—most of the laughter is that she is not in on the joke. And yet the sisterhood publishes this book, reviews it, and is silent.

In *Between Women*, edited by Sarah Ruddick, Marie DeSalvo, and Carol Ascher, we bring together a fine collection of essays on the relationship of the biographers to the famous women whose lives they have chosen to write about. But believing in the myth of motherhood, many of these biographers, not satisfied with status by association with these strong famous women of the past and present (such as Virginia Woolf, Simone de Beauvoir), proceed to turn their subjects—most of whom chose not to have children—into their mothers. This is no equal association between women. This is ageism, and as though these women had not given enough, the biographers (women in their 50's) in page after page ask to be mothered, nurtured, and have their lives blessed by their subjects. And still the sisterhood reviews this book, finds nothing offensive about it, and is silent.

In her essay, *Half of a Map*, Sandy Boucher, in speaking of old women who have been helpful to her, writes: "I would be *them* one day, and if I could be . . . as generous of myself as they were, then I could be proud to be old." Apart from the intolerable patronizing, only a male myth of motherhood makes this feminist think my pride in being old consists in my generosity to younger women. And still the sisterhood is silent.

I have to say of Women's Studies that when you make the lives of women over 60 invisible, when you see us as your mothers and fail to examine your oppressive attitudes, you are letting the parameters of Women's Studies be defined by men— by the man in your own heads. But more than that. In the consciousness raising of the late sixties and seventies, in the contributions made to feminist theory that grew out of those years, in the development of Women's Studies that followed, we planned curriculum with an entire piece omitted — that of age and the oppression of ageism. We cannot now patch up those structures in twenty minutes to cover the gaps of our ignorance. We have no choice but to go back once again, as we have had to do before, cover old ground in new ways, and rebuild this time with a wholeness that includes all women and all the years of our lives.

BARBARA MACDONALD

Young Lym Wong   *1975*   IMOGEN CUNNINGHAM

No words can describe old age as well as the photographs reproduced in After Ninety, *which is a direct result of Imogen's own confrontation with life after ninety. This is surely one of the most unusual projects ever undertaken by a photographer, not only because few artists live or work to such a fine old age, but also because in our culture it is the rare artist of any age whose work confronts this stage of life without fear, without condescension, but with self-identification and compassion. Imogen herself, as she turned ninety ... [was] still making new portraits, printing almost every morning, and keeping up with the latest work of other photographers near and far. Her work was not just her picture-making; it was people as well.*

By Margaretta Mitchell, from the Introduction to *After Ninety* (University of Washington Press, 1979).

Martha Ideler   1975   IMOGEN CUNNINGHAM

She was a famous pianist, and she's ninety-some. She had just undergone an operation for cancer, and she refused further treatment. She said, 'I might as well die when I'm supposed to,' and I said, 'You're right.'

Haru Asawa   *1966*   *IMOGEN CUNNINGHAM*

Grace Bauder   1968   IMOGEN CUNNINGHAM

This is Mrs. Bauder, the goat lady.

Jessie Luca   1975   IMOGEN CUNNINGHAM

She said, 'When we were young we were all puritans, and all we talked about was whether it was right or it was wrong. And then I married a man from Sardinia.'

Three Ages of Women   1972   *IMOGEN CUNNINGHAM*

The three ages of woman, on Fillmore Street.

Reprinted from *After Ninety* by Imogen Cunningham with permission of the Imogen Cunningham Trust and the publisher, University of Washington Press.

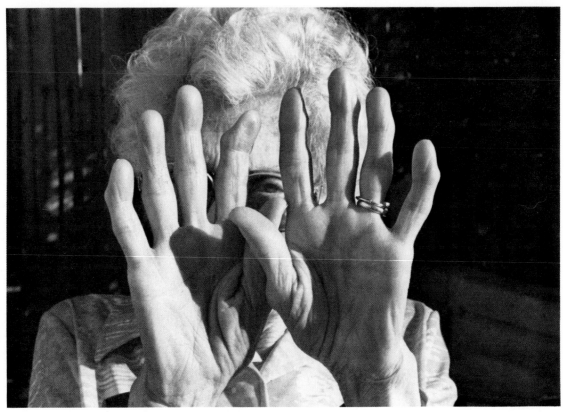

Tushu   1985   ANN MEREDITH

For the last fifteen years I have been photographing people, mainly women, in their eighties, nineties, and hundreds. As a lesbian photographer, I am concerned with dignity, beauty, and love for women.

Elizabeth Ann and Martha Jane   *1985*   *ANN MEREDITH*

Face-lift   1975   ANNE NOGGLE

YOUTHENASIA

I photograph people, mostly older women, focusing on the tension between the iron determinant of age and the individual character of the subject. Trying for an image that gets beneath the surface into that unchanging arena of the human psyche, formed in early life, which grows into maturity but does not relinquish its basic character thoughout one's life, and is discernible only to one who is patient, and watchful, and perhaps older oneself. It is of youth betrayed by age, of spirit strong but fragile with time. Old people already belong in the past . . . . historical objects occupying space. I want to show who they are and how damned difficult it is as each of us in our time becomes one of them.

Yolanda in Fur Hat   1983   ANNE NOGGLE

I did not start to photograph until I was in my forties so it was my own life's experiences that I drew on. Later I discovered Julia Margaret Cameron (19th C. photographer) and knew immediately that we were kindred spirits, for her people are alive today and vibrate that aliveness. The past is not dead, it has just already happened. I want my photographs to be alive forever if I could do that, and I try. Somehow the energy you put into it can make that happen to some extent, and I pursue it singlemindedly. Other photographers whose work has affected me to some degree are August Sander, Disfarmer, Judy Dater, and Diane Arbus.

Agnes in Shower Stall   *1976*   ANNE NOGGLE

I am filled with dread that I will wake up and find I have become a completely rational being with a finite set of values within whose framework I must mind my manners and dream my dreams.

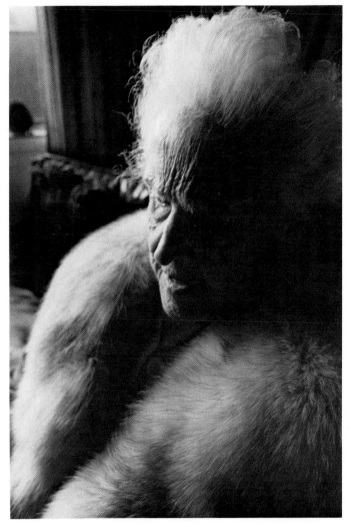

Agnes in Fur Collar   *1979*   ANNE NOGGLE

As a romantic, intent is subservient to expression.

Laura Cumming   *1983*   ANNE NOGGLE
from a series: East Texas Faces

   To look straight into a face and find the pulse of what it is to be human, that is what fuels me, that is the sum of my mind and longing.

Shelly and Her Sister Mim   *1983*   ANNE NOGGLE

I am more interested in what the image means than in what it looks like.

Always Looking   1976   DEBORAH KLIBANOFF

As a Buddhist practitioner for the past eight years, I find great benefit in always looking for and finding the dharma in all situations. I find photography an interesting medium for showing these processes.

Nun and Tatting   1980   DEBORAH KLIBANOFF

Using my camera as a reflective format allows and reminds me to understand the human experience more artistically, clarify perceptions more objectively, and to always carry a quality of compassion, awareness, and stability. I choose my subjects as teachers—they always show me the way.

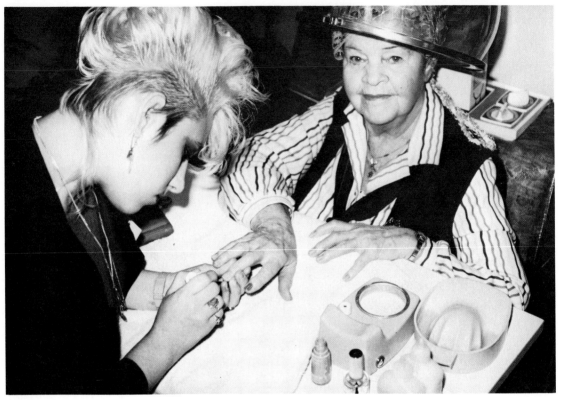

Styles   *1985*   *DEBORAH KLIBANOFF*

Has Anyone Seen Coretta Scott King?   1980   *DEBORAH KLIBANOFF*

Acoma Woman   MARGARET RANDALL

The photograph is evidence, evidence of that point of contact on the margin of sight, off center of the eye, just beyond consciousness, just before "truth"— as we are conditioned to know it—clouds our vision. Photography is a language of its own, so the less said ABOUT it, the better. I do not want to engage my subjects before the shutter speaks. I do not want

Anna   MARGARET RANDALL

anything else, the language of speech, of intent, of temperature or memory to get in the way of what will be said in the image itself. I should also say I make pictures of women because woman is my closest identity; I make pictures of women aging because I am a woman who is aging.

Elsa Gidlow   1983   MARCELINA MARTIN

My work has evolved from portraitures of inner visions to a method I call "pho-tomythology." In my work I seek to expose outdated myths, explore life-affirming images, and cultivate a dynamic vision of wholeness, integration, and empowerment.

VOICES: ON BECOMING OLD WOMEN   *BABA COPPER*

> *When we ask for a chance to live our old age in comfort,*
> *creativity and usefulness, we ask it not for ourselves alone,*
> *but for you. We are not a special interest group. We are your*
> *roots. You are our continuity. What we gain is your inheritance.*
> Irene Pauli, Some Ironies of Aging

How can old women define the subjects of age and ageism so that false understanding of these issues does not dominate the interactions between women and keep us forever separate? Aging is a natural and universal personal experience that begins the day we are born. It is a process of challenge—not necessarily growth and development when we are young as opposed to loss and deterioration when we are old—but learning through change. Ageism is the negative social response to different stages in the process of aging and it is a political issue. The ageism that old women experience is firmly embedded in sexism—an extension of the male power to define, control values, erase, disempower, and divide. Woman-to-woman ageism is an aspect of the horizontal conflict that usurps the energies of the colonized—part of the female competition for the crumbs of social power.

How can the same word be used for the experience of teenagers, old women, and the most powerful men in the world? Yet we say that all these are subject to *ageist* attitudes—stereotyping and denigration because of age. But each age group—children, teens, midlife women, old women, old men—have radically different expectations of their due, their rightful social place. For an old woman, ageism is a killer, because her sense of worth has been eroded by a lifelong pursuit of youth/beauty. Age passing—passing for young enough—is part of all female experience. The foundation of lies built into passing and the fear and loathing of female aging are what keep the generations of women—decade by decade—divided from each other.

I believe that age passing is one of the primary learning arenas of female competition, as well as an apprenticeship to hatred of old women. When women pass easily, we gain comfort knowing that we do not have to identify with the woman who, in our view, is not passing. "I am not like her" translates easily into "I am better than her." In our thirties, we do not want to be mistaken for forty. In our forties, we do not want anyone to assume we are fifty. Somewhere in our fifties, the mass of anxieties about age, and the increase of rejection and invisibility we are experiencing, becomes critical. This is often a time when our trained inability to identify with women older than ourselves reaches its climax. Old women cannot rely upon the midlife woman as ally. The midlife woman, in her rage and fear, may unconsciously discharge all kinds of covert aggression against the old woman as the personification of what is threatening her.

Can women afford to ignore issues that surround the aging process? When I have asked younger women what they thought ageism was all about, they talked about the aura of death and decay which permeates age for them, the oppressive power/over of the mythic Mother figure, and the deplorable neglect exhibited by the authorities in making adequate institutional responses to age. None have seen ageism as a problem of prejudice or bigotry on their part. With a righteousness reminiscent of the anchorman on the evening news, most of my young informants have advocated more and better government support for the old. But government subsidies for medicine and institutional care have created a highly profitable industry of geriatric technology, with the elderly aid recipients captive to the modern Grail, longevity. Just staying alive is a false goal. Acceptance of age in women has not kept pace with our increasing life expectancy. It is the quality of that extra time that is important. As long as women allow themselves to be brainwashed into worshiping youth and plasticized beauty, increased life expectancy (and the institutionalized responses to it) will remain a burden for both the young and the old.

How can ageism be defined by women; how can we develop clear vocabulary and theory; can we afford to ignore it? For me these questions are more than rhetorical. I am an old woman living in a highly politicized community of women. I find struggle and change taking place in relation to all the differences between women except age. I need to divert some of that political consciousness toward ageism.

I am an *old* woman. I am sixty-six. Part of the reason I self-identify as *old* is a need to escape the prissy category of "older woman." This label claims descriptive power over women from eighteen to eighty, depending upon the age and consciousness of the user. I used to wear a button that said "I like older women." When a young man accosted me in a supermarket to ask where he could get a button just like mine, I realized that *his* older woman was probably twenty-three. But what are my choices? I get called "little lady" by strangers, although I am neither. I found that the decision to abandon "older woman" was easier than claiming the identity of *old. Old* was without hope, ignored, invisible, trivialized, patronized, limited, powerless. If I didn't want to embrace all that, how was I to speak of myself?

After lots of internal arguments, I found a rationalization that made me comfortable with the label. Calling myself an old woman was the radical way out of my dilemma. At sixty-six, it may be presumptuous of me to assume a label that is descriptive of women in their nineties, but I have noticed that many of them avoid the term. Like other words that feminists are reclaiming by proud usage, I would take to myself the word everyone seems to fear. My *real* circumstances would not suffer more than they have from the visual impact of my years. Nobody but radical women would stand there beside me, honest and angry about the distortions that surround the time of life all women dread. I would walk through the door-of-no-return and from the other side name the politics of age instead of waltzing around pretending I am just an "older woman." The lies of age passing would not save me from the stigma of age. In fact, it has been my experience that the invention and practice of feminine lies keep women forever in harness, laboring to be someone who fits in, who pleases, who is chosen, who earns (and therefore deserves) love. I have grown sick of the harness.

Among my friends, lesbians like myself, the line between older and the shunned identity of old is fuzzy, indistinct, avoided. Having found my personal path over the edge, in resistance to the degrading dance of age passing, I discovered a burning need to share my insights with others. Isolation is part of the punishment of age. With high hopes, I set out to gather together a group of women committed to the discussion of ageism.

It was not easy to find women willing to focus on this subject. Most movement women see the problem as peripheral to "real" political issues. Ageism often is not even politically acknowledged, much less analyzed or confronted. Sadly, very few women recognize that ageism is the name of their emerging experience. Fewer still are able to separate ageist experience from the subtle changes in the content of their expectations and responses due to their real aging. After many discouraging conversations with women whom I mistakenly assumed would be interested, seven of us agreed to do consciousness raising together. As women involved in movements for social change, all of us had experienced the erasure of age from the very political issues that engrossed our energies. Women's control of our bodies, racism and anti-Semitism, rape and battering—all are issues important to our political lives, which are treated as if they had no specific impact on midlife and old women. We talked about our anger at feeling unwanted within the ranks of the activists. It was my hope that we would use our own experience to dispel those ageist afflictions of attitude that society adds to the process of aging.

Some of us were friends of long standing; others were new to each other. We had no pretensions of being a "representative cross-section" of midlife women.

Although the majority were white, able, middle-class, and middle-aged lesbians, one woman was Black; two, Jewish; two, disabled; one, fat; one, heterosexual; one, old. Two had never had children; five were mothers of grown children. All were college-educated; our economic resources ranged from fair to marginal.

From my point of view, our age differences were too large. I was the only one of the group over the edge (no longer able to pass for middle-aged), visually and by years. The others were from five to twenty years younger than I. I was the only one who didn't identify as "older." But even for me, the other differences between us seemed more obvious, more dangerous.

From the beginning of our group meetings, the differences between our points of view muddled our communication. Although the others were eager to describe the ageism they experienced as midlife women, only I seemed sensitized to the uses of relative advantage in the dance of passing. Our first get-together regressed quickly into a gripe session. It is my hope that readers will listen carefully for the tension between the perspective of the *older* woman and the *old*. Hearing that differentiation may help one to become more finely tuned to one's own age enslavement. The voices of the other women are in italics.

I am constantly infuriated by the assumption people make that there is a kind of watershed after which you are old. What they seem to mean by this is that one becomes part of a category which exhibits certain physical characteristics, has similar concerns and generally thinks alike.

You can't have a stereotyping without categories, right? Therefore there HAS to be an ultimate category called "old."

I don't feel old unless I am sick, or hung over a little, like I am today.

As I winced at this derogatory cliché, I began to recognize the magnitude of our group problem. All of us had accumulated enough years to have experienced some ageism. Each woman in that room was old in somebody's eyes. But unlike the others, I regularly got feedback from a great range of sources in my life which told me that I was perceived as part of the "old" category. This was not true for the others. Looks are the primary criteria by which women are judged, by women and men alike. I looked my age. How were we going to be able to communicate with each other, when *old* meant so many things? The vocabulary of aging was mined with sometimes unintended negative innuendo.

Younger is not better, it is simply different. Embracing one's years means that old is good. Not better, just different than young. Years are an accumulation of experience that one does not deny, either in the changes they have made upon our enduring bodies, the lines they have furrowed on our faces, or the quirks and strengths they have forged into our personalities. Typical uses of the words *young* and *old* ignore the disadvantages of youth and emphasize the negative aspects of age.

When I have trouble getting up off the floor, for instance, I say, "Oh, I'm getting old!" It is a way of covering up other problems. It is easier to say than "I can't because I'm disabled."

Or out of condition. The fact that I can't do it doesn't mean that another woman my age couldn't do it. In fact, when I say that, I am laying a trip on someone else.

If you are older, you are in charge.

If you are older, whatever you have belongs to whoever asks for it because "your mother never turns you down."

I was talking about being old, the others were talking about being middle-aged.

There are great differences between old women as a result of our work background, what career adjustments we have gone through, whether or not we have Social Security. Sensitivity to these anxieties should be part of the awareness of all women, not just old women. Among the differences that divided the group was our relationship to employment. For women still engaged in the work world — no matter how problematically — the psychological impact of the forced dependency, economic insecurity, and denied productivity of old women was a distant problem. When one is part of the category *old*, one is expected to be retired, i.e., not working. Manual labor is not associated with old women; neither is remunerative employment. No matter what old women do, or don't do, we are seen as non-productive. Yet all over the world old women do much of the undesirable unpaid labor designated in the culture as female work — agricultural work, child care, household maintenance, cooking. When younger women "escape" this work into the cash economy of factory or office jobs, it is largely old women who inherit what the younger woman can no longer perform. If women are the mules of the world, the grandmother is the mule's mule. And I do not mean just taking care of the grandchildren. The streets of the Soviet Union are swept by old women. In a socialist country, old women are paid the lowest wages within the system for the hard, cold labor of cleaning the streets with twig brooms.

Employment was not the only subject in which our emphasis or priorities differed. We were describing to each other our particular experiences in the erosion of youth privilege. Youth privilege, like male privilege or heterosexual privilege, is made up of all those reactions and expectations that we were taught to take for granted throughout our twenties, thirties, and into our forties. It is a privilege of youth to expect a minimum sensitivity to equal sharing of responsibilities, to be able to demand some respect for differences, to know you will get a certain level of attention. Midlife women correctly identify the erosion of these expected powers as age-related. But their solution is to develop further strategies of trying to remain "deserving" of that privilege. Women mill around in this trap of self-loathing, trying to avoid thinking about the inevitability of the ultimate category of the unforgiven, "old."

In the group I struggled to give examples of my own confusion over my experience and how to interpret it: "Recently I went to the women's bookstore, where I found there were two whole shelves of different books in the category *Age*. I was pleased, until I discovered that they were 'How-to' books about 'getting old graciously.' 'Be positive! be content!' say these books written by young or middle-aged gerontologists, 'even though you are getting older.' But what about the societal constructs that make getting older hard? Take me. I will soon be sixty-seven. I am becoming invisible. I am seen as asexual, although that is not how I feel. I am condescended to and socially segregated, as if I had a condition that was catching. And to top it off, I might be finding myself suddenly poorer, if my situation were like those of most women my age. We are inundated by responses we cannot explain. To ourselves, we aren't all that different than we were in our midlife years. It is not physiological aging or psychological aging that is troubling me. I am experiencing social aging—ageism. A generalized image is being projected upon me that does not correspond with my self-image. I must continually internalize this feedback, or adjust to it, in order to retain my sanity at all. It is disorienting, and very hard to not lose confidence and blame myself. But this is not named for me in all these 'How-to books on Age.'"

I wonder, if we went through and looked at a little girl up through all the years of her life, would we find a time when ageism was not a factor or aspect of the sexism which had an impact upon her life?

As women, certain restrictions are put on us at certain ages. All of those things accumulate. The pressure I may feel in being treated differently as I get older must be understood within the whole dynamic from my birth till now.

Young and midlife women tend to see ageism as a continuing oppression of women throughout their lives. The point of view I tried to voice as an old woman sprang from my new experience, which revealed abrupt changes in the degree or intensity of stigma, when, for whatever reasons, one could no longer pass as middle-aged. I am uncomfortable with the absence of differentiation between the kind of ageism I can remember experiencing as a teenager and what I am experiencing in my sixties.

I felt confused. I did not know how to integrate these concepts into my present circumstances. Was the pain over the ageism I experience intensified by the fact that my youth privilege had been augmented by the privileges of being white, able, thin, blond, tall, middle class? And how did all this relate to age passing, for many women try—and some even succeed by the use of repeated plastic surgery—to appear forever middle-aged? For instance, the small, thin old woman—especially one who plays the "cute" social role—does not receive the same direct hostility that big "motherly" women do. Was the pain of ageism relative also, or was there a pall that settled over an old woman (the year varying for different women) which was similar for all whether or not they had been pretty or middle-class?

I began to recognize that no one in the group ever said to me, "Maybe you are experiencing more ageism because you are older than we are." As movement women have discovered, imaginary hierarchies of oppression can be very divisive. It was evident—and disturbing—to me that my investment in the issue of ageism was much greater than that of the others. When I challenged them directly, as I did one day, there was some acknowledgement of this difference: "When a collective I worked with was meeting once a week to work on our differences, the youngest women acknowledged, after a lot of very painful probing of their inner realities, that some part of their minds was blocked when trying to think about their own aging. They said things like: 'Oh, I'm not going to get old,' or 'I'll be dead by then,' or 'I'll commit suicide before I get old,' or 'My life just isn't going to last that long.' Needless to say, I wasn't going to let them get away with such an attitude. But while they were mulling over the irrationality of their position, I must admit that I sat there thinking, Wow! They believe that they would rather commit suicide than to be like *me*! We carry around a shield that protects us from identifying with women much older than ourselves, and hence, of seeing them at all."

Women are so afraid of age that we erase any image of our own future while we are still young.

I can remember when I was about thirteen, watching my mother and her sisters partying, and saying, very indignantly, "Why don't they act their age!" I am their age now and I party the same way. Who's to say what I am supposed to act like when I'm this age? "I never thought about being this age."

I can remember having fantasies of things I wanted to do or be in my twenties, my thirties, my forties, and even my fifties. But now I have trouble fantasizing exciting new sexual encounters or imagining meeting Ms. Right who I want to spend the rest of my life with or projecting adventures I want to have or believing that there are windmills worth tilting.

My fantasy life is twenty-three years old. I feel trapped. I stay here because I don't know where I am going or even where I want to go. I can't visualize what I will be doing when I am eighty years old. It's just not there. Knowing, as I do, that my future is shaped by whatever my image of it is, I've got a REAL problem.

Some terribly negative images have been substituted for my fantasies. My mother has been sick for about a year in a nursing home. I have been taking care of her and her affairs. The strength of my identification with what is happening to her is absolutely terrifying. When I forget or lose things, it is like her *mind going. When I am not steady on my feet, it is* her, *not me. My fantasy of the future is to be in that nursing home. I want some of my old fantasies back!*

Fantasies and the role models are *tied together!*

Because we were talking about our fantasies, we were merging real issues of aging with the ageist diseases of imagination which we inflict upon ourselves. One of the things that women do when talking about these issues is to blur the distinction between aging and ageism. Aging is a real process, which takes place differently in each individual. Ageism, on the other hand, is a constriction that rearranges power relationships, just like any other kind of discrimination or prejudice. When one ages, one may gain or lose. With ageism, one is shaped into something that is *always* less than what one really is.

There is the ageist cliché that all older women are mothers in disguise. Thus, when we exhibit leadership, competence, or political skills, we become psychological threats to other women.

Older women are seen as a burden to the patriarchy, never as a threat! One of the reasons that older women are invisible is that men define female purpose as reproductive or for sex. So what are old women for? *Old women are always reminiscing about the days when they had a little power as mothers or wives. Memories do not constitute a threat to anyone.*

But older women who have resisted on the basis of both their past and their present oppression could be a threat. There is *a potential which older feminists are beginning to discover.*

Death is an extremely important subject that our culture has mystified, professionalized, sensationalized—and at the same time, made taboo. Everyone needs to make his or her peace with the meaning of death. However, the assumption that death is a preoccupation, or subject of expertise, of midlife or old women is ageist. I understood that we might want to talk about death. But the old should not be seen as standing with death at their elbow. Nor should they be expected to help others on the subject or allow the subject to be age segregated. Repeatedly, younger women make assumptions about my relationship to death. One woman said that she shared identity with me because she had had many losses of people close to her in her life. She assumed that I had too. In reality, other than the death of my mother when she was ninety-three, no one I loved has ever died.

I have been thinking about old women living together and helping each other to die. I don't know that we can discuss age without discussing death.

Those who are dying are not supposed to admit that they are. We who watch them die are supposed to pretend that they aren't. This denial has a trickle-down effect upon aging.

One of the ideas which is important to me is the concept of having more control over the dying process.

Here it was, that virulent stereotype—the age/death connection—unabashedly expounded in a group committed to exploring our own ageism! Apparently only old people die. Death does not hover near the cradle, the motorcycle, the toxic workplace, high bridges, or battlefields. But around old women, everyone is reminded that they have given their own possible mortality insufficient attention. Death is a forbidden subject with all but the old, who are expected to bear the burden of this social suppression. Since my own demise is as distant from my conscious mind as it was when I was twenty, I have come to recognize that it is my looks that evoke the age/death connection in others. Death has become a private buzzword for me, warning me of the shoals of ageism before me.

Talking about choice in relation to dying always makes me very nervous. I reminded the group that we were at the beginning of a world-wide demographic boom of old women. It is easy to predict that our society will soon be subject to all kinds of "new looks" at death and dying. I read a clipping from a futurist magazine suggesting that a demise pill be available to the elderly (but not the young, of course). The old are seen as half dead already. Old women, like everyone else, buy into the prevailing concepts surrounding both worth and death—we are as easy to brainwash as the next. When one believes that one has done everything one wants to do, it may be a way of expressing the feeling that what one has to contribute from a wheelchair, for example, is not valuable.

Our conversations about death were a good example of the divisions between us based on age. Only one woman, nearer than the others to sixty, expressed recognition of the oppression of the age/death connection. As time went on, I became acutely aware of the "voices not present" – the perspectives of women in their seventies and eighties and nineties. We know next to nothing about what it is to be an old woman in this society.

How can old women begin to change this? First, we have to name our circumstances more clearly, identifying the root sources of our denigrated place in society. Feminist analysis and the concept of ageism are not used as tools by most old women to explain the increased negative content of our experience. Old women tend to see problems as personal – interpersonal or physical or economic – instead of political. The time of life that should be a final ripening, a meaningful summation, a last chance for all the risks and pleasures of corporeal existence, is all too often deadened by emotional isolation and self-doubts. As the average life expectancy for women keeps creeping upward – almost into the eighties now – the quality of that life-to-be-expected keeps deteriorating.

The "natural alliance" that old women have a right to expect with midlife women will not emerge until all women begin to recognize the pitfalls of age passing. Separating the perspective of the barely-passing older woman from some of my concerns as one-who-no-longer-is-able-to-pass has taken all my confidence and a great deal of hindsight. The midlife woman feels increasing pressure – internal and external – about aging as well as the rejections of ageism. It is natural that she rushes forward to define the problem. In asserting her power over the insights of the old woman – the complaints, the accusations of ageism, the naming of the universal hatred of the Old Woman – she unconsciously silences the inherent radicalism of the only one who can tell her how it really is.

The problem for old women is a problem of power. First, power over the circumstances and directions of our own lives and identity. Second, power as an influence upon the world we live in – the world we have served, in which we have such a large, unrecognized vested interest. This is, of course, the rub. Patriarchal institutions are, without exception, designed to exclude the vision of old women. Most old women have little experience in leadership, influence, or even respect. Mostly, old women know how to serve. The roles reserved and expected of women in old age – grandmothers, self-effacing volunteers to the projects and priorities designed by others, or caretakers of old men – are custom fit to our powerless status.

But there are ways that all women can begin to prepare the way for the empowerment of themselves in the future, when they are old. These changes can first be brought about in the women's community, among lesbians and political women. The first step is for women to recognize that they have been programmed to hate old women and to deny them power. This brainwashing is so subtle that its eradication will take an effort equal to that which we have made and still must expend upon sexism. Further, this brainwashing extends down through our lives, making us fear the processes of our own bodies within time, so that our energies and attention are constantly undermined by ageist competition and self-doubts. These are attitudes and expectations that we can change now, if we decide to. Empowerment of women will come when we identify with women older than we are and not before.

BABA COPPER

GROWING TO BE AN OLD WOMAN: *SHEVY HEALEY*
AGING AND AGEISM

Presented to the National Women's Studies Association Conference,
Seattle, Washington, June 21, 1985; edited for CALYX.

In my late fifties, and then my sixties, I heard, "I can't believe you're that old.
You don't look that old." At first that felt like a compliment. Then I became a bit
uneasy. It reminded me of early pre-feminist days when I was complimented by
some men for being "smarter," "more independent" than those "other" women.
What was I now – a token "young"?

Slowly other experiences began to accumulate, reminding me of a real
change in my life status.

First, I moved. And while I found easy acceptance among older people in the
community, when younger people talked to me they invariably would say something like, "You remind me of my grandmother." Grandmother?! I felt labelled and
diminished somehow.

Recently, I have, in fact, become a grandmother. I found most young friends
expected me – automatically – to "be" a certain way. Many of those expectations
were in accord with what I felt. Some were not. I did not instantly fall in love with
my grandson. I was much more drawn to my daughter and what she was
experiencing. I must admit that I am now a doting grandmother, but being put in a
particular slot about that was a bit disquieting, as though all of my reactions could
be gauged in advance and belonged to the generic group "grandmother" rather
than to me.

I attended a Women's Action for Nuclear Disarmament (WAND) meeting at
which a young M.D. spoke about his research with children all over the world and
their responses to the atom bomb. His talk was stimulating, and after the meeting
I went up to him to comment on his research. I had the most peculiar feeling of
being looked through, as though, what could I, this gray-haired woman in very
casual dress, know about research design. I felt patronized, a feeling I wasn't used
to.

I lost some money recently through bad judgment and suddenly had the
realization that I would never be able to replace it. I do not have enough time left to
be able to earn that money again.

I looked in the mirror and saw lots of wrinkles. I had a hard time fitting that
outward me with the me inside. I felt like the same person, but outside I looked
different. I checked into a face lift, with much trepidation. What a seduction took

place in that doctor's office! He told me he would make me less strange to myself. I would look more like I felt! I became frightened by the whole process. Who was I then? This face? What I felt like inside? How come the two images were not connected? My own ageism told me that how I looked outside was ugly. But I felt the same inside, not ugly at all.

Finally, death entered my life as a direct reality. My oldest friend died of cancer three years ago. My father died two years ago after what turned out to be needless surgery. Another close friend died last month after a year of struggling with cancer. My mother is dying slowly and painfully after suffering a massive stroke. The realization hit me that I can expect this kind of personal contact with death to occur with greater and greater frequency.

Not just my chronological age, but life itself was telling me that I was becoming an older/old woman!

Just at this time I found Barbara Macdonald and Cynthia Rich through their book *Look Me in the Eye—Old Women, Aging and Ageism*. I join with May Sarton who said, "*Look Me in the Eye* is a tremendously stirring recognition of what we are doing to ourselves as we grow older and a rousing attack on what is being done to us . . . . To me personally as I enter my 72nd year, the book has come as a revelation, hitting me hard with the shock of recognition."

But why am I, a woman in her sixties, who has explored the stereotyping of sexism, racism, of the physically disabled, just now looking at ageism? Even to pose the question goes a way towards answering it. Because, in our society, to be old is so awful, one best not think of it. "Old" is equated with "awful" in every respect, with regard to function, thought, action, appearance. I mentioned the Old Woman's League (OWL) to a friend and her instant response was, "What an awful name!"

Think of all the adjectives that are most disrespectful in our society. They are all part of the ageist stereotyping of old women: pathetic, powerless, querulous, complaining, sick, weak, conservative, rigid, helpless, unproductive, wrinkled, asexual, ugly, unattractive, and on, ad nauseum. There is, by the way, an exception to this, and that is the stereotype of the wise old woman. She, of course, never complains, is never sick, and although no one really would want to *be* with her, occasionally it might be fine to sit at her feet!

How did this happen, this totally denigrating picture of old women? To understand this phenomenon we must look at sexism, for ageism is inextricably tied to sexism and is the logical extension of its insistence that women are only valuable when they are attractive and useful to men.

Under the guise of making themselves beautiful, women have endured torture and self mutilation, cramped their bodies physically, maimed themselves mentally, all in order to please and serve men better, as men defined the serving, because only in that service could women survive.

Footbinding, for example, reminds us how false and relatively ephemeral those external standards of beauty and sexuality are. We can feel horror at what centuries of Chinese women had to endure. Do we feel the same horror at the process which determines that gray hair, wrinkled skin, fleshier bodies are not beautiful, and therefore ought to be disguised, pounded, starved to meet an equally unrealistic (and bizarre) standard set by the patriarchy? Women spend their lives accepting the premise that to be beautiful one must be young, and only beauty saves one from being discarded. The desperation with which women work to remove signs of aging attests only to the value they place upon themselves as desirable and worthwhile, in being primarily an object pleasing to men. Women's survival, both physical and psychological, has been linked to their ability to please men, and the standards set are reinforced over and over by all the power that the patriarchy commands. The final irony is that all of us, feminists included, have incorporated into our psyches the self-loathing that comes from not meeting that arbitrary standard.

As we alter and modify our bodies in the hopes of feeling good, we frequently achieve instead an awful estrangement from our own bodies. In the attempt to meet that arbitrary external standard, we lose touch with our own internal body messages, thus alienating ourselves further from our own sources of strength and power.

What does this have to do with aging and ageism? Having spent our lives estranged from our own bodies in the effort to meet that outer patriarchal standard of beauty, it is small wonder that the prospect of growing old is frightening to women of all ages. We have all been trained to be ageist. By denying our aging we hope to escape the penalties placed upon growing old. But in so doing we disarm ourselves in the struggle to overcome the oppression of ageism.

To deal with our own feelings about aging we must scrupulously examine how we have been brainwashed to believe that three-inch feet are beautiful, or whatever equivalent myth is currently being purveyed. The old have done what all oppressed people do: they have internalized the self-hatred embodied in the ageist stereotyping. First they try to pass, at least in their own minds if not in the minds of others. They separate themselves from those "others," the old people. They are youthful. I know a woman who at 80 described how she visited the "old folks' home." She was not "one of them." That's not cute on her part. It is simply an expression of how she has incorporated that "old" is "awful," and she wants no part of that powerlessness and marginality. She has found a way to affirm herself, but it's at the expense of others. For all people who try to pass the price is high. In passing you are saying that who you are at 60, 70, 80 is *not* o.k. You are o.k. only to the degree that you are like someone else, someone younger, who has more value in the eyes of others.

It is difficult to hold on to one's own sense of self, to one's own dignity when all around you there is no affirmation of you. At best there may be a patronizing acknowledgment; at worst, you simply do not exist.

The oppressed old woman is required to be cheerful. But if you're smiling all the time, you acquiesce to being invisible and docile, participating in your own "erasure." If you're not cheerful then you are accused of being bitter, mean, crabby, complaining! A real Catch 22.

Old people are shunted off to their own ghettoes. Frequently they will say they like it better. But who would not when, to be with younger people is so often to be invisible, to be treated as irrelevant and peripheral, and sometimes even as disgusting.

What then is the reality of being old? With all due respect to the problems of younger sisters, to lump older women from 40 to 90 is more than inaccurate. It perpetuates the ageist assumption that there are no special conditions, problems, dilemmas for old women worthy of being addressed. When discussion of aging begins and remains primarily about women in their 40s and 50s, it reinforces the invisibility of the old woman, and diminishes the importance of the last 25 years of life.

We need to begin the systematic examination from a feminist perspective of the issues involved in women's aging, the condition of old women and our society's ageism. As the pervasiveness of ageist thinking becomes apparent, both in our culture and in the feminist movement itself, we will need to carefully scrutinize many of our basic assumptions, attitudes, and values.

We have systematically denigrated old women, kept them out of the mainstream of productive life, judged them primarily in terms of failing capacities and functions, and then found them pitiful. We have put old women in nursing "homes" with absolutely no intellectual stimulation, isolated from human warmth and nurturing contact, and then condemned them for their senility. We have impoverished, disrespected, and disregarded old women, and then dismissed them as inconsequential and uninteresting. We have made old women invisible so that we do not have to confront our patriarchal myths about what makes life valuable or dying painful.

Having done that, we then attribute to the process of aging *per se* all the evils we see and fear about growing old. It is not aging that is awful, nor whatever physical problems may accompany aging. What is awful is how society treats old women and their problems. To the degree that we accept and allow such treatment we buy the ageist assumptions that permit this treatment.

What then does it really mean to grow old? For me, first of all, to be old is to be *myself*. No matter how patriarchy may classify and categorize me as invisible and powerless, I exist. I am an ongoing person, a sexual being, a person who struggles, for whom there are important issues to explore, new things to learn, challenges to meet, beginnings to make, risks to take, endings to ponder. Even though some of my options are diminished, there are new paths ahead.

Secondly, I subscribe to Macdonald's view that "age in our society gives us a second opportunity (or places the demand on us, if that is how it feels) to finally deal with our difference, if we have not done so before; to move out of that safe harbor of acceptability." Here the difference we have to deal with is our own aging. Neither to run from being old nor to succumb to being more acceptable as a "young" old. We have the opportunity to deal with what is different, special, unique about being older and old, to find a belonging with other women as they examine the issue of aging, no matter what their age.

Finally, for me the largest issue of all is to deal with the appropriate task of my own age, to learn to live with loss and death, to prepare for my own death. Do I frighten some of you? I have just spoken the unspeakable. In our culture, death is to be avoided at all costs, to be struggled against, and when it comes, to be hidden—in a funeral parlor—away from sight. We so fear death that we have permitted our medical establishment, which neglects old people in life, to keep them from death beyond all reason and dignity. To face the challenge of dying with grace—that is power.

As an old woman I am approaching what in some respects is the greatest power of my life. I am truly freed from the role of wife, mother, daughter, career woman. I can in truth seek to take charge of my life. A bit scary for one whose whole life has been lived subject to external disciplines, now to explore what is important to me, not simply to respond to others. I perceive for myself a two-fold task: to attend to the current business of living with vigor and involvement, while at the same time attending to the unfinished business of my life, putting old rancors in perspective, letting go of pettiness, acknowledging love.

To the degree that I deny my aging I cripple my ability to deal with my living and my dying. To deal with both means most particularly to find and accept my own place in the world, in the universe.

SHEVY HEALEY

BEYOND HAGS AND OLD MAIDS:
WOMEN WRITERS IMAGINE AGING WOMEN   *BARBARA HORN*

When we think of how literature typically presents aging and aged women, we have reason for alarm – even for despair. Negative stereotypes are everywhere. Remember the witches and evil stepmothers in fairy tales, the school mistresses of Victorian novels, the sour widows and grandmothers in modern fiction? But where are the realistic portraits, the women who confront and even triumph over the difficulties of growing old?

Perhaps the most maligned of these aging women are spinsters. Writers traditionally depict unmarried females as ugly, cantankerous, frigid. Literature does them a double disservice: it turns them into unpleasant old women before they reach middle age, and it sees them as menaces. Often single females are little more than household retainers – there to assist with child rearing or emergencies, or to test the endurance of anyone younger. (We might recall dotty but protective Betsey Trotwood in *David Copperfield* or pushy Aunt March in *Little Women.*)

Aging widows in fiction receive similar treatment. Their unmarried state signified unworthiness, just as their advanced years curtailed experience. These women's lives go largely unexamined. And rarely do we find an older widow or spinster engaged in worthwhile work, unless that labor is part of an often oppressive family structure.

This superficial picture of unmarried women is but part of the larger issue of ageism in literature. Because most authors either refuse to write at all about older females or simply present these women in stereotyped ways, readers have very limited exposure to the realities of growing old. As Simone de Beauvoir argues in *The Coming of Age*, literature has always buried old age "under a heap of preconceived ideas, hiding it instead of making it apparent."

Obviously, this negative bias comes from Western culture's attitude about aging. Generally, old is ugly, unnatural, fearful, powerless. Therefore, old should be avoided, disguised, or denied. Because popular opinion holds that aged women are eccentric hags, sweet but crazy octogenarians, devouring stepmothers and mothers-in-law, or grotesque former beauties, such figures continue to dot our fictional landscape. And these unfavorable images contribute to the even less-than-second-class status of old women.

What is perhaps most discouraging is that the current women's movement has done little to improve the portrayal of aging females. In the recent book *Look Me In the Eye: Old Women, Aging and Ageism* by Barbara Macdonald and Cynthia Rich, Rich reminds us that, with few exceptions, today's women are unenlightened about aging. Contemporary women's art and literature, Rich argues, "tell us less about old women than about how thoroughly we younger women have absorbed male society's avoidance (masking a deep underlying terror and hatred) of our aging selves." Even a media star like Jane Fonda complains about the difficulty of finding worthwhile film scripts that treat women's transition from middle to old age. May Sarton's novels *Kinds of Love* and *As We Are Now* do provide sensitive handling of elderly characters in key, believable roles, as do Tillie Olsen's *Tell Me a Riddle* and Margaret Laurence's *The Stone Angel*. But we can count on one hand other such books.

We need fiction that counteracts ageism. We want stories that present older women as individuals, not as stereotypes. We would like to avoid stale, popular notions and read about spirited, capable, resilient aging females. We are not interested in romanticized portraits of sweet old things aging gracefully. As Cynthia Rich warns, we should not deny, infantilize, or trivialize old women's anger. The angers, frustrations, and fears of older females are as important to capture as are their courageous acts and hard-won pleasures.

We can, fortunately, find valid depictions of aging women, struggling for and maintaining their identities—if we turn to an earlier era in American letters.

We should make or renew acquaintance with four of the best-known women writers of their time: Sarah Orne Jewett (1849-1909), Mary Wilkins Freeman (1852-1930), Willa Cather (1873-1947), and Ellen Glasgow (1874-1945). Each author produced an impressive body of fiction, dealing frequently and powerfully with older women's lives. Known originally as regionalists (therefore, often called minor), these four artists present candid, positive portraits of aging females. Even when in their early work their elderly women disappoint, these writers attempt truth. Often their older females inspire.

The productivity of these authors as they themselves aged testifies to the vigor of old women. In her autobiography, Ellen Glasgow admits, "In the past few years I have made a thrilling discovery ... that until one is over sixty, one can never really learn the secret of living." One can then "begin to live, not simply with the intenser part of oneself, but with one's entire being."

As their careers advanced, these four writers believed increasingly that aging women could have stature. Impressive elderly women appear as protagonists in Glasgow's comedic novel *They Stoop to Folly*, Jewett's well-known New England tales, Freeman's stories, and Cather's late novellas. The older heroines in these works exhibit competence and strength. Often holding to unpopular convictions, they contrast sharply with the confused young people at the center of much mainstream, turn-of-the-century fiction.

Let us look, then, at some of these testaments to women's lives. Jewett's short fiction concentrates almost exclusively on solitary old women, undefeated by pinched situations. Upholding simple rural values, these characters also display lively independence. In "The Flight of Betsey Lane," a 69-year-old inmate of a poorhouse takes an unprecedented trip alone to the Philadelphia Centennial. Although her daily life is limited and impoverished, her imagination is not. Touring the vast Exhibition, "this plain old body . . . rarely found anything rich and splendid enough to surprise her." She speaks to and delights strangers, squanders her small savings on presents for elderly friends, and comforts herself in realizing she is not too old to have a remarkable experience.

The Country of Pointed Firs is Jewett's most sustained treatment of energetic women who are dignified and secure in their old age. The central character, Mrs. Todd, an elderly "land-lady, herb-gatherer, and rustic philosopher," is also an expert healer. Her 86-year-old mother, Mrs. Blackett, lives a rigorous life on a desolate island off Maine where she treasures rare visits from a network of supportive women. This capable, healthy matriarch is respected by all in the outlying areas. She even heads the procession at an annual holiday. But her most important role is within a community of women. Jewett's novel brings to life the benefits (sharing activities, making visits, recalling experiences) of a supportive feminine network.

Aging women in Freeman rarely have such sympathy and support. In asserting strong, unconventional personalities, Freeman's older females encounter pity, scorn, and even ostracism from the larger community. Rebels, Freeman's heroines fight their battles essentially alone. "A Mistaken Charity" is one of many stories showing old women triumphing over ageism. In it, a pair of frail, elderly sisters escape from an Old Ladies' Home, where others assume the two belong. But in their own ramshackle cottage, preparing modest meals and gaining strength from each other, these two take a stand. They choose a way of life they believe best for themselves. Freeman's women do not easily allow others to dictate their behavior.

In Freeman's "A Poetess," an aged woman is not as able to overcome small-town pressure. When her one meager talent—writing maudlin occasional verse—is called a silly waste of time by community leaders, this old woman takes to her deathbed. She has too long sacrificed her physical needs for impracticalities (nurturing a flower bed and pet canary take precedence over growing enough vegetables for sustenance). But the reader realizes that the structure of this old woman's life is her best poem. Freeman depicts the virtue of following one's lights, even when such action leads to a solitary, tragic end.

Freeman's most celebrated story, "A New England Nun," shows another steadfast woman whose seemingly heedless action stuns the community. Because she has "almost the enthusiasm of an artist over the mere order and cleanliness of her solitary home," she chooses spinsterhood over a marriage in which her fastidiousness would be neither understood nor valued. Throbbing in "genuine triumph at the sight of the window-panes which she had polished until they shone like jewels," she rejects a "coarse masculine presence in the midst of all this delicate harmony." While many non-feminists of the nineteenth century and our own pity this "nun" for what they see as her rejection of life, Freeman does not. The reader, instead, is offered a clear, memorable portrait of a middle aged woman whose temperament makes her unsuited for matrimony.

Willa Cather's women do not have opportunities for such acts of independence. Usually immigrants to the Western frontier, these aging females, while supporting families, must deal with displacement, loneliness, and poverty. Yet Cather's characters exhibit emotional and physical strength, often responding to the prairie landscape in restorative ways. They keep the homestead solvent— in the face of hardships that defeat males—and then face the future revitalized.

In her early novels, Cather follows her heroines into their productive middle years. The aging protagonist of *O Pioneers!* becomes one of Nebraska's most successful farmers and land owners. At the end of *My Antonia*, Cather praises her favorite heroine, a mother of eleven, because "she still had that something which fires the imagination, could still stop one's breath for a moment by a look or gesture that somehow revealed the meaning in common things." Her actions show "the goodness of planting and tending and harvesting at last."

Cather also includes many older immigrant women who find ways to nurture the seemingly unproductive soil and who serve as models for the following generation of women. Characters like old Mrs. Lee in *O Pioneers!* and Mrs. Kohler in *The Song of the Lark* are energetic, life-affirming, confident. Rather than try to conquer the wilderness, they embrace it by planting gardens and orchards. These women have energy, the ability to guide others, and a spirit of adventure.

In "Old Mrs. Harris" and "The Old Beauty," novellas written twenty years after her first work, Cather focuses solely on elderly women. The world-weariness and empty lives of these grievously ill characters initially shock us. Seemingly defeated, passive, and out of touch with modern ways, Cather's heroines see the "gravity . . . of human destiny," respond to the grandeur of nature, and remain steadfast unto death.

None of these authors covers the sum of women's lives—her ages—as thoroughly, as convincingly as does Ellen Glasgow. Early in her career (when she concentrates on young men's struggles), she tends to present older females as weak, minor figures: brow-beaten mothers, ostracized fallen women, eccentric spinsters. As her skills as a novelist ripen, however, Glasgow turns more to aging women as major characters. And she gives them dozens of believable roles. At Glasgow's mid-career, she writes of women protagonists who gain control of their lives as their years advance. By the conclusions of *Life and Gabriella* and *Barren Ground*, Glasgow's aging heroines have undergone painful but constructive self-scrutiny and have carved out—on their own—successful professions.

Glasgow's characters are the most modern and complicated we have discussed. That they establish independent lives and hold to clearly defined identities— both in their small Southern towns and in New York City—affirms their powers. These heroines do not merely endure difficulties, they enjoy the rewards of their labors.

One of Glasgow's final depictions of an old woman is Victoria Littlepage, co-protagonist of *They Stoop to Folly.* Approaching 60 when the novel begins, she has been the perfect Southern wife and mother: self-effacing, polite, devoted to worthy causes. As Victoria recognizes her impending death, however, she—like Cather's elderly heroines—takes stock. She dwells on matters which outweigh the petty or even jolting concerns of daily life. For the first time in her life, this old Southern belle becomes introspective. In her musings, she realizes that during her marriage she always held back "some inviolable sanctity of the spirit." As she sits at the head of her family table, she knows that "time, like a shallow stream, flowed on without her," that she is "scarcely more than a ripple in the current of being."

Glasgow almost parallels Virginia Woolf in this attention to feminine stream-of-consciousness. Before her death, Victoria becomes truly wise, self-analytical, and generous to the various women around her. In her picture of aging women, Glasgow shows a growing understanding of their concerns and an increased ability to present them as distinct individuals.

In contrast to today's fiction, that of Jewett, Freeman, Cather, and Glasgow would seem to provide older women with options other than the accepted, stereotyped ones. These writers teach us that what is a natural, inevitable process can also be a valuable one. Their important legacy to modern women is a vision of a graceful, productive old age.

BARBARA HORN

LOVING LEO   *SANDRA SCOFIELD*

Age is a desert of time…one has ample time
to face everything one has had, been, done;
gather them all in. We have time to make
them truly ours.
Florida Scott Maxwell
The Measure of My Days

Mrs. Boll built her house on Porter Street in 1953. It was at that time the last house on the street, only blocks from the city limits. She already owned and lived in a one-bedroom stucco bungalow at the opposite end of town on an unpaved street that flooded every spring. There had seldom been a season she had lived alone. In 1953 she was housing her daughter Laura and granddaughter Lucy, Laura's husband Charlie, and their daughter Faith, who had none of her mother's features whatsoever. Mrs. Boll would have been satisfied with the house she had—she had fine neighbors on the right, and an open field on the left, with wild berries and mint—but she built a new one to make a better life for her family. She had thought three grown and married children would not depend on her for much of anything anymore, but she had been proved wrong too many times to count.

Mrs. Boll and her granddaughter Lucy went to watch the house's progress on a long series of consecutive Saturdays. They planted rose bushes that had been shipped from Jackson & Perkins in Oregon, a sycamore for shade, two apricot trees, and a pecan tree later on. Mrs. Boll's parents and grandparents had been farmers (wheat, pigs, and the miscellany of self-sustenance in harder times) and had always had such trees, though never roses.

Mrs. Boll bought the house (plan and construction) at a discount, and one cost to her of the bargain was that she could make no changes. The house was a little over nine hundred square feet with two small bedrooms. She had hoped for a long sleeping porch in the back, because she knew there would always be family there in good months (if not in bad), but the contractor told her she would have to take care of it later. This she never did; there were always other matters, greater needs. Her children and their children, her brothers and their wives, her oldest daughter's husband when he could not avoid it (or when he could not himself provide), all managed, on camp cots, the three twin beds in the larger bedroom, an extra mattress that was stored against the wall behind her bed when not in use; all made do and never tempered their visits with concerns about space.

On an early summer day Mrs. Boll goes outside to pick apricots. It is her lifelong habit, kindled by spring, to scan the sky, one hand shading her eyes. Beyond her to the south the city sprawls with miles of houses, a shopping center, drive-throughs for movies or food. The sky is a clean bleached blue, the blue of a Panhandle summer.

There is so much fruit at once. The branches bow toward the ground. They are golden, sweet this year, and bigger than she remembered. She barely touches them and they drop into her upturned hat. She empties the hat into a basket and fills it again. Her idle day is suddenly full; she will pit and freeze, make jam and syrup, stew a bowlful for her dinner tonight. In twenty years, there have been only a few seasons when the apricots failed her. Once it was bugs, another time a drenching spring. It is the nuts that have been unreliable; some years the meat was dry and bitter inside, and there were others when the clinging hulls lost their grip in high wind.

The year the house was built, Lucy was with Mrs. Boll all the time Mrs. Boll wasn't at the mill. Lucy was a quiet, dreamy nine-year-old who liked to read and to follow Mrs. Boll into the garden behind the old house. Mrs. Boll thought a child needed more than silent companionship, so she often talked of family, especially her beloved grandparents. They had been kind German immigrants who never raised a voice, let alone a switch—Mrs. Boll's mother was inclined toward willow branches—and sometimes Mrs. Boll would get lost in reverie. Lucy stood nearby with her bonnet upside down, collecting the beans or okra her grandmother picked with her fingers while her heart wafted away. Mrs. Boll told Lucy how her grandfather wouldn't let any of the children kill a bird. He said that farmers know birds look after the land. He taught her to fish, in the quiet cool hours of night or early morning, and he taught her songs in German, away from her mother who forbade her to speak a word of the old tongue. It was her grandmother who braided her hair and taught her to make bread—Mrs. Boll's mother had been widowed young and was slow to venture out again—and it was her grandmother who taught her the sweetness of love between the young and old. Solemn Lucy took it in and touched her grandmother often, especially on the soft flesh of the upper arm and along the jaw where it came up under the earlobes. Mrs. Boll was a skinny woman until she was past sixty, but she had that German dapple of cushion in odd places, like fat stored for hard winters.

Mrs. Boll has more to do this day than apricots. She knows she must try to make up her mind about her life.

She never thought there'd be another man, but Leo Clark has worn her down.

She has told him she'll think about his proposal, not because it isn't fair to put him off, but because she doesn't know what she truly feels. He says he'll call every few days, to see how he's doing. His smart-alecky confidence makes her mouth twitch, where once it was annoying. He has been talking marriage for half a year, since he left the rest home where Mrs. Boll works, part-time, when they need her. He was recovering from glaucoma surgery that had not gone well. He wrote her a note in a wild hand, *I can't keep my eyes off you*. The silly old coot. "What a silly thing to say, Mr. Clark," she said; her voice was high and reedy. "I know you can hardly see at all!" He said, "I can see the girl under your belly fat." She was so angry, so humiliated, she wouldn't go in his room for days. It was awkward, getting what he needed to him, with the lazy help she had. He was sweet as sugar when she finally went into his room with her lips pressed tight. "We're not too old, Greta," he dared to say.

It is a very long time since Mrs. Boll has talked about the past. Lucy calls from Seattle on a whim to ask some small detail that troubles her. "Remember that time we lived with you and then moved out?" she says. "And there was this quarrel, and Daddy pushed you off the running board, backing out?" Mrs. Boll's breath turns leaden in her chest. "What was it made everyone so angry?" Lucy wants to know. Mrs. Boll doesn't remember, and says so. She doesn't say she doesn't care for Lucy's asking; she lets her silence take care of that. Another time Lucy calls to ask if it was true, as she remembered it, that her great-grandmother always made three pies on Sundays? Mrs. Boll can reply to that. It wasn't three pies, but three *kinds* of pies. One was always custard for Daddy Luke whose farm it was. One was apple, or some other fruit in season, and one was lemon with a frothy meringue. They told the story a hundred times about the time they all went to the farm for dinner and Lucy ran straight to the counter to check the pies. She lifted the soft worn feedsack towels that lay across the pastries. "Custard!" she called out; it was this caught their attention. Then, "apple!" The grownups turned back to their talk and left the children to one another. Lucy wailed. "No lemon! What did we come over for?" Mrs. Boll knows, when Lucy calls, that Lucy wants to hear the story again. But Lucy calls long-distance. She hasn't been to Texas in over two years. Stories are for telling over stringing beans or kneading bread; stories aren't for blessing absence from one's home.

Now, at sixty-five, Mrs. Boll sees the past more firmly, with a clearer eye, and in it, unchanging, her scattered and lost menfolk, ungrateful children, and at work and large, despots, bumblers, liars and thieves. She remembers the names of those long dead, some the others have all forgotten, and those that knock against her skull, desperate to be named. She remembers catastrophes and plays them late at night, watching Johnny Carson with the sound down low: tornadoes like the one that laid her husband Ira's head against a silo, or a later one that wrapped a pickup around a pole like putty; all the early deaths; the flood that took the Red River bridge out and two buggies full of churchfolk with it. She has built her memory on a scaffold of regrets. She no longer mourns the loss of unreliable men; grief is for her abandoned painting and the roses she had to leave at the other house, for not seeing Laura's madness for what it was.

She wonders if she and Leo would ever speak of death, being the same age. She feels sure she would lose too much in marriage. She needs her privacy and the company of ghosts. Leo would use the soap bar and leave it gummy. He would stumble, getting used to a crowded house, and knock the pictures haywire on the wall.

Mrs. Boll's daughter Opal wants her to move to Lubbock. Opal is still reeling from her divorce. She wants the company, and Mrs. Boll's small income wouldn't hurt, either. Mrs. Boll tells Opal she can come to her, the way she did when she came home from Florida with a fourteen-month-old baby and said her husband was a devil. Opal expects her mother to understand that Opal's life is in Lubbock. As if Mrs. Boll's life is lint in the wind.

The house is paid for now. Nobody seems to understand what that means to her. Paid for, and taxes forgiven for age and low income. She can't be put out. You would think Opal would remember what it was like after her Papa died. They lived in an old settlers' cabin on the farm of Mrs. Boll's parents. Like itinerant pickers or tenants. Like white trash.

Mrs. Boll's mother remembered about the pies. She said, "She really loved her lemon pie, didn't she?" Her soft, floury face was plumped by remembering. "Where is she?" she asked. She meant Laura. She thought Opal and Laura were girls. She had lost twenty-five years in a clutch of blocked blood. She died in Mrs. Boll's house, waking in the early morning to mew like a kitten, then curling like a baby back toward God, who begins things, and ends them. Mrs. Boll's mother was a harsh woman, badly treated by fate and abandoned, after her first stroke, by Mrs. Boll's stepfather, who went to live with *his* daughter. He sold the farm and stole it all. Mrs. Boll's mother was like a baby. Mrs. Boll forgave her everything and took her in. For almost two years, she was her mother's whole life. And in this house.

Leo always has something to show her. Once he gave her a rock he had polished for days on his pajama sleeve, and then a photograph of himself as a boy in overalls. She saw how his hand, quiet on his thigh, caressed. He admitted that he could not really see the features of her face. He said it was something in her stoop that smote him, that her shoulders sloped like a girl's, poised for touch. He'd been a farmer too, but he'd always read.

Before, only Ira had called her "sweet." Ira had called her "twig," and "my lovely," phrases their families would have never thought could pass between them. He had plucked her from her hard girl's life and made her tender. Then he died.

She washes the apricots one by one. It is a luxury of old age to have no hurry. It isn't being done, but doing, that matters; who says an old woman won't drop dead with her spoon in her soup?

Whenever anyone comes, they take jars away with them, but they take apricots for granted, and her time. Once she found a jar of jam, crusted by half an inch of mold, in Opal's refrigerator. The waste made her feel sick. Opal has forgotten all the years they lived like beggars. She needs two closets for her clothes. She wants Mrs. Boll to live in a trailer in back of her house, if she won't just live inside. Mrs. Boll says she won't leave her roses and her fruit. Already she wonders who will care, when she is dead.

Leo says she'll have more income married to him. She'll get her own check from Social Security, only more, on his record. He sold his farm early, then sold hardware, and made more than she ever did. He doesn't understand how this wounds her. She has worked fifty years, on farms, in railroad cars as cook, packing flour in a mill, and lately as an old lady looking after folks in worse shape than she for now. She wants what she has earned; she'd never let it disappear like smoke, to get a better deal.

Leo says he'll put a trailer on his lake lot and she can fish to her heart's content. He is divorced. He says his wife took everyone with her, two generations of kin, all blaming him for wanting a little chance at life before he died. He says he'll teach her to like football and he'll listen to her soaps. Already he's started, turning on "As the World Turns," just to show his intentions. "Look at that," he says. He is legally quite blind.

None of these things matter. What matters is what they have become inside her. Vanity and discontent. Her heart has been diminished by so much loss, it isn't heart that rises to his song. It's something wilder, young, long ago given up for dead. It has a cloak of laughter, an apron of shame. It's this that wears her down.

She imagines lying awake in her bed in the dark and listening to Leo moving around. She imagines herself thinking, *it's my house, he ought to go to bed.* He will annoy her, and want things changed. He will think he has something to show her, because he is a man.

Dozens of washed apricots lie on towels on the cabinets. Mrs. Boll scoops up the last handful from her basket. Suddenly she fears she is going to be dizzy. She goes in to sit on her couch, hardly aware that she still carries the apricots in her hands. As soon as she sits down she knows there is nothing wrong, nothing at all, except that she is getting old. After all these decades on her feet, her legs are crisscrossed by heavy mottled veins. It is hard to remember that she once played basketball on a team that went all the way to state.

She drops the apricots into the space her sitting makes. On one she finds a brown spot. She looks at it more closely. The mark is only a discoloration and not a bruise. She decides to eat it. All morning she has moved in a cloud of fragrance, and not eaten even one.

The apricot, opened by her teeth, exudes a warm sweet odor. She saves the dark spot until last and eats it deliberately, thinking there is some slight difference in texture, a kind of brownness, after all. She eats the flesh of the fruit and drops the pit into her lap, onto the mounds of apricots in the apron cupped between her spread thighs.

There is nothing to compare to the sweetness of apricots, nothing to stir her like that sweetness, their fur and pulp, the way they have come, year after year.

SANDRA SCOFIELD

i.

This morning I went out to work in my garden. I thought I'd put in more glads or maybe tulips. I don't know. Something with color and a little excitement. The daisies are taking over. Not that I mind a daisy. I come out in the morning without my glasses on, and I feel like I'm looking at a bush of fried eggs. But too much is too much. And they don't even smell good. If I'm going to be blind, I may as well see a little fire. So I bend over and grab one of those plants expecting it to come right out. I'd even soaked the ground beforehand. I pull and pull. I pull until I could have dragged the whole Empire State Building up by the roots, but the damned thing won't let go.

Then Gina calls. She heard on the evening news that some old woman over on Cypress Street was beaten to death. Whoever it was broke into her house late at night. There was silver and jewelry missing.

"Mama," Gina says, "I won't stand for it. I won't have you living someplace where you fear for your life."

"My life isn't much to fear for," I say, but the statement is lost on her.

Then she begins to talk about Johnnie. The kids in the neighborhood don't want to play with him, and he's having trouble in arithmetic. Yesterday he came home crying, and, when Gina asked him what was wrong, he said that his teacher didn't love him. "Of course she loves you," Gina told him. No, the teacher probably doesn't, I think to myself. And I feel ashamed because I know I have never liked the kid. Johnnie is too much like his father.

Then Gina returns to her theme. "Mama," she pleads, "why don't you come and live with us?"

Maybe I will, I think to myself, but it won't be for the reason you think. I may be nearly blind, but I know there are sharks cruising in these waters. But the sharks don't scare me that much any more. No. It is the house itself. I need to cast off the shell of this house.

Ernie would be outraged, but Ernie no longer lives here. He worked on this place the way some people climb a mountain. "Just wait 'til I strip those moldings," he'd say. He'd bring home samples of tile and paint chips from Sherwin Williams that he'd fan out on the table like a poker player laying down a full house. I'd be in some other room, and he'd rush in waving a paint chip. "What do you think of this pink," he'd say, "for the upstairs bathroom?"

"Sure," I'd reply, "it looks good."

Even after Ernie got cancer, he asked me to bring the Sears Roebuck catalogue to the hospital. When he wasn't in too much pain, he'd sit there thumbing through the home improvement section. I brought his things home after he died, and I found that he'd marked the catalogue with pieces of kleenex. He must have had toilets on his mind. He'd circled three of those new sleek models. You know the kind. They look like you could take them out for a drive.

This afternoon Max shows up with a real estate woman. She comes in with her talons out—a shiny red that matches her jacket and the red of her lips. She is dressed in red, white, and blue. And she waves her little banner in front of Max as he marches her through the rooms.

She is decked out, but she's hungry. Otherwise, she wouldn't look at this place. But Max is starry-eyed as usual. He never was any good at distinguishing the minnows from the pan fish.

They sit on the sofa—she with her binder of carbon listings and Max dressed in his three-piece suit with the Countess Mara tie. Ever the bigshot. And I bet he and Gina are two months behind on their light bill. I fix them coffee and pull out a Sarah Lee cheesecake. And they sit there discussing whether it would be better to fix the house up before listing it.

"I'm of the opinion, Mr. Pavese," she says, "that it's better to fix a piece of property up before putting it on the market. Of course you don't want to do things that don't show. Don't rewire the place or put in new plumbing. But a little paint and carpet will bring you two or three times as much as you invested." She bends toward him, and the enameled white anchor pinned to her red jacket flashes in the light. "A few thousand would do wonders with this place."

She might just as well have said a few million. But Max nods and smiles as though he could pull out his checkbook at that moment.

And, if you ask me, he isn't the only one who is bluffing. Miss Campbell's teeth are bad, and the white enamel anchor she wears pinned to her red jacket is chipped. It's a leaky boat, Max. Why can't you see that?

ii.

This morning I was again tempted by gladiolas—tall green stalks with bursts of flame on either side.

And I thought of Ernie and his tomatoes. He would rush into the kitchen with three or four on his arm next to his body like he was carrying a baby. "Look at the *pommodori*."

Every year he seemed to grow more. I gave tomatoes to all the neighbors. I put them up in jars. I made tomato sauce and tomato chutney. I fried them and chopped them. Still every summer they piled up on the windowsill. They seemed to multiply overnight.

"Ernie," I'd say, "what am I going to do with all these tomatoes?" But he never seemed to hear.

"Look, look at the *pommodori*," he'd say bursting into the kitchen year after year. "They're bigger than last year, don't you think? And this year they set on earlier."

I don't grow tomatoes. For a year or two after Ernie died, I put in a couple of plants. But they never seemed to do very well.

I cared about food once, but these days there is little that tempts me. Some milk and cereal, a chicken pie, a banana—that's enough for me.

What I want now is flowers—gladiolas, tulips, roses. I want to step out on my back porch and see their colors blaze against the fence.

Gina calls to tell me that Max and the real estate woman will come by again this afternoon. She has another story of an old woman who has been robbed and beaten to death. I listen and then say that I'm going to go visit with Father Lombardi. I hadn't planned to, but the idea is as good as any other.

When I am pawing through my underwear drawer, I come across that watch they gave to Ernie when he retired from Washington Elementary. "To Ernesto Pavese," it is inscribed, "with loving thanks from faculty and staff on the date of his retirement, June 3, 1970." I pull it out of the box where it has been padded with two squares of cotton wool. I twist the stem between thumb and forefinger. My joints are swollen, and my thumbnail is thick with little ridges running its length. I can't hear the watch ticking, but I know it must be because the second hand is moving.

The pale face, circled by gold, stares complacently up from my palm. The reliability of its little cogs and gears enrages me. I raise my arm and fling the watch against the wall. When I pick it up, the crystal is shattered, but the second hand is still moving. Just like Ernie, I think. Always steady. Always responsible. Never a doubt. I was the one who lay on my half of the bed having bad dreams.

Father Lombardi is turning into a tortoise. His shoulders become more hunched each year, and he carries his head bent forward as though it were an intolerable burden ducking out from beneath his shell. He is nearly bald, and his features are angular. When he speaks, I sometimes forget to hear the words, and I see him swimming behind aquarium glass, his jaw snapping at prey.

The housekeeper brings us toasted scones and tea. Father Lombardi has moved the riffraff into the church basement, and even in the rectory kitchen you can hear the heavy beat of the music they play. The electric heartbeat throbs in the floorboards. "Do you really think it's doing any good to have them down there?" I ask.

Father Lombardi retreats into his sanctity. His face has the pallor of a saint.

His hands are oily with good works. "They're all God's children, Maria."

I take a scone. They are heavy and sweet and dotted with currants. They've been buttered and toasted in the oven so that they're a bit crisp and the butter has sunk in. My foot vibrates with the beat below. "Maybe they're not God's children," I say. "When the shepherd invites the wolves into the flock, the sheep had better look out."

"Maria." I can tell by the way his jaw goes slack that he is genuinely shocked. "Maria, I don't know what's come over you."

I look down at the table and then eat the rest of my scone in silence. What's come over me? Could he understand I am only being myself?

I glance across the table at Father Lombardi. Once again, he is in the aquarium. Only this time he is struggling. His belly is exposed, and his small feet claw at the glass as though he senses there is another element beyond his watery world. "You know, Maria," he says, "old age is not the time to be self-indulgent. Quite the opposite, in fact. It is a time to be on our guard against new vices."

"And the lilies of the field," I ask. "Were they on guard?"

Father Lombardi's jaw snaps. "And you," he says, "you call yourself a lily of the field?"

When I leave, I go down the back stairs. The basement door is open, and I can see them in there. The room is filled with smoke, and the music is blasting. Before, they were standing around on the corner. Now they stand around in the church basement. They don't think. They feed and wait to strike. Father Lombardi has let the sharks into the church basement, and pretty soon they'll be nipping at his heels up there in the rectory. And even if he knocks out their teeth, it won't bother them. They'll just grow another set.

After I have been home for several hours, Max and the real estate woman stop by again. Today they are through impressing each other. They're working together. And she has given up red, white, and blue and is dressed in flaming pink. When she sits down and crosses her legs, you can see the bony knobs of her knees. All knuckle and bone and ambition.

Max has a bag of doughnut holes. "Now let's just sit down and have some coffee and talk," he says.

The Flamingo hops up from the couch. "If you'd like, I could make the coffee, Mrs. Pavese."

But I shoo her away. I go to the dining room cabinet and take out my china cups and put on a pot of coffee. Then I go to the backyard to cut some daisies. The afternoon sunlight is on the daisy bush, and it seems to glow from within. I bend down and thrust my face forward and breathe deeply. Even their acrid odor pleases me.

I bring out the cups and saucers and flowers on a tray. Max beams as he rushes toward me. "Ah, she's going to cooperate," his smile seems to say.

But, if I cooperate, it won't be because Max or Gina wants me to. And it may not even be because I want to. I want less and less.

The Flamingo loves doughnut holes. She tries to go at them slow and in a lady-like fashion, but she's hollow inside, or maybe she hasn't eaten for months. Her intestines are plastic tubing.

"Now, Mama," Max says when he feels the proper moment has arrived, "let's talk about selling this house. I know you're attached, but you're in too much danger."

"Who says I'm attached, Max?"

He gives the Flamingo his you-see-what-I-mean glance. Silence descends. The Flamingo dives for another doughnut hole.

Will the mystery guest sign in please? Enter Father Lombardi. They twisted him by his conscience. I can tell the moment he walks in. He blushes when he looks at me, and he doesn't wait for the cue before he begins his lines. "Max and Gina are concerned about you, Maria. They feel you're not safe here. They want you to move in with them. If you can't bear to sell the house, you could rent it for a while."

"*Et tu, Brute.*"

Father Lombardi looks down at his cup.

"Mama," Max says, "what's wrong with you? You used to be so reasonable."

"Mrs. Pavese," the Flamingo says, "your son and I have talked this matter over. Even as it is, I might be able to get fifty thousand. You could buy T-Bills. With the high interest, you wouldn't be losing much. In fact, you might be the winner. Property values aren't appreciating in this neighborhood. As you probably know, they haven't done so for years."

"I wouldn't trust my money to a flamingo. As far as I can see, flamingos aren't good for much besides standing on one leg."

It's Max's turn to blush.

"Maria," Father Lombardi says, "what's come over you? You've got a son and daughter-in-law who are trying to protect you. They're worried about you."

After they leave, I take a cup of coffee and go sit on the back porch. In the late afternoon sun, the daisy bush is a blur of green and white against the fence. Yes, I think, I will have gladiolas and red and purple tulips and narcissus with little yellow noses in the middle of their faces and daffodils on slender green stems. And along the walk I'll plant row after row of chrysanthemums.

BETTY COON

Louise Mattlage, 1985

GETTING THERE   *LOUISE MATTLAGE*

So I'll be eighty. Eighty! Great heavens, I've passed four score and ten. I'm old. Old? I've known younger women who were only forty and older than I was when I was at fifty. Fifty? Who's talking about fifty? That's youth. That's at the very crest of success. No, not the crest, for that would indicate the subsiding, the demise. Fifty is simply young. It has health. Beauty. A rich background of talents, and the means to express them. Fifty is strong. Fifty is the end of the burdens of retarded childhood, one's own and one's children's. It is freedom from menstruation. It is being richer than Croesus because it is full of life, it is full of power. It is being totally alive and having plenty of time to be alive.

But eighty? Holy smoke! This is DEAD! Or supposed to be. This is the end, or supposed to be. This is not rich, it is dying. This is not time to make new friends, it is time to settle in warm and cozy by the fires of remembrance. Time to enjoy one's children (and theirs) who have wandered off into a world too big to travel, too far away to communicate without artificial methods clutched to the ear. Isn't this what the phone is FOR, the ads ask? Well I'll tell you what a phone is for. It's for not looking someone in the eyeball and saying I love you. It is talking over air waves or wires or little bleeps saying a lot of shit that doesn't carry any weight beyond dates and figures. A telephone is for poorly disguised falsehoods. A telephone doesn't carry any weight and is boring. It has no body. It has no warmth. Never mind the telephone.

So I'll be eighty. Eighty! Mercy me. (That's the way I'm supposed to talk, I think, and quaver a little when I say it.) Well — at sixty one worries. Age is creeping up. One thinks about it, rather like thirty. At sixty one is taught to be careful. Look at all the men who have dropped by the wayside at sixty! One is advised to watch out. Get biannual physical exams. Take care, take vitamins. Look at all the women who are so fat they can hardly waddle to the next meal. Look at their sallow skin, their atrophied muscles. Who? Me? Am I talking about me? Nice little me?

Well, no.

But yes, I am talking about me at sixty. At this ripe age I was rushing around the world performing, dancing my head off. Giving lectures in schools, universities, giving workshops, having my portrait painted. I was assured. SELF assured. I was not afraid to speak up and say what I believed at sixty. I wallowed in it. (Let me add that at eighty I wallow in it too. With a difference. At least I think it is a difference, in as much as I am a little kinder to older people and a little harsher with the young.) I did T.V. shows (still do), read on radio. You name it. I did it. And loved every minute of it. At eighty I think I have a right, and I do it all still. Of course I may be wrong. Maybe I just ought to be quiet and look dreary and sigh now and then for things past. Like I'm eighty!

But I mustn't leave out seventy. Seventy is bursting with imaginative energy. I started a new career. Tentatively, of course, as I continued to perform. I needed time too, time which is always of the essence. However, now that I am eighty I will soon have my first exhibit of the books I make, design, illustrate, many with my own poetry. These are made for poets all over the world for their heritage-one-of-a-kind museum pieces. So let's go on to eighty and accept it. It's O.K. dear darling people out there. I still make my books and there is never never never enough time to finish one before the idea comes for the next. And besides, now I'm doing DANCES FOR PEACE. And although a precedent has been set for giving up and throwing myself under the hooves of whipped horses rushing about the streets of London, giving up one's life for a Good Cause, I personally would rather dance, rather live.

The obstacles I have to overcome! First and most important I have to tell people how old I am. Never *before* I go to perform, because THEN I'd never get the job ... because I'm OLD. And being old I'm nasty to LOOK at, right? And it reminds people that they too (women mostly) will be old (men get handsome, women get messy and nasty and wrinkled and pitiful.) Then I have to overcome this *numero uno*, and go on to the next which is not only how I look, but the prejudices people have about OLD people *dancing* (and I'm GOOD at it and will be for a little longer). Youth is the thing. And how boring youth gets performing *ad nauseum* the worn clichés of boy meets girl, girl runs away, boy catches girl, all is well and variations of same. To say nothing of the vacuum heads break dancing, or the contemporary dancers staring at me from empty stages in old blue jeans. . . . However, I'm slim. So that helps. I also have a dancer's body so *that* helps. I have small boobs. That's the best part of a dancer's body. I've been blessed with these two little nothings that don't get in my way, and don't flop around. But what about that FACE, I feel them asking when I say I am a dancer . . . Well it's not too bad. I still look out of wide eyes and use Louise-Nevelson eyelashes. I have wrinkles and "mouth" lines and wattles. And my hair is getting quite grey, but that's easy. I bleach it and tint it and who cares. Once I get on stage it's what I have to *say* that's important and good. I've all my teeth, too, and I guess that helps although I must admit eating is last on my list of things not to waste time over. So I eat. But I must add that it is at the bottom of my list of priorities in life. It's my mind I think about, and what goes into it and what comes out of it.

Have I said what eighty has to live for? There is so much. The mystery that awaits us is near. Tomorrow is never there. Now is the most marvelous thing in the world. The future is delicious conjecture. And the absolutely sure, unshakable conviction that life is only a part of being. The continuing certainty that the beyond is full of marvelous surprises. The conviction that whatever is there is what is useable, as I use artist's materials for color and laughter and joy. And it fills me — me, this agnostic atheist, this disbeliever in her dotage, in her old age — with a great longing for its wonder.

How can I tell you that I know this? Know that there is something beyond what is already accepted? Taken for granted? Difficult, but yes, I will try.

When I was less than four I nearly died. I was held, lifted up, embraced by death. But I remember how I returned to my body knowing that it was not time for me to go, and knowing that it, whatever it was, that held me close and dropped sweet tears on my fever ridden body, gave me another chance, another dream, a glimpse into a splendor of a place where I have never been but will surely find when I am ready for it.

Bless you all! I have talked too much. I have work to do, and so little time to do it that I am appalled at all the time I've wasted writing this treatise for this intellectual magazine that probably thinks I'm batty. Well maybe I am! But oh, the joy of it!

Won't you join me at my next birthday party?

LOUISE MATTLAGE

From the moment of my birth, tradition and society forced me to become a patient, loving, kind, feminine, possessed thing. I accepted that role and the fact that the male role was dominant. For years (it seems like thousands) I almost destroyed myself as a person trying to live up to that role, never taking any time for myself even though I continued to grow inwardly where no one could see. Everything I did centered around my home, husband, and sons. Sometimes to relieve my feelings I would write them down. I was a closet writer.

After a "good" marriage of forty-two years, my husband died suddenly after being retired only one year. My life changed completely. I was never prepared to be on my own and be responsible for myself. I thought I needed someone to take care of me. But I soon discovered resources I never knew I had, and through this experience I was evolving again into who I really am. I liked myself more than I ever had.

For one year I kept *very* busy but hurting internally because of the loss of my mate and battling my loneliness, needing male companionship and sensual fulfillment. One morning when the hurt became almost unbearable, with tears streaming, I started to write to my deceased husband. I wrote and wrote, pulling out all of the memories and what I was feeling. I discovered it was great therapy and I am still writing them.

I attended a poetry workshop on the campus of West Virginia University in Morgantown where I live. When I found myself actually in the room where the workshop was held I wondered what on earth I was doing there. I vowed to sit in the corner and just listen. My experience in Maggie Anderson's poetry workshop was earthshaking to say the least and such a tremendous release.

I could write and it was not too bad! It was as if I were born again into another body and for the first time in my life I felt good about being me, a unique, interesting person with some talent of my own. I don't think there are any words to describe that "mountain-top" feeling which continued for about three months. I saw poetry everywhere. I wrote and wrote and wrote about everything. I would awaken early in the morning with phrases, ideas, and whole lines pushing me out of bed to grab a pencil and paper. I wrote on grocery lists, church bulletins, scraps of paper or anything available. All of the feelings held back for sixty-two years were pouring out and it was wonderful and exciting. I didn't feel inferior to others and could converse with people easily for the first time in my life.

I am still learning, growing, and evolving into my real self. I find I am happiest when I am in any kind of a learning experience, be it a classroom, lecture, or just reading or writing. Time passes swiftly and I started late. It is so great to continue to grow. I do not expect to be a great writer and do not write for a living but write in order to live!

I would like to write about the problem of sexuality and the older woman. I am still trying to deal with that and welcome any answers. This poem speaks of these feelings.

HIS PILLOW

Once you cradled the head of a prince
and I rested and rocked in the strength of him.
Red and ripe were his lips
Trembling twin apples
tempted me to taste
and I did
again and again
I consumed.

Now my appetite reaches out
to enfold you into my body
to quench my thirst
and you are empty
A bucket without cool water
once so full
spilling over
Damn! Why did he die?

Woman, past your prime
Why is there still a need?
I should be in my burial box
Why do I feel so young
trapped in this wrinkled vessel?
A seed not fertilized
withering of thirst
among new pregnant orchards
and green growing grass
Still holding soft young dreams
within my barren pod.

BETTY DONLEY HARRIS

THE LIGHT

The light is eating me
and has eaten my Peruvian   letter by letter,
        as it ate the horses   word by word.
        of my childhood.
            It has eaten   By answering strangers,
the spare parts of my soul   by displacing anger,
and the planetshadows
        I used to hide in.   and by good works,
                I feed the sharks.

        It has eaten bone
            and opal.   Not faith and not good works
                but good work only
    It is eating syntax.   casts a shadow.
    It has left me only   How shall I do that? —

            an old woman talking
            in a dark house.

URSULA K. LE GUIN

AT THE PARTY

The women over fifty
are convex from collarbone to crotch,
scarred armor nobly curved.
Their eyes look out from lines
through you, like the eyes of lions.
Unexpectant, unforgiving, calm,
they can eat children.
They eat celery and make smalltalk.
Sometimes when they touch each other's arms
they weep for a moment.

URSULA K. LE GUIN

SOMETHING TO LOOK FORWARD TO

Menopause — word used as an insult:
a menopausal woman, mind or poem
as if not to leak regularly or on the caprice
of the moon, the collision of egg and sperm,
were the curse we first learned to call that blood.

I have twisted myself to praise that bright splash.
When my womb opens its lips on the full
or dark of the moon, that connection
aligns me as it does the sea. I quiver,
a compass needle thrilling with magnetism.

Yet for every celebration there's the time
it starts on a jet with the seatbelt sign on.
Consider the trail of red amoebae
crawling onto hostess's sheets to signal
my body's disregard of calendar, clock.

How often halfway up the side of a mountain,
during a demonstration with the tactical police
force drawn up in tanks between me and a toilet;
during an endless wind machine panel with four males
I the token woman and they with iron bladders,

I have felt that wetness and wanted to strangle
my womb like a mouse. Sometimes it feels cosmic
and sometimes it feels like mud. Yes, I have prayed
to my blood on my knees in toilet stalls
simply to show its rainbow of deliverance.

My friend Penny at twelve being handed a napkin
the size of an ironing board cover, cried out
Do I have to do this from now till I die?
No, said her mother, it stops in middle age.
Good, said Penny, there's something to look forward to.

Today supine, groaning with demon crab claws
gouging my belly, I tell you I will secretly dance
and pour out a cup of wine on the earth
when time stops that leak permanently;
I will burn my last tampons as votive candles.

MARGE PIERCY

THE SEASON OF BITTER ROOT AND SNAKE VENOM

It is the season of bitter root and snake venom,
the season when the children vanish,
returning as adults (their dreams tumbling
out of suitcases they re-pack and take with them,
my home a pit-stop on their way to newer stars),
familiar strangers whose child-faces
they have eaten up whole, small traces of the old lustre
but the children are gone. And it is the season
of the dying parent, strapped to a bed,
shouting obscenities, staring at me with white eyes
when I say "Papa" and he replies, "I don't understand."
The season of the 120° flash, a rock wall
surrounding me with blasts of heat
that coils into a steamroller
and mows me down. Panting I lie in the pit
of this rock valley, my rescuer a witch
of the hidden moon who offers herbs. I open my dry mouth
to sip and chew her bitter root and snake venom.
Slithering into a shady crevice in the rock
I survey the valley, the mountain peak.
I survey and I sip and I chew.
And I learn how to hiss.

PESHA GERTLER

HOW I'LL LIVE THEN

The wave hits and troughs
between the slim rock walls,
carving its channel, ten feet to go.
I try to guess how old I'll be
when the cut's done. Orange
and faded purple starfish slow it.
Their night is water, day is air.
Grip vertical rock and wait.
Everything comes.

Stone's nothing. The soft green flesh
of anemones muscles into it, dies
and leaves the first concave.
Years of water deepen into tide wells.

When I dip my hand, the crabs play dead.
Only crows and gulls on sun-dried kelp
want carrion. Anemones suck any finger
like a nursing rock.

Stay wet and dead, you live.
Some smooth stones know this,
drop inside the pools and won't
be washed on shore. I won't be stone.
I'll be a starfish when this channel's
finally cut, my arms in pinwheels
like some constant joy. Under any hand
I'll feel like beadwork. I'll kiss
a rock hard. I'll let the days
and nights come.

SIBYL JAMES

POEM FOR SAMANTHA AND ME

*i know my upper arms will grow
flabby it's true
of all the women in my family*
                    Nikki Giovanni

Samantha, I hate women with good bones.
The face talks money. Years of it,
a litany of great-greats, mothers
receding in a high-cheekboned mirror.

They won't age like us.
Those bones will hold them up
like tents, that look of webbed silk
stretched on poles.

We can't beat down the Midwest
Catholic Friday nights of macaroni
basted in our skins.
The nose will spread.
The elbows flap and fold
like rhino's knees.

Red nails and diamonds just spell floozy
on the wrong bones. Better to set rubies
in our gold teeth, wing it on a neon grin.

The future's full of skeletons.
I'll love you like your mother then,
we'll weave our own bones
from these roads we've travelled
and let the cornfields tassle in our thighs.

SIBYL JAMES

FELLED SHADOWS

There are shades of light
where sun is moon to you
          is layers of faraway stars.
Widow's pay keeps out no mice
          no winter out cracked glass
no velvet from deep-etched eyes.
Cater-cornered neighbors and
distant relations unlearned
          in the salvation of touch
whisper
          you are too old
          to sit alone
          being fierce
          with your life.
They watch you dive
at the altar of your husband
a starving gull
          tending a bone-ache
          from your god
not knowing the long shadows
cascading down wall and lace
          bear you through
          all the sorrow.

TERRI L. JEWELL

SISTAH FLO

She carried
one daughter
four sons
nine grandchildren
before a stroke
smoothed her clean
as the white lady's sheets
she scrubbed by hand
for thirty years.
She graced the pews
of Gethsemane every Sunday
sang in tongues to Jesus
about catching arthritis
from between the cracks
stretching less than pennies
sewing thread over thread
laying a brutal husband
to fitful final rest.
She loved through
the eye of a needle
and let Jesus soothe her
as she knew he could
even though she
could not hold a note.

TERRI L. JEWELL

THE POWER IN MY MOTHER'S ARMS

My mother stretched dough thin,
thinner, to its splitting edge.
All that certainty gripped her
wrist, while she sieved
bread crumbs through her fingers,
nuts, sugar, apples, lemon rind,
laying down family legends
like seams in a rock; then
she rolled it all up
the sweet length of the dining room table.
Beaten egg glazed the top, and still
aroma to come, cooling and slicing.
I didn't mind her watching me
eat: I'd give back the heat of my
need gladly, fuel to keep the cycle
elemental, if you've watched birds feed
their young.

To every celebration, she matched a flavor,
giving us memory,
giving exile the bite of bitter herbs.
God's word drifted in fragrant soups,
vigor in the wine she made
herself, clear and original.

      My mother's death
changed the alchemy of food.

        Holidays run together now
like ungrooved rivers. I forget
what they are for. I buy bakery goods.
They look dead
under the blue lights.

I don't do anything the way she taught me
but I get fat.
I don't look like her and I don't sound
like her, but I stand like her.

There must be rituals
that sever what harms
our connection to the past and lets us
keep the rest.
If not, let me invent one
from old scents and ceremonies.
Let me fashion prayer from a
piece of dough, roll it out,
cut in the shape of my mother,
plump, soft, flour-dusted,
the way I once played cook with clay.
Let me keep the cold healing properties
of female images,
and heated, their power
to hold fire.
Let me bake her likeness in vessels
made of earth and water.
Let me bless the flames
that turn her skin gold,
her eyes dark as raisins.
Let me bless the long wait at the oven door.
Let me bless the first warm dangerous taste of love.
Let me eat.

FLORENCE WEINBERGER

MY GRANDMOTHER'S HANDS

In the cracked October morning
I watch my hands rim
the edge of the pail.
Numb with the hard tap water
they redden as the sky does.
When did this happen, my hands
become furrowed like an old burr oak,
an after image of yours?

How clearly I see your slow body
thicken into the light
haloed by the hollyhocks
as you etch your way to the coop.
My fledgling hand held tight
in the sinew and bone clutch
of yours.

At five, I cluck to you
like one of the hens
you won't let me touch
for fear I'll become as marked
as you. You speak of yourself
as a coat ready for the junk heap,
and not that Polish daughter
I saw pictured once high on a hay rick,
the men looped around you.
Did you think you could keep
the world from flicking its knife-edged
tongue at me anymore than yourself?

At thirty and alone, I'm world-bitten,
these hands you worked so hard to save
scarred as old barn wood
and dry as the husks of corn
blown by September.
They do what they must do,
as yours did, and I won't mourn
their passing youth.
When do we learn to hate age,
to think of it not as growth,
but as a falling away?
This curse notched in us so tightly
there is no forgiveness
for what is only the self becoming
the self. My hair grays into a mirror
of yours. One day, I will lie down
next to you, my hands
dissolving into your hands.

ELIZABETH WEBER

FALLING, GLORIA LOOKS UP
for G.M.Y.

Decay sets in before death as nerve cells
rot away; sensation becomes a stranger—
Limbs prickle as though the thistle bloomed
inside the skin; the skin itself is numb;
touch reveals little about the texture of the world.
Walking becomes difficult; legs stumble,
feel unattached; she can not find her feet
unless she looks; she steps across the floor
as though wading through mud and becomes
exhausted; she collapses in a chair knowing
there is no way to look normal standing up.
The body is betrayed; time is measured
by loss—she becomes sensitive to sad events;
today she dropped her fork three times
and wept at the sight of food in her lap—
her whole body shivered like poplar leaves;
tears shimmered on her face and ran
down her chin dropping on her breasts,
a strange salt rain. She comes to think
of change as a flower rotting in a vase
with no one to throw it out. Only tenderness,
a visit from grown children who hold her, the touch
of her husband in bed distract her enough
so she can remember why she is still alive.

Conversation becomes an exercise in memory;
"Remember when I could still walk the beach,
the time we found the agate with the dark red
lines that put bars around the sun when I held it
to your eye. Remember when I rode the gray mare
with the face like a sheep and we saw the hawk
dive, his soft body a blur suddenly caught on wings,
feathers arching against the blue. Remember . . . . "
Her children learn to cherish her past
as surely as their futures. Alone they cry
that nothing lasts — life seems as tenuous
as snowflakes melting in the hand, elaborate
patterns breaking down before the eye. Gloria
tells them of a hundred yesterdays that time
has swept away. Alone she struggles to cope
with losing simple skills. The day she can no longer
button her blouse, she cries, resolve melting,
she feels herself slipping away, no frame
of bone strong enough to keep her from falling
to the floor. She lay and looked at the ceiling
seeing the shadows of leaves in the light
from the window as delicate brush paintings
transformed to moving pictures in the wind, the present
moment contained in images as startling as the pain.

GAIL TREMBLAY

COUNTRY HOSPITAL

Row upon row of rooms contain us
we survivors of numerous small deaths:
burns, bones bracketed in steel
breath fractured, blood
falling into confusion with itself.

Henry is next door. He has spent
his seven ages but still his chest
moves air that whispers the
lost sound of trees. The nurse
rustles in with instruments for ears

eyes that record but don't see.
Her stethoscope beeps the life
in our lungs but some hearts are
crazy, dancing like madmen in
her ears. Others the slight

sound of a pinfall. A broken
leg says *Damn* but knew it was
a chance meeting with a stone
too bare, too early for snow.
He'll be back, this Tom, give

it hell again. His blood is caged
and angry, it paces his body's corridors
wanting action. Unspent it boils
over. Millie (we are first names only)
is out of ICU. Her hair forgot

what color it was. It is the stubble
left in the spring field. In front
of the morning window the wisps
are dazzled white as a star. Bare
limbs of the tree behind her

branch out of her head, one with
last leaves falling into winter.
Her hands are blue twigs holding
her face which is the color my eyes
give her, the color of nothing

fading. She faces me knees to
knees, a hall between us. Hers
that once were white, caressed,
are spotted with purple, her
legs show ropes of blood trying

to climb home. Sandy's adolescent
appendix nearly burst but didn't.
She is petulant and feels cheated
not to have felt danger, denied
the thrill of death that brushed

her by, her voice, instead, a
dying light, it makes mothers cry.
We are rooms of hope standing
like ninepins. We want but do not
want to know who stands, who falls.

ARLENE S. JONES

RHEUMATOID ARTHRITIS

for Drs. CLS, CSR
(The Hospital for Special Surgery, NYC)

Parts of my hands, my left
knee, are dust. They were
incinerated in the hospital
dump. Ashes already.

We work together, decide
which bones have expired
their use, talk about them
like old friends now dis-

tanced by their going off.
Now the shoulders' turn: their
sockets once so gleaming
remarkably like giant pearls

in their oyster cases,
the bluebone now bruising
as beachstones with the sea
gone, leeched away. Its

synovial sheath corroded, it
scrapes the pearl metamorphosed
into sponge gone fossil-rigid.
We talk about them as though

they are a raspberry garden
brambled by overgrowth, by
canes which must be thinned
to save the strength of berries,

to fatten the purpling mass,
sweeten juices; as though they
are bittersweet gone beyond
into a neighbor's orchard,

climbing trees, choking apples.
It is easier to lose parts
bit by bit than have the earth
greet you whole, and suddenly.

ARLENE S. JONES

VINTAGE
On Being in the Hospital

I have gone beyond the desire
        for a case of good wine
that you promised, my dear,
        (if I ever get out of here)
disparaging, even insulting
        as I have been, not to your
tastes, but to your value
        of tastes, as you have measured
it, in hard cash. Currency
        outlives us, and endures.

        I am already into the new wine,
listening to the New World
        Symphony. Dvorak was once,
too, new to it all . . .
        Now it is my ears, my eyes
that hunger, more than my
        tongue thirsts, for a country
I have never explored:
        Homesickness and longing

are not currency for any
        endurance—no *place*, not
one inch of earth, one flower
        can promise that it loved me:
Earth's love was always un-
        requited. I have never
explored this new continent
        but I will soon
I will soon.

ARLENE S. JONES

RIGHT ON

Friends die, family moves to California,
And, worst of all, the friend we loved the most
Changes for the worse. She who knew
What we meant almost before we said it,
Now talks only of herself, takes wrong
The little jokes that used to send her off
Into gales of helpless, teary laughter.

But the feathery scales of the Emperor Concerto
Are just as feathery now as, when a child,
We heard them first. Mahler's Ninth means more,
Because if death is like that, with its crystal ending
Pure and precise as a hummingbird's needle tongue,
If death is at all like that, why, right on.

BARBARA MOREHEAD

WAITING TO SORT THINGS OUT

She would sort it all out later when she had time:
God's unsettling jealousy, embarrassments of blood,
the last sight of her little brother alive, but
patterns were as hard to find as in the nailheads
scattered down the wall. Jesus called, but he was
contradictory as her husband (and the Jews, she had heard,
were still waiting). She had her daughter baptized
for the time being, moved her fading quilt top from house
to house to finish piecing, kept everything in boxes
to sort later. To catch up with her decisions, she ran
and ran, one of Picasso's heavy women on the sand.

And if her heart had not stopped—
(Did it seem to her then that she inflated,
a large, light woman, and hung weightless,
saw the salmon glow on the cloud was sunlight
on its soiled edge, saw everything below
pieced and patterned, but couldn't reach?)

They sorted all her things. That was her grief.

REVA LEEMAN
1978, 1985

Though not occasioned
to mirror watching
        I stopped
and saw delightedly
        star streaks, grey lights
moving through my hair.
I was mother-reflection
then, my mother watching me
becoming old as she had not
lived to do.
        I cannot know
what she would have felt
as age came on in silence,
but I dance elated on seeing
touches of silver
        appearing unasked
but earned by living
as widely as I dare.

KATHIAN POULTON

OCTOBER

I know a winter bird rustles
    in the dry leaves
        but I deny it.

I hear only the silence of root
    and stem, of fur
        and feather

after the harried summer of a year's
    increase. The evening
        sets down a cold chill.

I relax in the pouches
    of a baggy sweater and sit
        on a rotting log.

Gray flannel blankness erases
    the rest of the world
        and leaves me comfortable

and free to be old, big, and plain.
    Strangely, in October's cocoon
        I am still twenty-six

in love for the third time, joints
    perfectly meshed, muscles
        trimmed on metered lathes

and taut, all movement synchronized.
    Who says I've changed? Grown old?
        Not I, marooned

in time unmeasured, a soft tangle
    of all my secret selves
        the real night not yet.

Startled by a falling pignut
    I know that summer clings too long.
        It grows dark before I know it.

LOUISE MONFREDO

MIDDLE WOMON

i am a middle womon
life parades past me hoping
but i do not choose
my eyes are sharp
and i never tire of looking
the world is waiting
to hear me declare my name
there have been sounds
but they take no shape
make no music
so i wear ties and shirts
and sit with my legs spread
my mouth is slightly open
i am ready

i am a middle womon
the chords of my voice have stretched
dissonant and sweet
and will no longer be quieted
i have been practicing these years
and can throw my voice across hills of bent trees
it can go farther than i ever imagined
i have been built with those hard woods
weight of my living
bears down against the grain
resting on knots that cause weakness
but add texture and beauty
fierce winds bend and move me
flexing
i am ready

i am a middle womon
half of me has been in the making
the next half lies in the morning just before dawn
i will enjoy this new sculpting
i have more tools for the cutting now
a more steady hand
my stomach has strength
when i swallow evil i can call it back up
there is nothing i have to keep down
i will taste everything
my belly will bear the load
these muscles are hard
i am ready

SHARON MOONEY

IS EVERY KITCHEN SINK UNDER A WINDOW?

washing dinner dishes
in scalding water
i see strong faces
of people i love
flashes
of car lights
on the window
but i who can remember
what they wore
what they said
cannot recall my own look

i find my reflection
and begin to recognize
me
digging for knives
picking at burnt food
getting lost
in stuck spots
i am surprised i like
my image
i look my age

dishes bump
muffled liquid sounds
i reach up
pull my skin lightly
toward my hairline
remembering
when i looked like that
soft textures
no lines not worn
i let go
my flesh falls back
i come home to my time
my place
i am my age

SHARON MOONEY

MI ESTOMAGO (MY BELLY)

Naked and as if in silence
I approach my belly
it has gone on changing like summer
withdrawing from the sea
or like a dress that expands with the hours
My belly
is more than round
because when I sit down
it spreads like a brush fire
then,
I touch it to recall
all the things inside it:
salt and merriment
the fried eggs of winter breakfasts
the milk that strangled me in my youth
the coca-cola that stained my teeth
the nostalgia for the glass of wine
we discovered in *La Isla*
or french fries and olive oil
And as I remember
I feel it growing
and bowing down more and more ceremoniously to the ground
until it caresses my feet, my toes
that never could belong to a princess,

I rejoice
that my belly is as wide as Chepi's old sombrero—
Chepi was my grandmother—
and I pamper it no end
when it complains or has bad dreams
from eating too much.

Midsummer, at seventy years of age,
this Sunday the seventh
my belly is still with me
and proudly goes parading along the shore
some say I am already old and ugly
that my breasts are entangled with my guts
but my belly is here at my side a good companion
and don't say it's made of fat
rather tender morsels of meat toasting in the sun.

MARJORIE AGOSIN
Translated by *Cola Franzen*

DON'T LAUGH, IT'S SERIOUS, SHE SAYS

At 55, I'm trying to meet men.
But though I look my best
(beautiful say some
of my friends) & am spirited
& very interesting (you can
tell this, can't you?)
most men look at me with blank eyes,
no part of them flickering.
At parties they talk around me
as though I weren't there,
choose less attractive
partners to dance or talk with.
Such a puzzle! I try
so hard not to let them know
that I am smarter, more
talented, classier & more
interesting than they. Nicer, too.
I cover this so well
with a friendly smile
& a cheerful word
that they could never tell
I want them to pursue me
so I can reject them.
Bug off, you bastards,
balding middle-aged men with paunches
hanging around women 20 years
younger, who the hell
do you think you are?
You'd better hurry up
and adore me or
it will be too late.

ELLIE MAMBER

From *The Poet's Job: To Go Too Far,* Margaret Honton, ed., 1985

MY STUDENT SAYS SHE IS NOT BEAUTIFUL

Who was it said
you are not beautiful,
to her, and flowers are.
Who was it
created the chart
ranking roses at the top,
all others under,
so that she would say
before us all,
the old men at the home
follow her
down their grey corridors
not because I'm pretty,
I am not,
but because the flowers
are her job.

Who was it told
old women
only youth is lovely,
and flowers,
and someone else
must do the choosing,
so that they too
follow the cart
on legs that barely walk,
as if on it rides
beauty missed or lost,
each one fighting
through the crowd
to clutch her sleeve:
Are they for me?
I know the roses are for me.

JUDITH SORNBERGER

FEBRUARY LETTER

Dear Mother,
my mother-in-law,
bled all January,
her spirits below zero
through the long Dakota winter.
Her son, who stayed
her bleeding once
for a period of months,
has moved south and can't
think how to help her.
The lithium no longer works,
or anti-depressants.
She thinks she should go off
it all, but the doctor's
recommending shock again.

Mother, my own soother,
apothecary of my first blood-
summer, what can a daughter
not of her blood do
when spring will not return
for months, and some things
never do?

You say your own law-mother
tells of hunching over dish water
each night for years, dropping
tears into its dark, not knowing
why. It took losing her uterus
to bring her to the surface,
and she rose clear
as her mother-in-law's crystal
when she dried it, but broken
in a way no one could see,
like the chipped pieces she kept
at the back of the buffet.

Mother, I will never prescribe
loss of any part,
I, who took her son,
her heart, her dearest blood,
I, who have sons to lose
and my own blood running out.
I can only write: *Come visit us.*
The cardinals you loved here
are returning just in time
to show against the last
swatches of snow.

JUDITH SORNBERGER

CAUGHT IN THE ACT

Christ doesn't fool around.
It takes just three dips
of the Easter candle
to make holy water.
My husband tells me
Christ is with us
each time we make love.
I buy a king-size bed.

Our seeds dance out of the wings,
cluster on the womb wall
bathed in infrared spots.
Christ gets the best reviews.
In seventeen years, we have
eleven shows, five hits.
Sitting on the bedpost,
Christ crows.

That's before the doctor
says I can't go on; cancels
my opening nights for good.
My husband's snores
counterpoint my fears
of starving belly, manta
rays and fat blue worms.
I push him on his side.

Dismantlers go about their work—
staunching, stitching, discarding.
Scene of triumph and flop,
no more than pulp. Morphine
comatose, I dream of erections,
walk the railroad tracks, cross
trestles with naked men.
My belly fills with lightning.

I party with four wardmates,
hysterectomy high; get out
in a week. Driving home
I delight in red roofs.
Christ has flown the coop.

LIBBY A. DURBIN

WOMAN IN DIALYSIS:
ENROUTE TO THE CLINIC

As her hips spread,
overlapping the years,
Mabel's legs move
to the outside corners,
accommodating,
like the eyes of flatfish.
She comes charging down
the sidewalk chute
three days a week.
Should she lose momentum
she'll kick up dust
like a bulldogged steer.
In salute, the special
mobility van dips
as she rises on its lift.
"If this was a cattle car,"
she says, "the cows would go
on strike." The seatbelt pinches
her middle; one leg stretched
in the aisle quivers constantly.
She chews nitroglycerine
like it was sen-sen and curses
her dead husband for never
letting her drive.
Handing her pocketbook
to Rose for safekeeping,
Mabel turns one eye on her;
brood hen watching a dog.
She raves on the way back
six hours later, hair flat,
sweaty from the couch. Pill paste
edges her mouth. She knows
her blood is killing her.
Driven hard, the van
rattles like a fire escape.
"My daughters want my money,"
she shouts above the noise,
"but they'll never get it."
She holds out her arm in pledge,
shunt gleaming in the dirty light.

LIBBY A. DURBIN

FOR WE ARE MANY

St. Mark 5:9

Late blooming dahlias brightened the entrance.
Our heels clicked over polished floors
to a cage dispensing information capsules
to visitors of the aging. "An attractive place,"
we said to each other, "the walls are pastel."

Down a hallway by a window our fragile friend
leaned on her cane, looked out on a garden.
"How are you?" "How nice of you to come."
"It has been so long." The amenities
labored against TV amplification.

She apologized, "Many patients do not hear well."
Her own hearing? It remained acute. My room?
No, it is noisy there also. We looked for quiet,
a place to talk: "You must get permission.
I have to have permission."

We sensed small fears creeping, nibbling,
while telling herself that something
she stood for needed to be asserted.
A nurse came, found a corner for our use.
She felt a draft. "Let me find your sweater."

Uprooted from her home with the chrysanthemum garden
this weaver of words and ways had buffed lives and silver
with equal grace in the richness of her days.
Her children were achieving; we listened;
she had followed our small accomplishments.

From the supper tray she tasted the institution soup,
tested the applesauce, ignored the peanut butter sandwich.
"They feed me too much," she whispered, looking weary.
"You do not sleep well?" "No. . . not with the talking."
Certified care was a shawl that covered but did not fit.

Reprinted from *Clouds and Keepings* by Ethel Fortner, Cascade Press, 1973.

We promised to come again. She was left to her own
private obstacle course, to lean on rhythms she had known.
Outside the orange shout of evening was fading to citron,
to dark. Like a haunting of crows in an ancient orchard
incoherent voices followed us home.

ETHEL N. FORTNER

IN NOVEMBER

A seedling survived summer drouth.
One pale pink hollyhock blossom
opened on Thanksgiving Day.
How brave and good, the late blooming.
I give thanks and take the stairs
one at a time, slowly.

ETHEL N. FORTNER

CALLING OUT THE NAMES

Mother, I am older than your picture.
Flanked by my aunts you pose
in dimity, batiste, and your names
repeat like testaments:

> Catherine, Esther, Marguerite
> Grace, Anne, Evangeline

Grandmother reaches out
with missionary eyes.
We never met.
Her mouth, her cheeks are yours,
are Marguerite's, are cousin Phyllis'
whose girls stopped by last summer
wearing your face.

Genesis, Exodus,
I have forgotten the order.
Once I, too, sat
in Grandfather's lap reciting
Leviticus, Numbers, Deuteronomy;
braiding the words like
Sunday school ribbons.

Mother, who would have thought
I could grow older
than your mother. I stare
back down the telescopes
of your eyes as you recede; wind,
rewind through my fingers
your lovely, silken names.

CAROL GORDON

SISTERS

We exhumed ghosts
of our childhood
exorcised them
along with past angers
then laughed
at family legends as we
laid to rest old antagonisms
She was no longer a threat
her beauty lost somewhere
in the two years
since we'd been together
She eighty-two
face a map
of many roads travelled
body bent withered
a dying tree
I seventy-two already
felt the imminent loss
of a sister
finally accepted
who brought me African Violets
to remember
she remembered
I always loved them

SUE SANIEL ELKIND

From: *TO LOVE IS*

iii

To love is
To desire the liberty
Of the one loved

And if I have desired
From my first moments of sentience
When I recognized that I ardently loved the world

The balanced radiance of its good and evil
And wanted to help
Unlock it to become

More and more itself
More and more alive
—What then?

As I grow older the evil seems
Uglier
Denser, more strangely skewed

And myself weaker.
Still I have my original loyalty
My memory

I have my task
What matter if I can
Never accomplish it.

ALICIA OSTRIKER

THE IDEA OF MAKING LOVE

The idea of making love   as sticking your tongue
into the calyx of the other   & licking up
its nectar   while being licked oneself   we
love this   because we are always manufacturing
nectar   and when someone sticks a pointy tongue
into us and takes a drop   on the tongue-tip and
swallows it   we make more nectar   we can always
     make more   of our own nectar and
     are always thirsty for the nectar of others

ALICIA OSTRIKER

NULIAJUK, A SEQUENCE

Old Man of all Oceans
loved Nuliajuk
dragged her under the sea
wrapped himself in her storm-black hair
named her Sea Mother.

with primal yearning
to find mystic roots
my tendrils blindly searching
again I enter the waters.
I seek Nuliajuk
beneath the green glacier

she rests upon
a couch of jade.
empty carapaces one by one
fall from her hair.
into its dark and cloudy coils
drift newborn creatures

from her stitching fingers
medallions crusted with beads
litter the centuries
around her.
no breath of sound disturbs
these unimagined rooms.

above, salt water is shining
sun throws fat noon shadows
vines hang heavy red.
women sing berrypicking songs
in late summer heat.
yet here I wait

rising from her
ancient dream she sings
Come to Nuliajuk, Nuliajuk!
She swaddles me
in a blanket of sea-anemones

MARY TALLMOUNTAIN

THE SILENCE NOW

These days the silence is immense.
It is there deep down, not to be escaped.
The twittering flight of goldfinches,
The three crows cawing in the distance
Only brush the surface of this silence
Full of mourning, the long drawn-out
Tug and sigh of waters never still—
The ocean out there and the inner ocean.

Only animals comfort because they live
In the present and cannot drag us down
Into those caverns of memory full of loss.
They pay no attention to the thunder
Of distant waves. My dog's eager eyes
Watch me as I sit by the window, thinking.

At the bottom of the silence what lies in wait?
Is it love? Is it death? Too early or too late?
What is it I can have that I still want?

My swift response is to what cannot stay,
The dying daffodils, peonies on the way,
Iris just opening, lilac turning brown
In the immense silence where I live alone.

It is the transient that touches me, old,
Those light-shot clouds as the sky clears,
A passing glory can still move to tears,
Moments of pure joy like some fairy gold
Too evanescent to be kept or told.
And the cat's soft footfall on the stair
Keeps me alive, makes Nowhere into Here.
At the bottom of the silence it is she
Who speaks of an eternal Now to me.

MAY SARTON

ALICE AT ONE HUNDRED AND TWO

Yes, she said, I want to live a lot more years
and see what happens, but

I want new fruits—a century of apples, oranges
and bananas is enough.

And I want new rooms. I want balustrades,
inglenooks, casement windows, and chintz!
Yes, I want chintz! Whatever happened to chintz,
with the sunlight or lamplight carving mother,
grandmother, aunt, out of its shadows?

And I want something to happen here, quickly—
the inexplicable death of a wealthy tycoon, six
likely suspects—midnight melodrama, love and
betrayal—a diamond robbery, fugitive in disguise—
a great-grandson eloping with a dancer from New Orleans.
Something!

Yes, she said, I want to live a lot more years,
but not so slowly.

ELIZABETH ALEXANDER

From: THE JOURNALS   *MARGARET RANDALL*

Age. Ageism. In a society rooted in a virtual cult to youth, the nature and circumstance of youth is often grossly distorted. But the nature of age is often invisible....

On the instructions for filling out a grant application, I note that "applicants should be between the ages of 27 and 45, although the Board is empowered to select some applicants below and above that range...." (On many grant applications I have seen, 27 is the cut-off age!) In my class on Third World Women, we deal with the idea of CONFINEMENT. Most of the women in the class link the idea of confinement to prison, poverty, gender oppression, marriage, childrearing, sickness, isolation, physical disability... but one woman, L. (who is about 45), speaks of age as the confinement she most fears. When we speak about it, it doesn't seem to be age itself so much as a kind of uncertainty at *where* her body and her mind stand, or a *contradiction* between her feelings and the image she has of her physical state. She speaks of retaining an "inner sense" of herself at 18 or 28 or 35, and continuing to dress and act and plan as if she were still one of those ages—and then suddenly looking in the mirror and feeling off-center (at best) or betrayed (at worst) by an image that does not coincide with the retained expectation.

I come upon age—as a member of a highly industrialized commodity-oriented society, and as a woman within that society—in different ways. Physically, I slow down, or forget. Fewer options seem open to me than before. Emotionally, my relationships change. As a lover, I look for a different kind of fulfillment than I once did. As a daughter I want to care for my parents rather than expect care from them, and my relationship with my own children is also different: no less loving, but certainly more distant, less immediate, dependent upon a different kind of space. I no longer control them. And I miss them! The dislocation created out of the contradictions between how I feel and look—and WHAT I KNOW—and how society perceives me—physically, socially, economically, emotionally—is a very real element in every day....

For a woman, menopause seems much less adequately dealt with than the onset of menstruation. True, the onset of menstruation is still often sadly shrouded in a lack of basic knowledge, a shame, a mystification. But increasingly there is a literature that speaks not only to the biological process but to the psychic and emotional process as well. This literature is not nearly so broadly available as it should be. But, with time, it will be. Menopause, even for the more conscious woman, still seems a mystery. Something is written of it in its psychological aspect; little seems written of it in other, equally important spheres. I am going through it now, and have found little, if anything, that satisfies me. Everything seems unexpected. One may fight annoyance, or even depression, with some degree of success. But I, for one, am left with a question about the POSITIVE changes, the unknown glory. . . .

Although aging, for me, has always been much more closely and immediately associated with a changing mind, a changing set of values (or values that firm themselves up somehow—*becoming stronger as they at the same time become less rigid*), I can understand how in this way of life we have created for ourselves, THINGS do become palpable "signs" of change. The clothing I wanted as a young woman is no longer important to me. The gadgets only clutter my life. My focus is much more centered. More and more I spend time trying to understand the so many moments or passages I once let pass me by in relative abandon.

Memory has a great deal to do with age, for me. In fact, the two words, memory and age, occupy a space in relation to each other that I never seem totally able to explain. As I grow older my memory changes. It is too easy to say "it gets worse." I forget a great deal, it is true, but I also remember things I was not capable of remembering before. My reasons for remembering have changed as well.

A great deal of what has changed in me, and I find continuing to change, is my relationship to others. Certain relationships are immensely important. And their importance has much less to do with expected ties (parents, children, sisters, brothers) than with affinities—affinities of thought, of value, of vision. Solitude is also more important—and more comfortable—to me. I have learned to be alone inside my skin and it seems to me that it took a very long time for me to learn that the way I know it now. No matter who I am with, no matter what the circumstance, conversation, stage diagram . . . it seems to me now that I am almost always alone. Alone in a way I cherish. As much if not more than I cherish "being with" those I love and need. . . .

Rejection of the absurdities of life is something that comes—to me—much more readily with age. I no longer have any patience for the things I once even cultivated, for reasons I then accepted unquestioningly. It is as if suddenly everything is made of glass, and I can see through objects and words and gestures and expressions in a way I never could before. . . .

Forty-eight is not 65, nor is it 85 or 90 . . . but there are physical changes now as well. One thing Barbara Macdonald mentions in her book *Look Me in the Eye* are "the brown spots of aging." I have them too, all over my arms and legs and chest. The flab, the stoop, the slowing down of certain movements. After having allowed myself to be enticed into coloring my hair back to its original brown over a period of several years—finally I simply said "to hell with always covering that line where it begins to grow out; I will broaden the line, and live with the two-tone consequences, until my hair is entirely my own again!" Now it has grown out to just below my ears, and when I pull it back and up and tuck the ends under with a clasp, I am grey once more!

The lines no longer speak of accepted beauty standards or their lack. They tell me about my own tensions, where and how I have been constrained in my life, where the pain was located, where and how I didn't do anything about that. They are like a wonderful gage or measure, telling me where and how I stopped short in my tracks, and also that I have another chance . . . another opportunity to learn to be who I am. That's a wonderful feeling . . . .

THE GLOVES

for Rhoda Waller

Yes we did "march around somewhere" and yes it was cold,
we shared our gloves because we had a pair between us
and a New York City cop also shared his big gloves
with me—strange,
he was there to keep our order
and he could do that
and I could take that
back then.
We were marching for the Santa Maria, Rhoda,
a Portuguese ship whose crew had mutinied.
They demanded asylum in Goulart's Brazil
and we marched in support of that demand,
in winter, in New York City,
back and forth before the Portuguese Embassy,
Rockefeller Center, 1961.
I gage the date by my first child
—Gregory was born late in 1960—as I gage
so many dates by the first, the second, the third, the fourth,
and I feel his body now, again, close to my breast,
held against cold to our strong steps of dignity.
That was my first public protest, Rhoda,

strange you should retrieve it now
in a letter out of this love of ours
alive these many years.
How many protests since that one, how many
marches and rallies
for greater causes, larger wars, deeper wounds
cleansed or untouched by our rage.
Today a cop would never unbuckle his gloves
and press them around my blue-red hands.
Today a baby held to breast
would be a child of my child, a generation removed.
The world is older and I in it
am older,
burning, slower, with the same passions.
The passions are older and so I am also younger
for knowing them more deeply and moving in them
pregnant with fear and fighting.
The gloves are still there, in the cold,
passing from hand to hand.

MARGARET RANDALL
Albuquerque, March 1985

THOUGHTS ON AGING   *ANN DOMITROVICH*

I remember the first time it occurred to me that time was not always going to be my friend, and that I was getting older. I was 34 and I was leaning over a mirrored table in the ladies room of a restaurant and I noticed that the skin under my chin was not tight. It was loose. That startled me. It wasn't much of a change— just a tiny little bit, but I was very aware that the world had shifted for me, and there was the beginning of fear in that insight.

After that I don't remember thinking much about age at all one way or the other. The 30s are, I think, the best years for a woman. She looks strong and healthy and beautiful with the confidence of that age reflected in her eyes.

My 40th birthday didn't bother me much. I had heard so much about it I was prepared for a jolt but nothing happened. I didn't melt or disappear and I looked exactly the way I had looked the day before. As I recall, it was around 43 that the real fear of aging, and what that meant to me, began. It started to attack in so many ways. Physically I was noticeably not as strong. My flexibility, which was just something I took for granted because I had always had it, began to go. I remember I started to get up from my knees one morning when I was weeding my garden and I felt like an old woman. And I know that I moved and looked like one. God, it seemed as though it took 10 minutes to get to my feet. I couldn't believe that this stiff, creaky old body belonged to me. I also became aware that my body didn't feel like me any more. Arms and legs, once sturdy and firm, now were saggy and flabby. And even if I lost weight (which I considered better than winning the Irish Sweepstakes) I didn't want anybody to hug me or touch me anymore because I didn't want them to feel my body. It had betrayed me. I didn't like the way it felt to me, so I was sure nobody else would either. I was beginning to relate differently to other people because my body had begun to age. The isolation of being an older woman in this society had truly begun for me. The prejudice of our culture was working on me and I was just as prejudiced as anybody else. I feared and hated these outward signs of aging, maybe even more than some other women as I have never had a particularly good image of myself. So the loss of my youth and the protection that gave me left me even more vulnerable than before. One more defense down.

And then there was my face. Oh God, my face. The lines, the wrinkles, the sags and bags. Every few months it got worse. Makeup only accentuated it, and, unlike my body, I could not cover it up. Your face simply cannot be hidden. Your eyes, your smile, your expressions—all right out there for the world to see and react to. And the world began to react to this middle-aged woman. My status as a citizen of this world we all live in began to waver. Women are desired and accepted because they are young. Middle-aged women lose rank fast just because they are not young. They are tolerated if they are bright enough, successful enough, and—this is most important—if they do not *appear* to be middle-aged. A middle-aged woman can still exist with some dignity as long as she belies her existence. If she looks thin enough, pretty enough, young enough, she can still be accepted. As long as she doesn't look like what she naturally is. For all those who have yet to travel that road, it is very frightening because you know the next day can only bring more of the same. And it will be that much harder because nature is taking her course. You can never catch up. Never. But I continued the chase because I didn't know what else to do.

Then there is the issue of sexuality. I have always wanted to have a fulfilling sexual relationship and took it for granted that I always would. But the chances of that diminish as the aging process accelerates. That was very frightening to me: the thought of not relating on a loving, sexual level to another person for the last 20 or so years of my life because nobody would want me. That nobody would let me get close enough to them because I was too old broke my heart. It was devastating. Another area of being cut off, shut out.

So that was my experience with aging in my 40s. I'm almost 52 now. Much of my life has not particularly come together as a whole the way I would have liked. I still do not have the confidence I could have wished for myself and for other women who have reached my age. I am still terribly afraid of the future, still neurotic and insecure and cowardly about many things. But there are a few areas where I have come a long way, and these few areas sustain me for the most part and get me through another long night. One is the fact that just by staying alive in this world I have acquired a certain wisdom and acceptance of life in general. I can look back now and get a glimpse of how people become who they are, and understand a little of how they got that way, and it's ok. It's also ok that there is so much I'll never understand. Life has so many questions and so few answers.

I am grateful that I was born a creative person—an imaginative person—and that I have let that part of me develop, almost unconsciously sometimes, all my life. By their very definition, creativity and imagination are synonymous with childlike, receptive thinking and open emotions. They also imply individuality. I have always liked that part of myself—my own individuality. I always wanted to be the best I could be—never have I wanted to be LIKE someone else (maybe I wished I could be them, but I never wanted to be like them). If, on a scale from 1 to 10, I rate a 3, then I want to be the most original, most unique 3 there is—not a pretender to 10. Even if I could convince the world I was a 10, I would know that "myself" had died, could never be realized and therefore never had any meaning.

Society today says that women should be young to be acceptable. And when we are not young anymore, we should imitate youth for as long as we can and then we should become invisible. I have never doubted that this is wrong for me. I will not lie about my age. And even if I had the money and the opportunity, I would not cosmetically alter my face or my body to look younger.

I will not apologize for my age. I will wear my hair hanging down my back if I want to just because it feels good. I don't worry anymore that some of the clothes I like to wear will be denied me because they are "too young" for me. If I like them and they make me happy and I'm not wearing them to try to appear younger, then I will wear them anyway. I will feel my feelings and think my thoughts and express myself as the sum total of my experience and my years. I will be who I am. And my looks will reflect that.

ANN DOMITROVICH

March 23, 1984

My external behavior in no way matches my moods, the mild, *Do you want lunch now, Ma? How are you feeling today, Ma? Do you want to go to the JCC?* But on the inside I'm dissolving away in anger. I know that her constant presence represents my own fear of aging, my own inability to live up to her selflessness, my own longing to get on with my life at last now that the kids are nearly grown.

* * *

March 25

Get dressed early for your Senior Citizen's party; sit in your chair all morning waiting for Claire to drive you to the JCC. Why are you so helpless, so fragile? Is it you I'm really upset with or something of myself? How sweetly and timidly you'll enter the room. Nowhere to sit; those old big babies all saving places for their friends, their names printed on napkins. No place for you, Ma. You'll have to sit next to that old man you don't like. You don't like menfolks now. Maybe too many years of waiting on them. Sing along with the group, eyes singing, voice still clear. *Oh, Ma, I want to cry.*

* * *

April 5

Ma sunning in the backyard. Why doesn't she come in to help? Everything falls on me. She says she "can't cook" anymore. Maury feels she is afraid to try. Meanwhile, I've got to get all this work done for my classes. She lies there on the chaise lounge as if she's afraid to breathe; the breeze blows through her thin hair showing her scalp. Suddenly she calls me. I jump up from my desk: there's something wrong.

"What's wrong, Ma?" I shout.

"Nothing, Claire darling. I'm just wondering where Mickey the Moocher is."

"You mean our dog? He died last year. Remember, Ma. You were here then visiting for a month before you went back to Florida."

"Oh, I thought he was still living. He had a soul, that good pet. I thought maybe he'd come and lick my hand like he used to."

* * *

April 7

Ma's feet terribly red and raw. She can't put on her shoes today. We've ordered special ones for her. They cost $400. If she knew she'd have a fit, tell us not to buy them. I brought her lunch in her chair. When I can accommodate, when I can be giving, I feel better. A sense of peace comes over me. Why do I keep fighting that? Is Ma somehow mixed up with my own ambivalent feelings about motherhood? When will I learn not to fear another's weaknesses?

* * *

April 8

Watched a TV show on senior citizen's rights with Ma. I've never seen her concentrate so fully on anything since she's arrived. I've learned one thing: I've got to begin my involvement now. A social protester of 60 has her seeds planted much earlier; and a bitter old woman of 70 has *her* seeds planted long before.

* * *

April 10

I'm leaving everyone tonight and going to the city to meet a friend, directed, focused, not allowing family to interfere with her academic work. Maybe I'll learn something from her. Why do I have to be the one to keep her, why can't she go to her daughter? I'm going to tell Maury I've got to have a break this summer.

* * *

April 12

Ma seems listless today.
"How are you, Ma?"
"Not so good. I'm kinda dizzy, but I can't complain. I have my legs, my arms, and I talk and walk. As long as I stay near you and Maury, I'll be all right."
I go into my room and silently rage. How desperately afraid she is that we will put her into a home. She'll never leave here. I will never get a chance to finish my damned degree.

* * *

April 15

By chance I met a young woman in the bookstore who works in a hospice in Oakland. We were browsing the same rack. She told me how she loved her job, that the only time she felt "real," that she felt any emotion, was at work helping the people who came there to die.

"At last there are no pretenses; I have a kind of reward knowing I ease them into their deaths while everyone else wants to keep them alive," she told me.

I finally mentioned Ma. "Try to keep her as long as you can." And then the beautiful strange dark young woman disappeared.

* * *

4 a.m.

I kill someone it is the kindly old queen. I kill her because I don't want to see her feeding her grown son at my breakfast table every morning I cannot find my freedom with her here I will never find my freedom I cut my hands that acted so evil without my will but of their own instead I cut a slice of darkness and wrap it around myself a shawl a cloak my poverty charity chastity I am a beggar woman from here on for the rest of my life I beg in villages only a bowl of milk a crust of bread I keep nothing for myself

* * *

April 19

Ma lying in bed deathly quiet. I come in to straighten her pillow.

"Claire, is that you?"

"Yes, Ma."

"I had a dream. My mother came to me. Her face was nice and pink. She had on her long blue dress. 'Hildy, you were always my favorite. Here is a bag of candy. Eat this and you will be well.' She knew already. She knew I am sick. She gave me the candies made with honey that she cooked for me when I was a little girl. She was trying to help me. Her cheeks were pink the way I remember."

* * *

May 1

Against my will I become the matriarch. Move in and out of roles, see the whole, the years passing, the once strong Hilda fading further and further into the distance. Hold fast, Claire. Know the meaning, see the richness, the blessing.

ELAINE STARKMAN

ANOTHER PART OF THE COUNTRY   *LAUREL RUST*

for A.W.K.

I've worked in nursing homes as a nurses' aide for many years and this piece is about one woman, Amy, whom I was privileged to know. I'd like to dedicate it to her with her full name, but I don't know where her family is or the legal implications. As it is, I have changed her first name a little.

Nursing homes are unique worlds, and I had trouble deciding how much of that context to include. My main intent was and is to share Amy with others, preserve some of her life. I asked her if she would allow me to do this and she was pleased. Originally I included only her words and not my own feelings and reactions towards her, but because one myth of the institutionalized, "senile" elderly is that they are not responsive to "reality," I included my presence to show how intimately she was. Much of the confusion, withdrawal, hostility, repeated phrases, etc., that are considered symptoms of "senility" are more accurately a reaction to an environment where seldom does anyone speak with them or listen to them or be with them in any kind of genuine, egalitarian manner: the literature on aging supports this as do my own experiences.

I feel that in feminist circles, when the subject of women and aging comes up, nursing home women, especially those who cannot or do not communicate or relate to "reality" as we do, are very often forgotten despite all the adulation of hags and crones. I get angry when others refer to nurses' aide work in nursing homes as shit work: the pay is certainly shit, but coming to know these women is like nothing else.

In Amy's room in the nursing home there are three identical narrow beds with metal rails, three small closets all in a row, three hospital tables, three small metal bedside cabinets, and three plastic water pitchers with three plastic glasses.

Amy's bed is closest to the door, which is only closed when someone has died. Next to her is Isabel, who repeats "lebalebalebalebaleba" with varying inflections and occasionally says a sentence, such as "I want to go home," and looks at you, amazed. "Lebalebalebaleba" resumes at fever pitch, her face tight with concentration, her thin hands patting her thin thighs, her bony chest. In the bed next to the window is Molly with her thick shock of white hair and her big, square face. When you feed her or turn her or dress her, Molly roars. Mostly she is in bed, moving her hands in front of her face and watching them. Outside the window is the big concrete parking lot.

Amy is "ambulatory" and one of the very few here who are labeled "self care." This means she can feed herself when the tray arrives three times a day. She can take herself to the bathroom. Unlike the others, most of whom are "heavy care" and nearly all of whom are women, Amy will not be spoon fed, not be tied in a wheelchair, not be changed and turned every two hours night and day, not be put to bed after lunch and remain there until morning. Within the institution's rigid schedule, Amy has some small choices because she can walk, see, hear, and talk. But like the sixty or so others, Amy has to take the medicine she is prescribed, which in her case includes mind-altering drugs. Her body is handled as though it is no longer hers. She has to stay in her bed all night; if she tries to climb out, she will be "restrained," which means tied into the bed until morning. She is not allowed into the kitchen. She is not allowed to leave the building.

Amy is awakened at 7 a.m. every morning, rolled up in bed with a tray on the table over her lap. An aide will hand her clothes to wear. By mid-morning, Amy will have modified her attire, perhaps adding another shirt, rolling up her pants, tying a scarf around her neck, putting on her coat. Throughout the day she may join the others lined up in the activities room where the television is always on. She will be allowed to range the halls with their fluorescent lights and linoleum floors; with women in wheelchairs, geri chairs, walkers; with rushing aides, laundry carts, medicine carts, and the loudspeaker with its constant commands: "Mary, Hannah needs assistance in the dining room," which means Hannah has wet her pants.

There is no space which is entirely Amy's own. Not even her self. Every two hours at night the light in her room will be switched on while Isabel and Molly are changed and turned, while the aides feel Amy's linen beneath her hips to be sure it is dry. Noise and light come in through the open door, which Amy is not allowed to close. Amy is allowed what personal possessions can fit into her tiny space, but if she has photographs or vases or nearly anything, chances are they will eventually be lost, broken, ruined in various ways. Any jewelry of value will be kept locked at the nurses' desk. If she gets any mail, it may or may not be read to her.

Amy's diagnosis is senile dementia. She is considered crazy. She talks non-stop, her face focused, animated, and attentive. Her expressiveness is considered insanity; her way of seeing, senility; her aging as an invasion, a rotting. Her life is considered to be over and because of this she is not perceived or treated as creative, adaptive, engaged—all the attributes of being human and alive. Instead, she barely exists in a limbo of invisibility where her body, her self, and her expression are not considered her own. She is entertaining to the staff not because she has a lively sense of humor and a quick mind that is sensitive to what is going on around her, but because she is crazy and everything she says is nonsense, because she does not know what she is saying.

Because Amy is ambulatory and self-care, she has certain advantages. But like the other women here, she is talked to and talked about and treated as though she were a child, a "cute little old lady," a deviant, a delinquent. Often she is talked about in her presence in the third person as though she is not here at all.

When I first began working here, one of the staff told me that "Amy is off the deep end." But where is the final edge in a place like this with its monotonous hallways, its identical beds, its artificial and unnatural oblivion? What is this if not a deep end?

Over the months I came to know Amy's ways well. I came to know her well enough to feel at times that I could follow her, to feel in moments that we understood something of each other. Her past remained largely inaccessible to me: her "records" include nothing of her experiences other than marital status and medical history, and because I am an aide I am not allowed access to them. If I were, it would be an invasion of her privacy, yet the nurses and administrators are free to say Amy is crazy in anyone's hearing. If they suspect she masturbates, everyone will know.

What I know of her past is that she'd been raised in Utah, that her father was a doctor, that she had asthma as a child, that she had been a dancer, that she was widowed and had two children. I write this as a record of one woman's creative struggle to exist in the world of an institution that regards her as a non-entity, where upon moving in a stranger to her will sit beside her for ten minutes and ask questions like "who is the president?" in order to ascertain Amy's "orientation to reality." According to her records, Amy exhibits none.

Amy ranges the halls all day wearing her own combination of clothes. Her body is very thin and slightly stooped, and she moves lightly as though floating. Her long thinning hair is tied up with a bright scarf: this is something she takes pleasure in doing every morning, coiling her hair on top of her head with her long arms as she sits on the edge of the bed. Her aqua eyes are deep and large, her bony cheeks red and her skin that light brown shade one often sees in very old white people. She talks nearly non-stop in a seemingly incoherent manner, nodding and often answering herself with "uh-*huh*, uh-*huh* dearie." All the while her face is animated with emotions, her eyes gazing directly into yours. She stops and chats with anyone, sometimes patting them or holding their hand, smiling. "Remember to laugh when you go around corners." Sometimes her rapid talk is filled with fury. "No sir, it's this one and that one and that one, uh-huh, and if I say yes they say well that's too bad. And if I stop talking I'll just stop." The staff laughs and smiles at crazy Amy who can talk circles around your head.

Amy keeps carefully rolled up pieces of toilet paper in her stuffed purse. They are tied neatly with shreds of toilet paper. Often she has one in her hand. She calls them her "little ones." She keeps them under her pillow, in her drawer, in her bed, until the housekeeper comes through and cleans things up, throws the little ones away and rearranges everything according to institutional order.

One day I made a little one and handed it to her.

"Here's another little one," I said.

"Well my my," she said, taking it, "you certainly cracked me." She laughed and made a face. "You certainly saw into that one, you blew the whistle on that little story."

Talking is Amy's way of knowing she is still alive. It is her intense, continuous engagement. It is one of the very means of creative expression allowed her. It is a way of creatively adapting to a monotonous and inhuman environment where no one really talks with her. If she stops talking, she'll "just stop." It's not so much death the very old fear as losing awareness of existence. It's our own fear of death, those of us who have the knowledge of a lesser number of years in the cells of our bodies and our consciousness, that often makes us oblivious to all the awareness in the old and makes it alien to us not because of any truth in the myth that the elderly are diminished, reduced to bare bones, but because it is so radically different and so unique to each individual.

Amy has a wonderful way of saying things. I often think of my grandmother, whose "hallucinatory" talk aptly described the undercurrents in my family that no one would talk about or admit. Like all of us, the very old have codes of their own: sometimes you can find your way into them and sometimes you can't. I struggled with the question of if I was intruding. Does an 83-year-old woman want to be comprehensible? Does she want me to follow her? How does one see and feel the world after living for 83 years? Working with the very old, one learns new ways of speaking, of listening, of communicating; new ways of seeing. Often the exchange is startlingly immediate and direct, a gut-level communication that transgresses the boundaries established by social conventions. Many of the very old have no use for such conventions.

Amy and I have developed an intimacy that is hard to describe, an intimacy that makes me think of companionship differently because Amy does not know my name and has never asked. We sit and simply take up talking, wherever and whenever we are. Talking with Amy who "exhibits no orientation to reality" is a wonderful experience in which we are always in the present, and the present could be anything we choose to create between us.

I asked Amy one day if I could interview her. She had been sick in bed for a couple of days. I wanted to be able to write down things she said. My pencil, though, couldn't keep up with her pace.

Amy was propped up in her bed, surrounded by her little ones, the crown of her head encircled with a tightly rolled bright pink scarf. She looked down at her long, bony legs stretched out straight in front of her and said, "My, it feels funny, it isn't mine anymore."

I asked her what it is like to age.

"I could tell it in one fell swoop, it is H-E-double L. It is because I am used to having my own way and when I see all of this and see I'm fifty and sixty and seventy years older than they are and I'm still not pushing through, doing nothing, monotonous—I say to my family, 'I'm just going to be here for this little time. Don't stop here with me, go on with yours.'

"It's not very nice when you think of what it used to be, what a beautiful thing it was, all of us running here and there. Beautiful. I've had a lovely, lovely living, myself, growing old, shabby, aging. When I get this far I have to look myself in the eye and say uh-*huh*, dearie, this is as far as you go: I have to think of myself.

"When I could dance I was happy. I used to dance on the stage in Salt Lake City and Europe and places everyone came. I could dance and I could count and I can still count, but this is too much for it. You girls are the ones keeping it going. If we didn't have you we wouldn't have a chance. You do things beautifully, you do things differently and carefully and there's a shine to it and don't you forget that."

I asked her what she thought about death.

"Oh I'm past that too. So many of them, I'm the oldest one of them in this creative thing. They're all crazy to be counted, and here I can take one look at it, read it up and down, know it from A to Z, but even with that I have to sit up to breathe and I have to be careful.

"But only the little ones can see it quicker than you. Some of the little ones can lead you better, because they don't feel things like you do."

I asked her if her consciousness had changed with age.

"Oh my yes," she laughed, "but the main things don't get thrown over. I just chow-chow-chow because it makes you feel more relieved not to take in too much. But it's wonderful when there's another voice in here."

"How do you like living here?"

"Well let me think how to say it. None of us had much in common. Oh I don't think I'd like it. It's too satisfied, it all has to be done on cue. They just leave everyone in here. As soon as you walked in and said hello, they'd say hello, and you could see how it would be, because you can't wait on them and they can't wait on you. Oh yes I'd rather be home. You see I'm spoiled to death. I had one brother and then another, I'd run up and down, but now"—she starts to cough—"I'm wishing I'd just stayed still. And not make my eyes move. Just close them quietly."

Over the next few days Amy grew increasingly weak and stayed in bed, her hands clenched, listless and quiet. I arrived one day to find her nowhere around: she'd been taken to the hospital, found to have pneumonia. I was afraid she was going to die, I'd seen it happen so often. I always feared coming to work, filling my laundry cart and starting down the halls, room by room, and finding a bed empty, stripped, a plastic garbage bag on the mattress filled with possessions for the family to retrieve. After work I drove to the hospital.

Amy turned and looked at me when I walked in. There was an oxygen tube in each nostril that looped around her ears and came together again at that place in her throat where in self-defense classes I'd been taught you could kill an attacker with your finger. Her fine-boned hands, the veins raised as cords, were clenched into fists and her breathing was shallow as that of a newborn bird. She took my hand into hers and smiled weakly. I realized that I had worried that she wouldn't recognize me in a different environment from that in which she knew me. I realized seeing her in a place other than the nursing home made me a little uneasy.

The shades on the other side of the room were open and we could see the mountains.

"It's beautiful outside today," I said, "I could even see Mt. Baker from the bridge."

"Well I'm glad you found a place for yourself," she said. "I hope you do it justice."

"How are you feeling?"

"Oh I'm not doing anything, lazy."

"How was your ambulance ride?"

"Oh it was wonderful being in the wild wide open. I've always loved that." She looked at the woman in the next bed. "I wonder how she feels, my little friend Virginia. I came over here to take care of her and then I fell down.

"Oh they don't leave you alone in here. They're always in and out. I was crashing in and out and couldn't get around this thing," she said, gesturing to her chest, "and dad said everything was fine. Everyone's been calling me but I'm too tired to chat and chat with all of them. But I'm glad you're here, I'll always remember that."

Amy tried to keep looking in my direction but her head would fall back and soon she would be turned toward the window where dusk was falling. The room was full of her struggle to breathe. Both of us were quiet, holding hands. She squeezed my hand from time to time as though to comfort me.

"I want to find my family and tell them I'm going over to see dad and where they all are. I just want this all to be over with. Why don't we just blow the whistle and all go home?

"I'm standing on a street corner looking up and down for somebody. I haven't seen anybody for quite a while.

"It's just too much, too fast."

Seeing Amy struggling for breath, fidgeting with her chest as though to free herself, so frail and quiet, her eyes gazing in an agitated way around the room, I started to cry. She looked down at our hands together on the sheet and said quietly, "I think this is all filled up. If we could just wait until Thanksgiving and start all over and have another big one like this."

The nurse came in and tried to give Amy her medicine.

"Come on," she said cheerfully, "let's be good and take our medicine so we feel better."

Amy looked up at her and said in the chatty style I'd seen her use so often in the nursing home, "Oh I'm busy with all the youngsters." She smiled but she wouldn't open her mouth. Finally the nurse had to force the medicine down her. As soon as she was out of the room, Amy spit it out and wiped her mouth.

"It's ridiculous," she said fiercely, "it's wasted. I don't want anything like this."

When I left that night, I told her to sleep well.

"Oh I'm saving sleep for when it is really over," she said.

I visited Amy nearly every day in the weeks she was in the hospital. Back in the nursing home they weren't sure if they should save her bed or not. The housekeeper had already steam cleaned it.

In the hospital Amy wouldn't eat, saying she was "full of goobly-gook from here to here, there just isn't any place left." She was given IVs, which she ripped out. Her hands were loosely restrained and she still managed to pull out the IVs. Yet she was pale and extremely weak, and referred frequently and in oblique but clear ways to the question of whether she should fight for her life or "close my eyes quietly," and if it was even right to wish for all of it to end. She was taken off oxygen. She moaned in pain often, turning away from me when she did. She continued to spit out her medicine. Her lips were chapped and I rubbed balm into them; she opened her lips and let me. I'd bring her coffee and ice cream and she'd eat a little and talk about picnics in the country, about driving the old car full speed on the back roads.

"But it's just too fast, too sudden and too much. I wish it would all slow down.

It's so quiet in here I feel scared sometimes. I just have to keep talking to keep myself from going to pieces.

"And when it was my husband and he was gone, it wasn't anything like this, it was so sudden, like a great rift. You just didn't know what to do, whether to see people or if you should say anything at all."

She looked at the t.v. her roommate was watching with the volume off.

"It's boring, all those people with their mouths open.

"I've been wanting to get ahold of my father, he always carried me through. It's ridiculous, all this, it all means *father*.

"It's so quiet in here. I don't hear the voices from down below.

"I ache all over. I just want everything to stop."

I asked her if I brought strawberries and peaches, would she eat with me?

"Oh that would be beautiful. I've always lived off that. But you might go your way and I another. We'll just have to keep our fingers crossed. I just don't know what to plan for; it all goes back to the dark ages."

I dreamt one night that I was driving my old sky-blue Valiant down a hot, dusty dirt road that was still under construction, down a long hill to a ferry dock in a small green harbor. The ferry had just left. I noticed the wake on the water and that it was dusk. Amy was sitting beside me, wordlessly, looking. I slowed down because I knew there wouldn't be another ferry for a while.

I took her a bouquet of daffodils and she stuck her whole face into them.

"Oh it's a crazy, crazy old world. It used to be so good and now it's slowly stopping and everyone is rushing here and there. Who would have thought I'd end up like this, an old lady. I just want all this back and forth to get over and be on the outside. But when I move just my little toe I ache all over.

"I'm afraid to sleep at night. They come in and go out. I just don't like all this coming down and landing, it just burns all through me."

She looked down at our clasped hands.

"It helps having something to hold. I'm such a coward. I was afraid it would be like this. If only we could fall back and sleep, and then it would be all over, just the two of us.

"It must be horrible for you, a young girl listening to me moaning. But it's nice to have somebody hear it. And if I'm not here when you come back, I'll leave a note on this door and that one.

"Tell me, what comes after the afternoon?"

As I left that evening, I heard her say quietly as I walked out the door and she lay gazing at the ceiling, "Hold on to me. Hold on to me."

I arrived just as she had ripped out her IVs again. Her hands had become black and blue. She was furious, talking non-stop as the nurse put in a new one, and in the middle of her furious speech I heard her say "and I'm tired of people who come by just to be nice and say hello, goodbye."

She drank a few swallows of the coffee I'd brought her. The energy of her anger made me feel she was getting stronger.

"I'm sick of being hovered over, pricked and jabbed. I just don't care anymore."

"Amy," I said, "do you think I come here just to be nice?"

"Well I think maybe you do, because I've seen you doing things you don't really want to do. But you don't know what this means to me."

I told her if she kept ripping out her IVs she'd starve to death. I said she probably knew that. I said starvation was a painful, slow way to die.

We talked about death a little: or I did. I asked her if she minded me talking like this, and she nodded quietly that she didn't mind. I told her the things I thought about it, the deaths I'd seen, near death experiences I'd read about, the light around Stanley's body when he died.

Sometimes she seemed to want to die and sometimes she didn't. What was hard was all the "crashing in and out," the "coming down and landing," the constant exhausting pain. What was also hard was daily being invaded, "hovered over," the daily things around her, as important to her as the possibility of death and "what to plan for." I found I had to remind myself of this.

I remembered how in the nursing home if I managed to leave her tray in her room long after the trays were supposed to be picked up, that within a few hours she would have cleaned her plate. She liked to take her time with things, she liked to do things "carefully" and "with a shine to them." And I realized she didn't need me to translate her, to drive her to the ferry dock, though I felt as I talked about death that she was willing me to talk. When I left, I told the nurse to try leaving her alone with her tray. It worked. The nurse said, "It's so hard with these old people, they don't tell us anything about them."

But I drove home wondering if Amy trusted me, if I was another intrusion, some kind of macabre voyeur. She was right: I often do what I do not want to do. She'd blown the whistle on my little story. But not this, not seeing her, not coming to know her. I began to see the ways in which I needed her. And the next day, the drift of her conversation made me feel she'd read my mind, that she'd been in the car beside me on the dusty road still under construction.

The inflection of her voice was a combination of anger and tenderness.

"There's nothing here that can conclude with anything. This is a children's rendezvous, just an ordinary thing, just a little chit-chat. I like things that I can chat about, that I don't exactly have to know what I am thinking. I'm too old to start in and think about it all, know what I think and what I want. My homecoming is entirely different from this place and I'm years and years older than you girls."

"Amy, are you talking in part about our friendship?"

"Well there's nothing here that has stirred me to the limits of anything. I just don't think there's enough of anything in me; I can't believe in it. It's just a question of what happens to come along, each man for himself. You can't make it be special. What I've always done is to take things with me and make something of them. Everybody does this and in their own way and with no one else. I wish you joy, you're young and if you move carefully and see what you want then there's no limit. Just keep asking anything that comes to your mind and keep pushing. But I just don't have anything to say to anyone who has bright ideas about changing things. I just don't have anything to contribute. It's a crazy old world. I don't consider this as in any way special except as a stop sign. Each one has to try and do what they want to do but they can't count on different people to show them different things. That's too bad, if it lets us down with a thud at the end of this. But each year is a little more truce than the year before, and I lose interest because I'm in another part of the country.

"Companionship is however you make it. You try to make it come back to you the way you like, and if it does, fine, and if it doesn't.

"But this is something that you turn back and toss into the wastebasket.

"And I never was one to go behind the curtains and do everything right.

"But there might be a time when someone will be needing something.

"All my family has gone home now."

A few days later, Amy was released.

I took her for a drive one day in my old Valiant.

"Just seeing things," she said, looking out the window, "makes everything different."

Sitting beside me as we drove, she chatted away out the window and suddenly said in a louder voice: "I've never been so sick as that, never this far, I just didn't know what to plan for and I could always figure things, read them up and down and in and out, and there was someone to say uh-*huh* dearie, there's the hill and there's the bottom and you could see how things would be, and when you go as far south as you can you have to stop and look around before you go on. And sometimes someone can help you see, they can read it better than you because you're lazy and you can't move just then, I'll never forget that."

Gazing out the window, she began to sing in a playful, exaggerated falsetto her own version of a Nina Simone song, laughing at the end of it:

> *I used to be the only one*
> *Now I'm the sad and lonely one*
> *Ain't I blue*
> *Ain't I blue.*

LAUREL RUST

ELIZABETH LAYTON   *LUCY LIPPARD*

Who says art is powerless? In 1977, at age 68, Elizabeth Layton saved her own life and added immeasurably to ours. The medium of salvation was large, colored-pencil drawings. The supplies were bought at the local drugstore in Wellsville, Kansas, where Layton—one of the most original (and most feminist) artists in the U.S. today—was born. Her drawings are not only "high quality," but offer a view of American life rarely reflected in contemporary art. Aging, depression, dieting, marriage, grandmothering, death, Jonestown, world hunger, the nuclear threat, capital punishment, and the ERA are only a few of her subjects. Overriding them all is the theme of hope.

Layton came to hope the hard way, through a difficult childhood, five children, a "shameful" divorce, bouts of manic-depression, mental hospitals, electroshock, contemplated suicide and the death of a son, after which, at her sister's suggestion, Layton signed up for a drawing course at nearby Ottawa University. There she was "discovered" by Don Lambert, a young reporter for the *Ottawa Herald* (a certain poetic justice here, since Layton is the daughter of a newspaper publisher and a columnist, and has been a journalist and managing editor herself).

Lambert saw two self portraits in a student show that made him laugh and cry and seek out the artist, who refused to see him. One of these drawings, in a spidery but forceful line, shows Layton and her granddaughter eating a Thanksgiving dinner of Kentucky Fried Chicken, while a happy turkey stalks outside. The other shows Layton, a very large old lady in a white veil and black slip, holding up in front of her bulk a dainty, old-fashioned wedding dress and displaying a red button that proclaims, "I am loved."

Don Lambert persisted. He eventually became the artist's friend and agent and introduced her to the World of Culture, which wasn't altogether ready for her. But to make a long success story short, Layton has been crowned with honors since 1980, including a full-scale retrospective exhibition that is travelling through 1986 under the auspices of the Mid-America Arts Alliance, accompanied by a handsome catalogue and excellent text by Lynn Bretz.

Pal Wright, who taught the drawing class at Ottawa, encouraged "contour drawing," where the artist looks at the subject rather than at the page. "Drawing this way is simply fascinating," says Layton. "Things just appear on the page. There they are. I don't really have any say about what goes onto the paper . . . . Contour drawing is a wonderful way to get rid of anger or whatever you want to get rid of."

"Elizabeth Layton had gone through the whole course of modern psychiatry, and it hadn't really changed her life. Then she takes up drawing and cures herself," marvels artist/therapist Robert Ault.

Wright said to draw large and "go to the edge" of the paper, and she suggested self portraits as the most available subject matter. But the sense of design Layton brought to her work is decidedly her own. Her compositions are as dynamic as the minute details. Unlike so-called "naive" or "primitive" artists, she is not a prisoner of the frontal view. Totally unafraid of odd angles, scale changes, and other "modernist" tactics, she draws bodies from strange perspectives, while never sacrificing her strong sense of realism. Her drawings are vortices into which she draws the viewer with all the force that she herself experiences in the process of artmaking. Freedom might be her middle name. She has the experimental courage not only of her convictions but of an avant-garde art education she never had.

Layton is a missionary for art as therapy, but the fact remains, she gave as good as she got. She has used art for exorcism, catharsis, an instrument of self-transformation, but so do all artists. Her art might not have been such good therapy if she were not such a good artist. At the same time, it's not as "high" above it all as art is supposed to be—it's right down here with us. Its breadth and intimacy must touch something in the lives of everyone who sees it.

In *Christmas Eve*, 1977, for instance, Layton offers a uniquely unsentimental image of domestic content with two old hands, just touching; the unseen couple faces a window whose crossed curtains form a wonderful visual pun—a triangular piece of starry sky doubles as a Christmas tree burning at the top like a candle. In *Death of a Child*, an aged, grieving Layton suckles a baby at her breast, while over her shoulder, her husband's hand offers a red bandana handkerchief.

Why is this kind of identification and emotion so rare in our experience of art? Is it not considered "exalted enough" because it *does* speak directly to so many people?

"For the most part, what I draw is for other people who are like me and may be troubled by their feelings," says Layton. "You'd never believe the wonderful letters I get from people who have seen the show. And to me that's the whole thing. It's not whether this is art or not. I don't care. . . . I think any of my family will tell you they would never have recognized this as art. And if they had, they would not have known what to do with it."

Nowhere in art have old age and marriage been depicted so honestly and yet with such emotional force—not as saccharine lies but with the true bittersweet-ness of experience. The faces that peer out of Layton's drawings are usually her own and that of her second husband, Glenn. They are long, lined, unabashedly spotted and battered by age. Glenn Layton is caught in his underpants on the bathroom scale, "just home from the hospital, struggling mightily to gain pounds." In *Last Rose of Summer*, he stands in the kitchen with an early morning offering of one yellow rose, while his wife's hand emerges from the corner with a slice of lemon meringue pie in return. One of Layton's eyes is half closed, so she has used this "wink" in several witty drawings, especially one where she flirts in a lacy, almost topless garment, a bottle of perfume, and a Cinderella-like slipper floating at the side.

I've begun to wonder why so few artists have pictured older people, aside from the occasional portrait or "how-quaint-what-a-wonderful-face" syndrome. (Photographers are the exception.) Feminists are increasingly interested in the process of aging, given the peculiar social stigmas borne by the "non-young"

The Eyes of the Law

Self Portrait as Nike, Winged Victory

woman, and the fact that some 75 percent of the aged poor are women. Yet like other personal/social experiences, it is an unspoken taboo in the high art world.

Elizabeth Layton is able to tackle such difficult content because she doesn't give a damn about the art world. She has unselfconsciously mastered the fusion of personal and political that so many progressive artists strive for. By using her own image to stand for all of denigrated, invisible, abused humanity, she has raised the universal from the particular. In *Pushing Up the Daisies*, she drew herself in the grave, attended by birds, animals, and insects (a worm emerging from her heart), and she drew her skin black, because "people of other colored skin have the same feelings."

Layton is Everywoman, resisting the evils of the modern world. In a protest against capital punishment, it is the artist with the noose around her neck; in *Garden of Eden*, she is an aged Eve, hollering in anger at "being blamed for all the sins of the world." In *Warning: The Surgeon General Has Determined ---*, she puffs a weed, a gun held to her head, while behind her pollution rises from a spiraling highway and a mushroom cloud looms. She is Pandora struggling to hold the lid on her box, to contain "No Hope"—a grimacing male head surrounded by bats labeled "age, poverty, apathy, bias, hate, war, waste." It is Layton who emits the *Nuclear Scream* and becomes *Liza Crossing the River*. It is her face reflected in the dark glasses of uniform rows of CIA types . . . and she is thumbing her ears at them.

It is Elizabeth Layton flexing her muscles in a radiant, grinning portrait, showing off a broad chestful of political buttons. And it is Elizabeth Layton whose arms and head replace the missing parts of the Winged Victory, with her Nike sneakers slung over her shoulder, who says: "Now she is where she wants to be and ready to fly. Scars, where the arms and head of the statue were broken off, now are only the hallmarks of the new and everlasting growth."

LUCY LIPPARD

Self Portrait (with Glenn) as Phyllis Schlafly   ELIZABETH LAYTON
colored pencil and crayon on paper
28" x 22"

*The worth of the pictures I draw is measured in empathy felt, in understanding of ourselves
and of others.*

Self Portrait as the Statue of Liberty   ELIZABETH LAYTON
              colored pencil and crayon on paper
                          30" x 22"

Self Portrait as Liza Crossing the River   *ELIZABETH LAYTON*
colored pencil and crayon on paper
28″ x 22″

Self Portrait as Noah's Wife   *ELIZABETH LAYTON*
colored pencil and crayon on paper
28" x 22"

Stroke   *colored pencil and crayon on paper*   *ELIZABETH LAYTON*
28" x 22"

Self Portrait (with Glenn) as The Old Indians
colored pencil and crayon on paper
28" x 22"

ELIZABETH LAYTON

Maria in Memory   *fabric and thread*   DEIDRE SCHERER
                        23 1/2" x 19"

I "paint" and "draw" with fabric and thread utilizing the techniques of cutting, piecing and machine-stitching in non-traditional ways.

In two years of on-site sittings at Linden Lodge I have slowly perceived a framework of aging as residents shared themselves and their experiences.

Freida *fabric and thread* DEIDRE SCHERER
10″ x 10″

In my portrait studies I wanted to make honest images of the elderly. This soft medium with its textural and detailed surface expresses the sensory, narrative and psychological aspects I have found in these lives.

The Waitress   *JORJANA HOLDEN*
bronze with wood base
9" x 4" x 4 1/2"

I want my sculptures to be like three-dimensional poems where forms and symbols combine to echo in another's heart and head.

Woman Dressing   *JORJANA HOLDEN*
bronze with wood base
17 3/4" x 9 3/4" x 9"

The ME Generation   oil   *MARJORIE RAEDER ALTENBURG*

I remember in art school they used to tell us to make these little thumbnail compositions. I never would get anything out of that. Things keep shifting until I know exactly where it's supposed to go. When it's there, it's there, and that's it. It's a process: one thing suggests the next thing . . . I'm always amazed that I don't seem to be painting my paintings. They just seem to happen.

How to Make It All Work　　　*oil*　　　*MARJORIE RAEDER ALTENBURG*
　　　　　　　　　　　　　　　　40″ x 40″

Lilies   oil   PAULINE STIRISS
                    29 1/2" x 23 1/2"

Alienation, oppression, despoliation—these are my obsessions; oil paints and symbols are my media for the expression of a humanism which means to me a caring about people, a belonging to the human race.

The Goddess   oil   *PAULINE STIRISS*

I don't mean to be destructive except toward whatever forces—ageism, sexism, racism—work to impoverish us and keep us and our environment from their richest and fullest flowering.

The Mermaid   oil   *PAULINE STIRISS*
35 3/4" x 19 1/2"

My use of visual metaphor is for enrichment rather than mystification: meanings, sometimes astonishing to me, are added to the work by the observers, contributing to its intensity.

The Mask   *oil*   *PAULINE STIRISS*
                                        19 1/4″ x 27 3/4″

THE LAST FRINGIE   *M. ANN SPIERS*

She lived in the dining room of a four-bedroom house, now divided into sleeping rooms for graduate students. The kitchen and bathroom were communal. She used deceit when she rented the room from the landlord. Her great-grandson was moving over from Ephrata. He was going to graduate school in hard-rock geology.

But she moved in. Once ensconced, she was ignored by the absent landlord. The students didn't mind her there. They only slept there, studied in their labs and libraries, and spoke to her at least once a month. She didn't like to chat.

She had dined in this room before. Before was when the focal point of the room was a stuffed turkey or a sheet cake with candles and animated space men stalking among sugar roses. Now only a small table held a coffee mug and a bakery sack, a white body bag for a dead napoleon.

The room still had the same physical points, the usual four walls. One wall was a bank of parallelograms crowned with leaded glass, the diamonds now bowled out with age, a wad of Christmas wrapping stuffed into a missing pane.

The second wall was French doors that once led into the living room. Now the doors were permanently closed. Each pane was covered with salmon and purple swirls of marbled paper. She liked to think she lived within the corners of an expensively bound diary.

A cup rim ran across the upper midsection of the other two walls. Once her cup collection was housed there. That is, until the pet indigo snake reptiled his way between the wall and cups. With each curve of his satanic tail, the cups and saucers toppled. The resulting tones delicately filled the house as Limoges, Royal Doulton, Spode, and Nissan cracked expensively on the hardwood floor.

The snake survived. She had looked at the brilliant shards; then at the snake and felt lucky. She never had to hostess another lady tea because she was the only lady on the block who had enough cups. Nor did she ever have to pack them up again and haul them over to a less-endowed lady's revel. She had lost her cups.

Now she placed her things there, the things she liked to keep, never look at unless to use as a mile marker if any visitor would care to journey through the spoils of her years.

Two squint-eyed newborns sleep in a double frame. Printed hurriedly across the photo are the words "boy," a note on the hour, minutes, poundage, and length. Her babies. Her boys.

Hung by a utility string on a golden tack is a small gathering of dried red roses, upside down, unopened clots of blood.

"Fringie" refers to someone who lived on the fringe of Seattle's University District during the early sixties.

The ledge holds lines of rocks: volcanics, not the measured stones of sedimentary time nor the heavy lumps of metamorphic eons. But pumice, basalt, lavas, tuffs, tephras, scoria found in the Cascade Mountains, sisters to other rocks she had carefully placed on the trails, a promise testifying to her future return, when she herself was a bundle of bones, ghost of the Cascade Crest, Wonder of the Wonderland Trail.

She was ready. Her calves still had the V worked into the back muscle. Her boots and backpack were vintage Eddie Bauer, and her binocs were definitely REI when REI was still up the stairs on Pike Street before Pike Street went whore.

On her ledge she had an all-day sucker. She licked it just enough to keep it dust free. That sucker had two more years, she imagined.

Then books, lines of books. She had spent hours at used book stores repossessing her favorite books: *Seaweeds at Ebb Tide, Tibetan Book of the Dead, Septic Field Practises, Childbirth by Lamaze, Joy of Sex* with its antidotes *Vile Bodies* and *The Principles and Practise of Sex Therapy.* Next in this display came the *Bible* in the right translation, *Options in Rhetoric, Least You Have to Know About English, Tales of a Fourth Grade Nothing, Upward and Onward in the Garden, Pigtail Days in Old Seattle, Where the Wild Things Are, Edible Incredible,* and *Good Night Moon.* And more.

She had plans to reread these favorites, working up slowly to her favorite passages. But she thought perhaps she didn't have that much reading time left to her. So she began to copy out her favorite passages longhand. She became impatient. So she tore out her favorite pages and kept them in piles next to her reading chair.

Her reading chair was an overstuffed number, The Crotch she called it. Warm, enfolding, it had interesting recesses.

She read there. She never read in bed. If she did, she would have stayed in bed all day, and it was depressing to be in bed all day unwashed, undressed, unbrushed while absorbing the adventures, physical, mental, sexual, of other people. Her vicarious joys were taken easier sitting upright, her teeth flossed, her hair brushed out and caught in a loose grey bun, and her cheeks scrubbed pink.

She had one tea cup. The balique reminded her of her own skin now: fragile, bumpy, the light caught and preserved in the milky whiteness.

She drank Earl Grey tea each morning. She would walk out on the porch, squint into the Seattle weather, and list up her day. Students would leap past her; she would sip and decide.

On her ledge was also a wine goblet. Waterford. Heavy, not appropriate for a white. She called this piece her portable decadence. Occasionally she would catapult and sign up for a Golden Age bus tour when their destination was the Chateau Ste. Michelle Winery.

She would pack her goblet, grab a seat behind the driver. She found his uniform, albeit pure polyester, spruced him up for a conversation. Upon arrival at the carefully placed lawns and token grapevines, she departed the bus and briskly went forward, kicking geese when necessary. She would ascend past the pond, enter through the tour's exit gate, bustle up to the sipping counter, pull out her Waterford, place its sparkling lip under a fine red, perhaps a Cabernet Sauvignon '79, expectable but trusty. She would raise her eyes to meet the eyes of the once-surprised tour guide, words of wine flowing from his lips. As he continued to list out the dead animals that should accompany the various wines, she would say in an undertone to the guide: "Fill it. I've come a long way." Then she would take her goblet, leave the fumes of the casks and tourists, exit the building to emerge among the greens, the bedding flowers, and wet smells of the Sammamish Slough, to take in the weather and to sip well.

Next on her ledge were five bayberry candles, numerous stubs of Advent candles, and two baptismal tapers. The tapers she associated with limbo which the Pope had lately cancelled in spite of generations of dead babies having been cast there unbaptised. The Advent's purples and pinks reminded her of the children's snickers as *Oh Come, Oh Come, Emmanuel* was seasonally rendered off key. The bayberry reminded her of Christmas at Frederick and Nelson when the perfect egg salad san and white clam chowder and Frango mint shake were served on real crockery and the sundae had hot caramel gooped all over the top, not served in a plastic thimble on the side.

Her bed was double, not a queen nor a king nor a waterbed. She had a double bed for herself to wander over feeling for cool places on hot nights, dry places on damp nights, unlumpy spots on restless nights.

She had a bad mattress: hollows, ridges, ravines. But she accommodated them. She curled her body around them, moved about as age and pressure moved them about the geography of her bed. She had done the same for men most of her life, moved herself about the bed for them.

She had only one lover now. He was eighty, a bone to be sure. He came to town twice a year. "Stay over at her place," he'd say. He never said he came "to sleep with her" or said "to crash at her pad," but said "stay over" as if she had the farm down a long road, a big porch, a few chickens and fresh eggs in the evening of his journey through the hen houses of this world.

With her, this was okay. She didn't so much like him, as like the night with him. This visit was a review for her. She had breasts, and thighs, and lips, and a vagina. He had all his spare parts, she knew. He never considered them spare. She did. A luxury like a spare bedroom in good times. Or a spare tire in bad times. Sparity had virtue.

Obviously when she thought about his parts, or more precisely, his part, she was ambiguous in attitude. The night was a review. He did well. She did well. But they both looked past the right cheek of each other and gazed into the kettle of their sexuality in the pattern on the pillow or the pattern on the ceiling depending on who had the most energy or ascendancy that night.

The door from her room went directly into the kitchen, a common kitchen for the boarders. She used the kitchen often. On the kitchen wall was a duty chart. "Deep Cleaning" it said in block letters. The tenants' names were listed in the right hand column. The duties, in multiple listings over the face of the chart, were listed by area: porch, hall, steps, bathroom, laundry room, garbage bins.

She liked deep cleaning: grey beards of mildew in the wizened cheeks of orange peels, tufts and tufts of baby-soft lint, forgotten umbrellas, fly specks, and in the bottom of the shower stall, pubic hairs, black, glossy, kinked.

She left her room and went on campus every day. Under the deciduous trees of fraternity row, she accommodated the irregularities of the root-tortured side-walk; she ignored the spring running of the sap in the form of chug contests, sorority serenades, posing and flashing. She'd hit campus with enthusiasm.

One day the lecturer in Kane Hall concentrated on the edges of dark holes. She preferred the dissertation defenses in Johnson Hall. Memorable was the paper entitled *Hydrothermal Alteration within Mt. Rainier, Washington.* The ordeal was followed by champagne. The poker game in the English Lounge in Padelford Hall provided an occasional witty aside. Imogen Cunningham's photos at the Henry Art Gallery were a mistake for her. They gave her cataracts. End-of-the-quarter departmental potlucks were tasty. Fisheries had great casseroles and engineering had excellent desserts.

The open air ministers on the greens gave her pause. She also wanted to raise her voice as witness. But she didn't. She adjusted her straw hat, picked lint from her gaberdine coat, then flapped away in her flip flops before her urge to orate became too strong, before the need to recite from *Cat's Cradle* became too deadening. As she moved away from the righteous, she would merely throw back her head and crow in delight.

Her last stop was the Burke Museum, the museum of totem poles, of North-west mammoths, of butterflies stretched cheaply across styrofoam. Inside she'd pause to look at her favorites. The welcoming totem, two stories high, had pendulous tits hanging down to the statue's waist level. The bottom plane of each breast had a carven face: a muskrat or a beaver, features in red and black. She had to turn her head and bend over to see the humor. She thought the breasts hilarious.

At this museum she'd always use the women's room whether nature called or not for on the way to the room was a reclining Greek male, a token wound in his lovely side. As she would pass by her dying warrior, she would raise her left hand on the way in and her right hand on the way out and briefly caress, only in passing, the cool scrotum of the statue.

Then she would attend the Boiserie, the museum coffee shop. The table and chairs here had arrived from modernized areas of campus as old-fashioned rejects. The tables were wood and heavy; the chairs large and comfortable. The walls of the coffee shop were a nut brown, their golden veneer peeled from a French hunting lodge and reglued here on the wall of this Northwest museum.

The music was insistently baroque. The coffee was French Roast. Expensive. Each day she ordered a cup. Each day they gave her a cup. And then she forgot to pay.

The coffee made her heart buzz, numbed her tongue, while the harpsichord made her fingers tingle, the bass her tongue throb. The chords thundered across her bones until the tears coursed down the scabland of her face like a spring rill on its rush out on dry dirt.

On her centennial birthday she would also come here, let them treat her to a coffee. But instead of egressing through the erratics and columnar basalt of the courtyard, she would return to the circle of totem poles, adzed from red cedar, potlatch images stretched up into the grey of the Northwest sky. She would place herself next to raven, bear, salmon, beaver, and whale. Also in her circle would be the poles of elongated human figures, raised high on occasion as ridiculers or greeters. In this company she, too, would stretch her legs, expand her chest, and lift her arms straight up in wild greeting, her mouth caught in a bellow of welcome.

M. ANN SPIERS

THE LIGHT WITHIN   *AUDREY BORENSTEIN*

for Hannah Leah (b. November ?, 1900, Plotelai, Lithuania,
d. Erev Pesach, April 5, 1985, Miami) with love

That spring afternoon in 1970, Ruth found Sophie sleeping in the back room of the bookstore. Her mother-in-law was lying back in Harold's chair, her mouth hanging open, a ruff of soft white waves encircling her face under her black wig that popped with electrical charges against the smooth naugahyde. Her shirt was unbuttoned halfway down; a thin brown line, the tender bruise of aging, divided her heavy breasts. The shadows of her nipples were dark under the limp, coarse cloth. Her stomach rose and fell with her deep breathing. Ruth saw that her mother-in-law was putting on weight again, her thighs were bulging against the denim. She thought of how they looked when Sophie came out of the shower, the purple markings on the furrowed skin, a relief map of woman's estate. She saw how tranquilly her mother-in-law's clever hands lay folded just now, how thick her nails had become—

"Too beeg!" she used to cry, holding Rachel's little fingers up for inspection. "Come, Grandma'll give you a manicure." Then they would play "beauty parlor," the stylish duenna from Miami Beach and her three-year-old likeness.

Sophie's face, the most beautiful face Ruth had seen in this life, her skin smooth as an olive's, her eyes—

Ruth knew better than to look at the eyes of someone who is sleeping.

A beautiful woman still, she herself often said it in self-mockery, her conversion to hippiehood had left no visible markings on her face.

You, who could spend whole afternoons talking about noses, Sophie, about which earrings to wear with this and that dress, shoes, shoes, you filled closets with shoes—

"What are you doing, giving all your money away to an orthodontist?" she had scolded that first day she had come to live in the Village, to *be near*. "Whatever you're born, that's what you should stay, you stay like how you come out. In the shtetl who heard of fancy dental work, surgery on noses, on breasts? In Miami Beach the old fools spend all they got stretching and wiring themselves, at eighty they still want to be movie stars. Making themselves handsome for the grave. Dot's the first thing I learned in my encounter sessions. You peel all that off, you stand naked in front of the world, dot's the beginning of real. To think I threw away all that money and time painting myself for those cranks in the Garden of Yidden!"

Was it that, Sophie, knowing, truly knowing that you were growing old, that you would die, that brought you to your second birth? That and the loss of your husband, the shock of your widowhood?

"Sex!" she would scoff, with that wry twisted smile, "Sex, Ruth! I never liked it, I never found anything in it, the little pleasure once in a while what good is it, it goes away."

"Sophie, *nothing* lasts. Nothing."

"So, nothing is worth anything then, simple as that."

"Not even having a child?"

"A child, ha! My Harold! Harold, ha! What was it all for? He went away. You'll see, ha, you'll see! Like little birds, they fly away. If you're smart, you won't love 'em so much, it doesn't pay."

"Sophie, they're not stocks I'm buying on the market."

"Nu, what are they then, children! Jewels you'll put away in your jewelry case? What, you're smarter than all the other millions of women who lived, you'll solve it? I see how you hover around 'em, how you watch 'em, you talk to 'em, you make 'em smart, you love 'em like crazy. You'll change what it is, Life, eh? You'll see, my big, educated one. You'll see how like birds they'll fly away."

Ruth could still taste that soft hair under her lips, she buried her face still in the nameless fragrance of his infant's head, she felt his weight on her shoulder, she opened her arms and saw Rachel running toward her, her chubby legs hurrying, hurrying toward her. She saw Rachel riding on her scooter, her starched dress of dotted swiss that Sophie sewed for her spread out all around her like a tutu, her soft hair parted in the middle, a pony tail at each ear. She could see the two of them, brother and sister, coming down the road from school, coming home, carrying their lunchboxes, she was stirring the cocoa warming on the stove, the door burst open. . . . *Bubbalas, I missed you*

Eternity, Sophie, we want eternity, you and I. If only we could go down that slope in a rush. Not this tortuous descent, with all the false signposts arrowing upwards again.

"If we could get past that, Sophie," she had told her once, in a very private talk they had, "if we could *just once* get past that wanting certain moments to last forever."

"You with your *farshtunkena* philosophies! A woman would be better off if she could make a statue. It would keep! It would keep!"

So we take photographs, we make films, record voices on tape. Holding on. Yes, that's our sin. Again! Always crying, Again! The male can go on, Sophie, no matter what he loses. He knows the trick of keeping a part of himself separate. If it weren't for that sin, Sophie, we could rule the world! We could civilize it in one generation, all of it, we Women!

The male, he has that itch in his privates, it's his nature, he can't help what he is, that itch that can paint a Mona Lisa, but also make holocausts. We are at peace, Sophie, we are complete, and therefore humane, and therefore just. Only think, Sophie, what a world we could bring to pass! If only, if only we would let go!

"Tell me, Ruth, what is a child? I'll tell *you*, a child is a *pish*, a nothing, he eats you alive when he's little, and then when he doesn't need you no more, he throws you away, the core."

She tumbled from me, Sophie, an apple so fair . . . . He used to sit in the grass, Sophie, with that wondering, wistful look . . . . They would crowd against me, one on each side, as I read to them, Sophie, they were so jealous of one another, then, everything had to come out even . . . . They would hold hands, trudging up the hill side by side in the snow, they would fall, and get up, laughing, and their laughter rang up the hill . . . . Play that reel again, Sophie, and again, and again—

Sophie stirred, almost came awake. Then, with a little crying sound, she took in a great draught of air, and her head fell down on one shoulder and she went on sleeping.

Now Ruth saw Sophie looking into the eye of the camera, her own huge eyes deep, shadowy with her history. Her father's eyes, she said, her brother's eyes, her son's eyes, yes, Harold's eyes. Her heavy hair was coiffed in soft curls around her face; her long, dark dress was gathered at the throat with her mother's brooch, put away, now, for Rachel's children's children. Her dress, falling in soft folds over her full breasts, gathered again at the waist with a velvet sash, falling away, again, over a body shaped, *formed* to be filled up with a minyan of Harolds. "My mother died like most women in her time, Ruth, in childbirth. With a prayer on her lips. Was it all so long ago as they say?"

She saw Sophie calling to her father as the ship moved away from the shore where he stood, weeping. And she saw her dancing with the captain, as in the story she used to be forever telling, the story of the young and beautiful Sophie with the milk and honey complexion and the huge, haunting eyes who danced with the captain on her way to America. Now she saw Sophie singing as her foot worked the treadle. And now the nurse in the maternity ward was bending down to kiss Sophie's soft woman-lips. And now Sophie was running, dragging Harold by the hand, to help her brother's wife in a time of need. There was Sophie, chasing after *Parnosse*. Scolding Abe, scolding Harold, ladling broth into gleaming bowls at a seder table set for twenty-five. And now she caught the Sophie-scent as her new mother-in-law pulled the measuring tape taut around her breasts, then her waist, then her hips. "A poor girl he married, come, let me make you something to wear."

She saw the quick smile of Sophie as she turned towards Harold's camera, both hands fastening the clothespin, in the back yard of the rooming house in Miami. She saw Sophie putting coins in the pay telephone at the end of the hall on the medical ward of the hospital, dialing their number, croaking into the phone, "You'll have to come, I'm in oxygen, it's very bad for me." She saw Sophie standing in front of the apartment, waiting for her grandchildren to run up the stairs and into her arms, calling hoarsely, "I'm a heart patient, don't forget, be careful when you hug me, my darlings!" She saw Sophie coming down the steps from the plane with her mottled face, in her Afro wig, a pea coat she had picked up at a navy surplus store, her sweatshirt, her patched bluejeans.

So many Sophies.

And now she saw her own mother, growing smaller every year.

And now she saw her own face. Aged, deeply lined. She saw herself as she would become. In a little time, a little time.

"The inner landscape," she had once explained to Sophie, "this is what you think about when you raise a child."

"For what? Will you get back? You'll get, all right, a hit in the face is what you'll get, a door slammed against you is what we all get, you'll see!"

"Sophie, all children have gifts. Do you know how few women in the world have this chance? This freedom not to have to worry where the next piece of bread will come from, what to do when you get sick? Do you know how grateful we should be? Think, *think* what it would be like, this world, if every woman who bore a child need have no fear of hunger, of sickness. Of war. Only that she must find these gifts and bring them to harvest."

"What about *us*, eh? You had gifts, too. So did *I*! Beauty, talent, you wouldn't believe what I had! Who cared about *our* gifts, eh?"

"It can't be helped, what's done is done, can we redeem the past? Look, look what we've been given; there's still time! Sophie, I feel it in my bones. That time is running out. For all of us. Unless we turn a corner very soon."

Sophie had laughed long and merrily. "Look who's gonna stop the world from crashing! With her two children, with their music and picture-painting, look who'll make a Utopia! Dreamer, you worked yourself to the bone, you made yourself half-blind for an education, and you throw it all away for your children, they're growing up right before your eyes, they'll go away, they'll forget everything you ever taught 'em and gave 'em. What, Rachel is gonna be different? She'll be the same dummy we all are, she'll waste herself on family. And she could paint Mona Lisa *without* having to make holocausts! It'll be too late for her, too, she'll get old, like me, with nobody left to care."

I used to think, Rachel had said to Ruth when she was six years old, *that when you dreamed you were in G-d's world, then. I used to think, there is the world under the earth, and then the one on the earth, the one we know. And then there's the sky-world. And above that, above the stars and the whole solar system, there is a blue sky, very small. And I used to think that's where G-d is. In there.*

"Her mind, Sophie. She let me in. She knows how to make me come back, the way I was when I was a child. She can fill anyone out again, she can make us ripen all over again. I remember the naturalist on our walk, how the years fell away from him when he saw her running ahead of us on the mountain trail. Her whole body was singing. He couldn't hear it anymore, Sophie, the song of the wood peewee, he was going deaf. And Rachel listened for it. And she heard it. She lifted up her field glasses, and her face was radiant. She turned to him, she put her finger up to her lips. And the bird stayed there, like a small miracle, it stayed on the ailanthus tree, and it sang and it sang. They became great friends after that, Rachel and the naturalist. He told her what it was like when he first saw the red-eyed vireo, he said, *The bird looked at me and I looked at him and O! what a red eye he had!* He chose your granddaughter to pass on all his secrets to. . . .

"Here, Sophie, here is my sculpture that I never will make, that will never stand in a museum so that in another century some madman will smash it to pieces because he thinks he's Jesus Christ . . . this is my debut at the opera house, the aria I never sang there, can you hear it, Sophie, this note I'm singing now, that can stop the earth from turning, that can melt the feathers off the breast of a nightingale? This is my leap, Sophie, so high that even Nureyev can't catch me . . . this is my orchard of white blossoms, red apples . . . my garden of roses . . . my silk tapestry . . . my symphony, my epic poem, my *obras completas,* look, Sophie, quick, before she disappears!

"Look, Sophie, at this osprey your granddaughter drew, only look at its wings! And look at this horse she painted, with hooves of gold and black, plunging into the fresh blue running water, I can taste its freshness, look at the black mane floating, the wet-loam color streaked with gold all down its back, and under its jaw, Sophie, are these shadows, Sophie, are we shadows?

"Sophie, Sophie, she is my bridge, she calls me, she can't wait, she wants me *now,* this *minute,* while she's taking her bath, please, Mother, come in here now, she *has* to tell me about the river otters, did I know what it must be like to be a mother river otter? Behind every tree, she says, there's some creature waiting to devour her young, she has to find somewhere to hide them, she lives only to protect her young, did I know, did I know what it must be like? Sophie, Sophie, will we *die* of this?"

"What for, what for?" Sophie screamed. "Who appreciates? Does Society appreciate? What, It won't crush them? It won't gas them? Do you know what It destroyed already, that nothing, nothing can replace?"

"I know. Sophie, I *know!*"

"Then, *meshuggena*, what are you doing? Making something beautiful, then keep it for yourself you crazy girl, the scraps you can throw away. That's all the dogs deserve, is your scraps."

"But you *can't* keep! It doesn't keep!"

"Is dot right? Is *dot* right? Watch me, you'll learn! You think I'll lay down and let Life take everything away from me? Ha, wait, you'll learn a few tricks from me yet."

Through her tears, Ruth saw Sophie's face as an image in a window looking out into the rain. Old, old, she was beautifully old, a magnificent ruin. What did she know, what secret, that she refuses still to tell? "I always thought I'll die young," she used to moan, and Abe used to tell her, "Don't look now, but I don't think you're gonna make it."

Sophie's eyes opened, closed, opened again. She looked around the room bewildered. Then she looked straight at Ruth, smiled, and shook off her dreams.

"How long you've been here? Why you didn't wake me up?"

Show me the way, Sophie, how to let go . . . with grace . . . It's your responsibility, to show me the way. You're my elder. . . .

"What are you staring at? *Oiy*, I'm stiff like a board from sitting like this, whyn't you wake me up sooner?"

"You looked so peaceful. I didn't have the heart to disturb you."

"You should've anyway. Listen, Ruth, I gotta make a poster."

"What poster is it now?"

"Since when are you interested in politics, you wouldn't even help your own mother-in-law get started in my own business, you refused me."

"Sophie, you know it was impossible, how many times did we explain it to you, it wasn't that we *refused* you, it was that it was *impossible—*"

"Impossible is a word for don't want to."

"Sophie, not today, please, not today. Don't you remember, this afternoon is the children's art exhibit. It's Rachel's Big Day!"

"All right, I'm coming, I remember. What is it, her animals again she painted?"

"Mostly birds this time, she said."

"*Oiy*, birds. It's the *people* we gotta think about, never mind, what's the use, *Oiy*, Ruth, my arms are so stiff, my legs. Wait, I'll get up."

"Here, let me help you." She held out both her hands, and Sophie took them thankfully, and pulled herself to her feet.

"I had a funny dream. My mother was coming to me, leading a woman by the hand, and she was saying to me, *Here, I'll give you a daughter.*"

"Who was she, did you know her?"

"Did I know her! Who do you think, Ruth? It was *you!*"

Ruth heard a loud drumming in her ears. Her limbs seemed drained of feeling, of strength. She sat down on the chair staring up at her mother-in-law.

"What's the matter with you, I'm not allowed to dream I got a daughter, you think you're the only one who knows what it is to have a daughter? What do you think I tell you everything for otherwise? I know I can depend on you to remember everything what's important. Ten, fifteen years from now already, I know I'll be gone, Kenny'll be a big shot musician some place, Rachel'll be painting Mona Lisas, your little birds, they'll fly away, but I know you, I know I can depend on you, you won't forget what I taught you, dot's what makes you my daughter, you'll remember."

"Sophie...."

"Never mind, it's enough talk, tell me what she's putting on for the show, Rachel, come on, I know you had the same old argument with her. Tell me if she won or did you, will she wear pants?"

"She's wearing a long skirt." Ruth laughed. "Mind you, not because of anything *I* said. She found out that the other girls are wearing long skirts."

"She should care what somebody else does? You used to yell at *me* about that, remember?"

"I remember everything, Sophie. Everything."

"Better sometimes for you maybe you shouldn't remember so much." Sophie ran her tongue along her lower lip. "What time?"

"Almost two. It starts at half past. I thought you might want time to change. I went over to your place first, and when I couldn't find you I guessed where you were. Harold and Kenneth are in the library. They'll go over from there. I'll wait for you."

Sophie started laughing. "Remember, I used to yell at you when I was in Miami, you should change your clothes, you should look just right for this one and that one when they came to visit, you should dress up like a doll. I used to care about such *narishkeit*. Now *you're* the square! You're worried I'll go in my jeans, eh?"

"I've given up worrying. Believe it or not."

"Given up worrying, *go vay*, I know you. You have to be all spic and span even when you clean up the bathroom. You. I'll bet you still got one of those harnesses with garters. You still put on lipstick, too, and put perfume in back of your ears. Don't tell you you're not worrying! You're still a slave, my dear. A serf."

"All right, call me a slave, a serf, anything. If you want to go to the exhibit like you are, fine, let's go."

Sophie laughed even harder, and pointed a finger at her daughter-in-law's nose. "You wouldn't allow it, that I should walk in there like this. Admit. Admit."

"Sophie, I swear I don't give a tinker's damn."

"Admit! Admit!" Sophie sang gleefully. "We're wasting time!"

Ruth reached down in her purse, brought out her compact, flicked it open, thrust the mirror at Sophie. "Do you think you ought at least to take a few minutes to wash the Magic Marker off your nose? And button up your shirt? *Well?*"

"The slave can't stand the free! You can't stand it that I'm free!"

"Sophie, just once look in this mirror. Just once. Please."

"Put away your dumb mirror. I spent most of my life looking in a piece of glass, what did it bring me? All right! So I'll wash!"

They hurried away in opposite directions, Sophie to the washroom at the back of the building, Ruth up to the front to see how the book business was doing on a warm and sunny Saturday afternoon when everyone, even booklovers, would want to be outdoors.

The light moved along the panelled walls, over landscapes and seascapes and a painting of a blue woman rising from a cairn of blue stones, over still lifes, over paintings of insects, horses, birds . . . it dusted Sophie's wig with amber resin . . . it burnished the red-brown hair of her granddaughter. . . .

When she brought the dead fox sparrow to me, and she was weeping, and I said to her that we must find what never dies, she answered that all our dream-birds, the phoebe she imagined perched on my wrist, the thrushes filling my many arms when we play that I am a tree, can never be as that one bird, never, that bird that had breathed and was warm and could move and could fly

Ruth saw that her daughter was standing at the edge of the light, there where all the children of the world were gathered, that they were beyond harm there, in the dreamforest of Light,

and that her own hour had come, now, and she must go down into the vineyard.

AUDREY BORENSTEIN

She first suspected that something might have changed when the yellow roses began to bloom in the weeds at the edge of her porch. She had never noticed the rosebush before, but she was delighted with it. Yellow was her favorite color. She began to water and coddle the roses, humming an old hymn as she worked.

"Here, Jana, you want a pretty flower?" she said to the little neighbor girl. Jana wouldn't look at the rose, only at Amalia's outstretched hand. When the girl turned and ran into the house, frightened, Amalia realized that only she could see the yellow roses.

Amalia had wondered what was going on for years, but the changes had been so small, so subtle, that there hadn't been anything she could point to with certainty.

At the old house, on Valley Avenue in East Los Angeles, nothing had changed for many years. Her brothers and sisters grew up and moved away, her parents died, one after the other, until only she and Rosetta were left. They never married, and the old house, with its musty books and broken-down furniture, was left to them.

At first, she gave piano lessons on the old upright, and Rosetta ran an old hand-cranked printing press in the living room. This gave them a little income and kept them busy. But as the paint began to peel on the house, and rain came through the roof and damaged the upstairs rooms, fewer and fewer students made their way past the old, drooping trees in front to study piano with Amalia. Rosetta's back got too bad to run the printing press, and they sold it to their church, the Spanish American Free Evangelical Church of the Resurrection, for sixty dollars. So the two aging sisters were left alone with their father's books and the mice which began to make themselves at home in the sagging house.

They lived on crackers, eggs and Ovaltine, and passed the time reminiscing about their younger days in Mexico and Texas, which remained brighter in their minds than the present. Once in a while relatives would visit, bringing used clothing or strangers who they claimed were their children, but otherwise the sisters spent days uncluttered by concerns from the outside world. Amalia was happy. As guardian of the family castle, she had a purpose in life. Rosetta's back grew more crooked, but she refused to see a doctor and still smiled radiantly, even if it was at an awkward angle.

Then the neighborhood began to change. Families with more children began renting the houses, and quiet Valley Avenue was loud with the noise of lowriders at night. This did not cause them too much concern until the children began to taunt the two old women.

"Bruja, bruja!" they would chant, and eventually the teasing was accompanied by a small rock or two as one or the other of the two women scurried up the long walk to the warped steps of the porch. Amalia wept with fear and frustration, but not until Rosetta was knocked down one day did Amalia dare to tell her brother.

"Carlos, something terrible has happened," she began when he came on one of his monthly visits. He was tacking plastic over one of the broken windows upstairs.

"The children hurt Rosetta."

"What children? What happened?"

"I don't know. A neighbor family. They're always in the street, saying things to us, but yesterday they pushed Rosetta, and she cut her hand."

Carlos went to see his other sister, wedged behind a bookcase downstairs where the sisters now lived, surrounded by the least damaged furniture. She told him the story, and showed him her hands. Finally she even admitted that the children thought they were witches.

Carlos was outraged. He wanted to call the police, but Rosetta and Amalia were afraid that it would just go worse for them. Nothing could be done to the children, and the parents certainly didn't care. It would just be taken out on the two helpless sisters. Reluctantly, Carlos agreed.

Later that evening, Carlos described the situation to his wife, Concha.

"Well, it's no wonder," she said over her shoulder from the sink. "They go around all summer wearing three sweaters and a coat, their stockings falling down, and they never comb their hair. It's no wonder the neighbors think they're witches." Carlos admitted that she had a point.

The family held a conference, and it was decided to sell the Valley Avenue house and use the proceeds to find the sisters a safer place to live and help pay their expenses. As it was, each family gave what it could now and then, but it was Carlos who made sure they had groceries and paid the power bill. It was getting too hard to heat the old place, anyway.

Amalia was incensed. How could they do this to the memory of her father? Who would keep his books? How could they even think of selling the family property? She and Rosetta, of course, would refuse to move. But in the end, the choice wasn't given to them; and Rosetta, it turned out, didn't really care one way or the other. She knew she was not in a position to say. Her back grew a little more crooked, and the two sisters were moved to a duplex on Loma Street. Some of the old books went with them, in a bookcase with anchors carved in the sides, just to help them feel at home. The piano was given to the church to use in Sunday School.

On Loma, things were a little better, but not much. The roof didn't leak, but the neighborhood was almost as bad. Amalia was so mad at Carlos for selling the old house that she didn't speak to him for four months. Her eyes were rimmed with red, and she sat in a straight-backed chair without moving for hours at a time. Rosetta did not bother her when she was like this, but went on about her business, moving like a gray crab with her shuffling, sideways walk. Carlos finally got Rosetta to a doctor, but she was told that an operation might or might not correct her ever-bending spine, and would certainly be very painful, if not paralyzing. Rosetta chose to keep her back as it was.

"It doesn't bother me," she said cheerfully. "If this is the way that God wants me to be, then that's the way I'll be. We all have our burdens to bear." Just as though she carried a great rock on her right shoulder, Rosetta continued to bend more and more sharply down and to the left.

Carlos did the best that he could to keep the two sisters looking decent, but Amalia would wander vacant-eyed down the street, her purse dangling on her arm, her coat buttoned up wrong.

When she finally resumed speaking again, no one paid attention to Amalia. Her sister Rosetta would nod and smile, but often not respond to her questions. Carlos would assure her that the rest of the family was fine and that he would be back in a week, no matter what she said.

"When is my sister Ruth coming to visit?" she would ask. "I have a present for her birthday, which was two weeks ago, and I want to give it to her."

"Ruth is fine," Carlos would say. "Save the present for when she comes at Easter." Amalia would hold the present, a necklace purchased at the five-and-dime, or found in an old purse, and sit at the window in her straight-backed chair, waiting for Easter.

When the rent was raised at Loma Street, Carlos decided to move the sisters again. He knew it was hard on them, but Amalia had already had her purse snatched once, and the street was too busy for Rosetta to cross alone. It was very hard for her to stand so stooped over and look both ways. She refused to use a cane, because she liked to have both hands free to fend off muggers or overly solicitous people. "Besides," she said, "a cane makes me feel old."

Amalia was angry again, at another move in less than three years, but this brought her to the duplex with the yellow roses. The roses appeared after they were living on Highland Street for almost a year.

"Look!" she said, running inside with a beautiful bouquet. "Yellow roses just like my mother used to grow in San Antonio!"

Rosetta smiled and went to fetch her a vase, but when the roses had wilted after two days for lack of water, she didn't seem to notice. So Amalia enjoyed her roses by herself, moving her chair out on the narrow porch on warm summer evenings to inhale the delicious fragrance.

One day, maneuvering her chair through the screen door, Amalia was startled to find her nephew Ezekial from Mexico sitting on the steps. He was turning towards the wall, trying to light a cigarette.

"Ezekial!" she said, scandalized. "Does my sister know you smoke?"

"No," he answered, puffing calmly. "But it doesn't really concern anyone anymore."

Amalia was too shocked to say anything, so she sat down on her chair for a minute. It had been so long since she had seen her nephew, years and years, and she tried to think of why he would come.

"What brings you to visit?" she finally said. "Did the others come, too? Where is your mother?"

"I've been coming here every day for a long time," he said, sprawled out on the steps, "waiting for you to say something to me."

Amalia was mystified. "I didn't see you!" she said. "Why didn't you say something?"

"It wouldn't have made any difference," he answered languidly, "you would have thought you were hearing voices."

Amalia sat and thought some more. "And how is your family? I haven't seen your mother in a long time."

"I guess they're okay," said Ezekial. "I really haven't seen much of them since I died. . . . My brother sells Cadillacs."

He blew smoke into the air while Amalia tried to figure out what he was talking about. Finally, she remembered that he had died rather suddenly of typhoid fever almost fifteen years before. All the young girls in Chihuahua had cried at his funeral. Yet here he sat, still handsome and young, his curly brown hair pressed back against the side of her duplex.

"Then how can I talk to you?" she managed to ask.

"I'm not sure," he answered. "But I noticed this street one day, and saw you outside, so I thought it would be polite to visit. We can go anywhere we want, you know."

Amalia didn't know. She sat and sat some more, but she couldn't think of anything to say. Finally, it grew too dark to see anything but the glowing tip of Ezekial's cigarette, so she took her chair and went back into the house.

After that, Ezekial came to visit once or twice a week, and Amalia would sit on the porch with him. He refused to go into the house. Eventually, other people came to visit, dear friends and relatives Amalia hadn't seen in thirty, sometimes forty-five years. She sat on the porch and discussed the old times with them, the places they used to go, and tended her roses. The bush had grown up and practically screened off the porch from the street, and new flowers of a kind Amalia had never seen before began to appear along the walk. She tried to make sure they got enough water to sustain them through the stifling summer days, but it was hard work.

Amalia tried to get Rosetta to go out on the porch and visit, but she refused, saying she was too busy. If Amalia tried to force her, taking her by the arm, Rosetta would hang on to the doorframe and go even more crooked. Amalia was afraid to hurt her, so she stopped trying to drag her out, apologizing to the visitors for her sister.

They seemed neither surprised nor concerned. "She's just not ready yet," shrugged Estrella, a childhood friend. "When she wants to see us, she will."

That was a wonderful year for Amalia. While before she had been drawn and pale, her face grew rosy and plump with smiles. She combed her hair now, and dressed properly for her little evening porch sessions.

One night, rather late, Ezekial and Estrella showed up and asked Amalia if she wanted to visit dreams. "Come on," said Ezekial. "It only takes a few moments. It's the best way to visit your living relations."

Estrella took her by the hand, and they dropped in on her brother Carlos, tossing in his bed. They stood by impassively as he relived a speeding ticket he had received that day on the freeway, and he woke up confused by their images mixed up with that of the California Highway Patrolman.

They went to two or three other dreams that night, a gardening dream, a church service, and food, and caught up on the nocturnal concerns of their living family. After that, Amalia went along with them now and then, just to see how everyone was getting along.

By the next spring, Amalia was transformed. She carried herself like a young girl, and chattered happily to her brother Carlos when he came to visit. He was relieved that the sisters seemed to like their new home. He gave the next-door neighbors fifteen dollars a month just to keep an eye on them, and this meant that someone often accompanied Amalia to the store, or got the groceries for them.

Rosetta seldom left the house now, self-conscious about her back, and now bent so far double that she mostly saw people's shoes, anyway. This took most of the joy out of outdoor walks.

As Amalia grew healthier, she ate less and less. She complained that eggs were too heavy for her, and subsisted almost entirely on crackers and hot cinnamon tea. Her skin was now so translucent, an egg would probably have been visible through her stomach. Her eyes and her curly hair shone.

That May, Amalia looked down the beautiful boulevard of green trees and formal gardens and knew that this wasn't really Highland Street anymore. In fact, it looked like Chapultepec Park, where she had visited as a child. The bushes were shaped like lions and birds, and there was even a statue of her famous ancestor, Miguel Acuña.

"Where are we?" she asked. "I mean, really, what is this place?"

"Purgatory," answered her deceased sister Julia, "a way station to heaven."

Amalia was stunned. "But we don't believe in purgatory, do we? That's Catholic!"

"Probably not," sighed Julia. "I've never seen our father here. But it might just be that we haven't been here long enough."

"It seems long enough," said Ezekial. "What's wrong with purgatory, anyway? It's not so bad."

"No, it's not," agreed Amalia, "but our family doesn't know."

"Know what?"

"That we're in purgatory, that purgatory exists."

"You're not, really," said Ezekial to Amalia. "You just visit a lot."

"Oh, I see," said Amalia. A cool breeze blew the scent of jacaranda blossoms across the porch.

"Not that we blame you," added Julia. "We love to see you. And we have plenty of time on our hands."

"But we need to tell them!" said Amalia. "They should know!"

"How?" asked Julia. "They wouldn't believe us."

"No," said Amalia, "no one pays any attention to what I say anymore, and I'm still alive. And they're concerned with other things, busy with their own lives. When we visit their dreams, they're full of new cars and work and the faces of children. Where did all those children come from, anyway?"

"That's what happens when you have a big family," said Julia. "Lots of nieces and nephews and second cousins. I'm sorry I never had children. Only Ruth's children were like my own."

"Ruth's children!" exclaimed Amalia.

An idea was coming to her. In their nighttime wanderings through the dreams of their relatives, they had come across Ruth's youngest, a young woman who lived in a part of the country where Amalia had never really been. The dreams were cool and wide, full of nights on the desert and luminous skies, rooms full of dusty books, and a fear of the color combination of pink and black.

"Rachel would believe us!" she cried, jumping up. "We can tell my niece Rachel, and she will tell the others!"

"Yes, Rachel," said Julia. "My sweet little Rachel. And she's smart, too. She'll figure out a way to tell them, and make them believe."

"Well, maybe," said Ezekial, doubtful. "Your relatives are all so stubborn," he said, as though they weren't his relatives, too, "that they may just call her a heretic and put her on a prayer list."

"Well, we must try," said Amalia firmly, "and Rachel is our only chance. We will all go to her in a dream," said Amalia. Her mind was made up now. "We will go and tell her that we are all right and we are in purgatory, and that we will see her on the Other Side."

So that's what they did, later that summer, when the last petals were falling off of the yellow rosebush, Amalia and Julia and Ezekial. Amalia held Rosetta's hand through the open doorway while they dream-travelled, so she was partially included, too.

Rachel got the message, loud and clear, and waking, was impressed that she could dream so well in Spanish, after all these years, for at first she thought that the dream had originated in her own mind. But the longer she thought about it, the stranger it seemed, so she got up and wrote the message down, word for vivid word, and listed everyone she could remember seeing in that swirling garden. It was hard to sleep after that, so she sat awake until the dream faded a little and she could return to her indistinct slumbers.

And so, not knowing how else to tell it, I have written this story. The Indians in this part of the country, the Northwest, have a term, sheel-shole, which means "to thread the bead." It refers to a way of travelling from inland to ocean by guiding a boat from one interconnected lake to the next. My aunt Amalia is still alive, but it's only a matter of time before she paddles her canoe, yellow roses and all, out into the open sea.

KATHLEEN J. ALCALÁ

MIRROR OF STRENGTH:
PORTRAIT OF TWO CHILEAN *ARPILLERISTAS*   *MARJORIE AGOSIN*
                                        Translated by COLA FRANZEN

The *arpillera* is a wall hanging, a small simple scene constructed from scraps of cloth appliquéd onto a backing cloth, often of burlap. The word for burlap in Spanish is *arpillera*, hence the name given to the wall hanging. The women who make them are called *arpilleristas*.

The *arpilleras* made in Santiago as a way for poor women to earn a little money have evolved into a surprising political phenomenon. Workshops to make them were set up in 1974—some months after the coup that overthrew the Socialist government of Salvador Allende—by the Vicary of Solidarity. The vicary, an organization of the Catholic Church particularly concerned with human rights and with helping those in most need, operates under the special protection of the Cardinal of Santiago.

Women began to make *arpilleras* that showed their own lives under Pinochet's dictatorship: the houses in the shantytowns, the church, the little school, the common water faucet often X'd out to show lack of water. Hunger: empty pots, empty bowls. Unemployment: closed and shuttered factories, lines in front of the unemployment office. The disappeared: empty chairs, empty rooms, a picture of the disappeared one with question marks embroidered all around. Political terror: arrests, beatings, burials.

The *arpilleras* serve not only as a source of income for the women but also as a way of rescuing their loved ones from oblivion, of exacting some small bit of justice by letting the outside world know what is really happening inside Chile.

In showing the stuff of their everyday lives, the *arpilleras* document the terror and provide a searing indictment of it. The *arpilleristas*, the poorest, most powerless group, have found a way to speak and the courage to do so.

One might say the *arpilleras* are the revolutionary posters of Chile. They are colorful and striking, their message is clear and immediate, they are moving and dramatic. They show better than any words ever could what life is really like under the dictatorship and they are a great embarrassment to the usurpers. On the one hand, the *Junta* does not like to admit that a group of poor women, using scraps of cloth, can do anything to unnerve them. But the *arpilleras* go abroad, through the efforts of the Vicary of Solidarity, and they spoil the image that Pinochet and his cohorts have tried so hard to build up. So the *Junta* tries various methods to curb the *arpillera* production and distribution. They spy on the workshops, most of which are in the basements of churches; they harass the women who make them; they confiscate shipments of *arpilleras* at the airport when they manage to find them, and they forbid their exhibition and sale within Chile. The final irony is that they have resorted to having "fake" *arpilleras* fabricated—same size, same technique, sometimes the same Andes in the background, but with Pinochet's slogans embroidered across them. These are prominently displayed and offered for sale in various locations throughout the country, for example in gift shops along the major highways where the unwary might be trapped into buying them.

* * *

I grew up amid grandmothers and great grandmothers. They had travelled the width of the sea to come finally to the faraway corner of the world called Chile, a slender and beautiful country lying between the imperturbable Andes and the impetuous Pacific, land given to wild storms and earthquakes. I grew and came to consciousness in the protective shadow of old women. Their age was not a misfortune; it had no stigma attached to it. On the contrary, old age was regarded as a serene and joyful time. I believe that old age in Latin America and in much of the third world is not a time of abandonment and destitution, years passed in old peoples' homes, the boredom of days interrupted only by occasional and dutiful visits of relatives. It is a time of tranquillity and reflection, living in close and warm contact with family members of several generations, in the same house or in the same neighborhood. This living side by side of members of different generations is one of the richest gifts the third world has to offer.

However, the lives of women of all ages have been turned upside down in Chile during the past twelve years, during the tragic epoch of the Pinochet dictatorship. As the nightmare drags on, uncounted thousands of citizens continue to be arrested, only to disappear, continue to be tortured and murdered. Women, particularly older women, are drastically affected by the terror and its destructive effects on family life. Women whose husbands and/or children disappeared were left to hold together and care for whatever remained of the family. They had to become wage earners, to learn to be both father and mother. In the process—at a time when men who openly oppose the government are dealt with immediately and harshly—the women have become a visible, courageous, outspoken, effective resistance force against the dictatorship.

Many women have coordinated the efforts to find the disappeared and to share information by forming the Association of Families of the Detained-Disappeared. Its membership consists almost entirely of women, whose ages range from 20 to 80. Anita Rojas is an active member of the Association. She is 75 years old, and she says she never misses a meeting of the Association. She has taken part in all the manifestations organized by them, including hunger strikes that sometimes last many weeks and take place on the sidewalks near detention centers or outside prisons.

Anita Rojas worked for many years as a maid to support and educate her only son, who graduated from the university with an engineering degree. He was arrested in 1975 and disappeared some months later. Even now, a decade later, his fate and his whereabouts are still unknown. The fortitude and vitality of Anita Rojas are incredible. Since the day her son disappeared, she has neither given up nor seemed discouraged. In the demonstrations she will always be seen carrying a big sign that says "WHERE ARE THEY?" She makes regular visits to prisons and morgues searching not only for her own son but for other disappeareds.

Anita Rojas also makes *arpilleras*. She says that her life goes into her *arpilleras*, but she receives strength back because every snip and every stitch is a way of feeling connected with her disappeared son. Her hands are vigorous and strong; they move over the cloth like knowing birds. It is wonderful to hear her explaining to the younger women how to cut the pieces, how to place the sawtooth peaks of the Andes to form the backdrop and set the mood of practically every *arpillera*.

Sitting next to Anita is Irma Miller, who is 70 years old. Her son, a film cameraman, also disappeared in 1975, along with his fiancée. Irma has tremendous strength and vigor. She speaks of her tragedy with boundless courage, but when she tells of her recurring dream, which is to see her son "running freely across the sand as he did when he was little," her voice trails off and she begins to cry. In a letter to me she says she had reached the age when she thought she would enjoy being a grandmother and having her children and grandchildren around her. But instead she finds herself in the middle of a fierce battle for social justice, marching in the streets and denouncing the criminals who have imprisoned Chile, and making *arpilleras* to send the tale to the outside world. Irma says she never thought that in simply continuing to follow all the clues and threads that resulted from her son's disappearance that she would end up in an arduous battle for the restoration of democracy in Chile.

These women are tireless, and the effects of their activity keep rippling out in wider and wider circles. Perhaps most impressive is their constancy and persistence in keeping up their search and their efforts day after day, year after year. I have been corresponding with Anita and with Irma for a number of years now, and in each of their letters they tell me of their daily political chores, and it is in the "dailiness" that their strength comes out. They are absolutely determined to keep going until they change the destiny of their country.

Although Anita and Irma regularly take part in activities of the Association, such as pilgrimages to known torture centers to conduct candlelight vigils or to sing freedom songs, they consider themselves first and foremost arpilleristas. In one of her letters, Irma says, "As members of the Association of Families of the Detained-Disappeared, we searched for various ways to denounce what happened to us, to tell about our tragedy. One method is the arpillera. Each woman chooses her own theme. In the beginning I only made arpilleras that showed the arrest and disappearance of my son, but later I began to show the problems and tragedies of other people, to illustrate a wide range of social problems of our people. . . . Every arpillera is made with a lot of pain, because each image has great significance for us, but while I can, I will continue to make them because that is our way of letting the world know all that is happening in Chile."

Anita writes about the arpilleras this way: "I thought about my moments of happiness when I was with my son and my moments of loneliness when they took him away from me, and those moments I put into images for my arpilleras. I thought about my life, how much I had sacrificed in order to educate my son. And just when I didn't need to work any more, this happened and there came over me all the anxiety that I express in my arpilleras."

For these women, making arpilleras also signifies a new creative process in their lives. The search for fabrics and patterns, the choice of colors, the communal activity, all are parts of a new way to begin living again, to tell about and comprehend their lives. They are no longer mothers caring for their children, they are mothers searching for their children, tenaciously, without respite, knowing that those they search for are probably no longer alive. But the search continues for the truth of what happened, so that the disappeared will not be forgotten, and all the suffering will not have been for nothing.

I ask Anita and Irma how they can keep up such an exhausting pace at their age. They tell me they never think about their age. They say, yes, they get tired, but they keep going anyway. They find the energy and vigor necessary for the next manifestation, for another trek around prisons and morgues; they find breath and inspiration for another arpillera.

To us they may seem like real heroines, larger than life, but they see what they do as normal. They say they never expected to find themselves working as political activists, that this turn of events in their lives was unplanned and unexpected, but they feel they are doing what has to be done. They will continue to march, denounce, search, go forward. Their official slogan is: "For life or for peace tell us where they are."

MARJORIE AGOSIN
Translated by COLA FRANZEN

Barbara Macdonald and Cynthia Rich, 1983   photograph by Avery McGinn

BOTH FEET IN LIFE
INTERVIEWS WITH BARBARA MACDONALD AND CYNTHIA RICH
by JEAN SWALLOW

I interviewed Barbara Macdonald and Cynthia Rich after their essays and narratives were published together in the book *Look Me in the Eye: Old Women, Aging and Ageism*. Barbara is a small, solid seventy-one-year-old white-haired woman. Cynthia is taller than Barbara, and her gray hair contrasts to Barbara's white. Cynthia is in her early fifties. In part because of the difference in their ages, they have come at the issues of age and ageism from different perspectives. They now live together in a small trailer on the Anza-Borrego desert in Southern California, writing and producing the crucial conversations which inform the book. *Look Me in the Eye* is the first book on aging, ageism and old women to come out of the lesbian-feminist sensibility, and it is intense, intelligent, angry, and hopeful, as are both these women.

TALKING WITH BARBARA MACDONALD:

JEAN SWALLOW: Tell me why you wrote this book.
BARBARA MACDONALD: I wrote the essays in Look Me in the Eye because I was taking in aging and ageism and I was so angry, I had to deal with it.

I put the essays together because they have a sequence. When I went to live in Cambridge I couldn't figure out what was going on. I had come from a place where everybody knew me and all of a sudden nobody knew me except as an old woman; that was all they could see. It was a matter of shock. When I wrote the first essay, I began to see that there was something operating; there was a politic; it was not just my personal experience. So then I wanted to put the essays together so that other women could start from where I was and go through the experience with me.

S: Tell me how you see yourself.
M: I think of myself as a woman who survived the Depression. One of the differences between women of certain ages is whether or not they lived through the Depression. Once you have lived through that experience in which there were literally no jobs, no money, there are certain things that you just can't take for granted.

For example, prosperity. I never really trust it. I'm not a consumer. If I decide to spend $50, I think of everything I had to do in the thirties to earn that much, or I think of the last ten years before my retirement, when I earned more but I had to waste years of my life just waiting to live. I guess I'm saying that money represents years of my life, so that even if I had a lot of money now, I couldn't throw it away, spend it casually, because of what it represents. I paid too much for it in order to survive.

I am a radical feminist. I think I really didn't know that I was always a radical feminist until I read Joan Nestle's work. When I read her description of the dykes of the fifties, it helped me understand who I was in the thirties. A lot of what earlier felt shameful to me in terms of the pain of being so different, I see now in just a very different way.

I define myself as an old woman. I think young lesbians define me as an old dyke, but I define myself as an old woman. The dyke is a given—doesn't need explaining, not that I want to minimize it. Part of the reason I say I get real pleasure out of growing old is because I'm a dyke. I'm not facing otherness for the first time, with all that discomfort that I once felt about being other. And now I have this brand new chance to find out who I am, facing now another kind of otherness. Almost in some ways I welcome it as a chance to know myself.

S: What else do you like about growing old?

M: I spent a lot of my life, as I think most women have, wondering, "Am I even going to really make it, will I make it through life?" I see now that I'm going to. I have that answer.

Some women I talk to are so frightened of growing old. I sense their desperation. They say things to me like, "I'm not going to live to be old. I'm not going to live to be dependent." The message young women get from the youth culture is that it's wonderful to be young and terrible to grow old. If you think about it, it's an impossible dilemma—how can you make a good start in life if you are being told at the same time how terrible the finish is? And this ageism encourages a sort of carelessness with life—fast cars, fast foods, drugs. There's a kind of toying with death. This is reinforced by the violence constantly portrayed, saying life is cheap—and for men, life *is* cheap, they don't produce it. These are male values, destructive to women.

Because of ageism, many women don't fully commit themselves to living life out until they can no longer pass as young. They live their lives with one foot in life and one foot outside it. With age you resolve that. I know the value of each day and I'm living with both feet in life. I'm living much more fully.

I like taking the measure of my own death—it was always part of my life. We miss a lot by not taking in the real jeopardy we are in. Every moment is important. We don't talk about the fact that you and I, despite the differences in our ages, may not live our lives out; that between what we are eating, breathing, and the risks of chemicals all around us, and the possibility of dying by nuclear bombs, your chances of dying in the next few years may be as great as mine. And if we are both going to go out by a nuclear bomb tomorrow or if I'm going to go out in the process of old age and dying, we ought to know the reality of our lives every day. To be conscious.

There is something about taking in the ending that changes your values—you are empowered by it. You are less willing to compromise. You are more determined to make your life meaningful and to refuse to distort in any way who you are in order to please. I have really almost no desire left to please and there is power in that. The power of the old woman is not being afraid to die, being conscious of all of her life, being in charge of her life, and these are in addition to the ways she is empowered by being less useful to men.

I was never useful to men, though I had to work for a living and so I had to work for men. But the message that I sent out was that I would not serve men, I would not be available to men for any kind of exploitation and to the degree that I could do that and earn a living and survive, I did. Now, I am out of the labor market and it is an understatement to say that I am not useful to men. I will thwart their purposes every way I can for the rest of my life.

And I think that in one sense, I can't say they are afraid of me, because they can't see me. I am invisible to them. But when I make myself visible, then they are afraid. The power of the old woman is that because she is outside the system, she can attack it. And I am determined to attack it.

One of the ways in which I am particularly conscious of this stance is when I go down the street. People expect me to move over. I noticed it particularly in Cambridge, where there is the University and there are groups of young people, and they are coming down the street in groups of two, three, or four and they expect me to move over, which means to step on the grass or on the curb. I just woke up one day to the fact that I was moving over. I have no idea for how many years I had been doing that. Now I never move over.

I simply keep walking. And we hit full force, because the other person is so sure that I am going to move that he isn't even paying any attention and we simply ram each other. If it's a man with a woman, he shows embarrassment, because he just about knocked down a five-foot seventy-year-old woman and so he quickly apologizes. But he's startled, he doesn't understand why I didn't move over, he doesn't even know how I got there, where I came from. I am invisible to him, despite the fact that I am on my own side of the street, simply refusing to give him that space that he assumes is his.

Another example. I have always liked to fix things. When Cynthia and I go to a hardware store to get something, the hardware man will only discuss it with Cynthia. It is inconceivable to him that I could use a screwdriver, whereas when I was younger they would talk to me. Sometimes in a store, I just make a great big scene. "What the hell do you mean," I shout. And they are kind of stunned.

By the very way that they shut me out, I have found my power. I've gotten a hold of my rage and I speak out and I define it for them. I go to women's department stores and I say, "What do you mean that there is not a thing in this store for me to wear? Don't send me over to that rack when you know there is not a thing for me on that rack." And I say so in a loud voice and I don't care if a crowd gathers. It's infuriating.

Clothes have been designed to separate women. Over here we have the young who are bonded with males. And the clothes are dykey; the pants have pockets; they are well-made. At least superficially, they are made to empower women. Then you have another set of clothes that are made to disempower. They have no pockets, are made of polyester, flouncy. They define you as other; they define you as mother.

When I can't go into a store and buy clothes, I want young women to know that I am angry. I know you have heard this before from me, and I am not through. I hope other old women will not give up their anger until young women walk into a store (and I don't care if they can wear a size 13, size 18, or a size 40) and say, "I will not purchase from this store if I do not know that *all* women can come in here and buy clothes that are comfortable, that allow for body movement, and that you do not have hanging on your racks Mother Hubbards, or any other clothes designed by men to set women apart."

I expect to see young women marching in front of those stores before I'll be satisfied. Young women really don't seem to take in that I and other old women are turned away at the door and that this is outrageous.

S: Is this what you want me to do? What you want women my age to do?

M: I want you first to form consciousness-raising groups and workshops to examine your own ageism, and I want that process to be ongoing. I think that out of that process women's collectives—publishers, activists—will see that they have not included old women. I want such groups to study the publications coming out and be sensitive to what is ageist. But yes—I want you to quit going into clothing stores that pretend I don't exist. Why would you go into a store that turns me away? Why aren't you out in front of those stores marching? If you were, you would be surprised at how many old women would come out of the closet to join you around other issues.

S: Now this brings me to a question that I have not asked because I was embarrassed and shy.

M: I understand shyness—believe it or not.

S: As a lesbian, I don't feel I have a history. I have a desperate desire to know that you were a lesbian in the thirties. I have a desperate need to know that there have always been lesbians. And because you are here now, I think that the tendency of myself and of my contemporaries, who also have that need for place and time and continuity, is to treat you as justification. If someone was one before me, then I can't be unnatural. I take immense delight in knowing that there are queer seagulls. I think that I, and my contemporaries, need to know that lesbians have always been. Except what happens is we don't want to deal with, maybe we even can't see, old women, women like you. And so we make up stories about who you are (and those stories are certainly published by a number of presses and magazines) rather than talk with you.

M: If you dealt with old women as equals, you would already know our stories. You would have already heard our stories, as you have heard all this morning around this breakfast table because you have engaged with us on a real level and know what the pain is like. And so I don't feel as though you are staring at us as though we were an animal in a cage. I feel as though you want to know who I am, that you see me as a woman in process.

S: *And to not make it up, not to have some 35-year-old out there making it up. I mean, it strikes me as obscene, in a way that Henry Miller is obscene, in that it is somebody else telling me what my story is.*

But the other thing that occurs to me is that I want to know how you made it through your life. I want you to be my parent. I don't have a gay parent, and I have had some negative parenting in some areas. I think I want to go to you and say, "What do I do now?" Which is probably okay if we are friends. But when I go to you as an old woman and say "Give me your wisdom" then I've trapped you, haven't I?

M: I haven't got any wisdom. I wish I did. I would love to be able to tell you how great I was and how I had this powerful stance and how I made it through and tell you I never had anything to do with men and I had a clear vision.

But I just muddled my way through as best I could and I am filled with shame at the compromises I had to make. It's a curious kind of reversal. When I was young, I was filled with shame at my difference and I tried to hide it, and now that I try to write about my past, my shame is in the way I did not reveal it, the ways I compromised myself. It is not easy. It is not easy for an old dyke to tell you about the early years of being a dyke. For me at least, it is filled with shame and now I begin to feel that I may be able to write about those early years, but only since Joan Nestle has helped me out.

Anyone can ask me, but I have no answers. I just muddled through. And I never thought I'd make it. Half the fun of old age is that I made it. And there is no magical way.

S: *What becomes clear to me is that out of my need, I am putting you in a slot. And I am separating you from me. It seems to me that the pain of ageism is about separating us. That you become this, and I become that, and we no longer are able to be together.*

M: That's right. And I think Cynthia describes that so well in the book: if we sit down to have coffee with each other, as long as we are two women talking together everything goes well, but at the point where one of us thinks this woman could be my daughter or my mother, the conversation is really over. We've gotten into roles that are part of the patriarchal caste system. We need to change the ways women talk to each other across generations if we are going to change the world.

TALKING WITH CYNTHIA RICH:

S: *How do you see age and ageism being dealt with in the women's movement?*

R: When I began to consider myself a feminist and first thought about "women's" issues, the image that came to my mind was of women in their twenties or 30's or maybe, like myself, just coming into middle age. In my mind's eye, I simply did not see old women. I think that wasn't unusual in 1970. It's painful to say, but—fifteen years later in the movement—it seems as if younger women still don't see old women as real women whose lives are ongoing, who face many of the issues and problems that younger women face, but also the women's issue of ageism.

When younger women are aware of old women at all, it's usually as women who *used* to be somebody. So from time to time we'll seek out some old woman to tell us how it was back in the days when she was still a woman.

But our level of awareness of how things *are* for old women now is very, very low in the women's movement. We've treated ageism as a luxury issue, or even a non-issue. The National Women's Studies Association has knocked ageism off its list of serious oppressions.

S: It was on, and now it's off?

R: At one point, NWSA at least gave lip-service to it. It's not as if ageism was ever significantly integrated into women's studies. You can go to conference after conference where it's simply not seen as important.* Yet it seems to me that you can't really have a feminist politic without looking at ageism, that ageism connects to every other issue that affects women's lives.

Barbara and I attended the National Association of Lesbian and Gay Gerontologists recently, and there was not a single workshop on ageism. The issue wasn't discussed. Here were younger lesbians planning social services for old lesbians without feeling any need to examine their own ageism.

S: Talk to me about social services, and how that relates to ageism.

R: It's a question of who defines whom. Old women are not the ones defining aging, old women are not listened to about aging and ageism. Right now, aging is being defined by all sorts of people who make a living from inventing goods and services for old women. So we get stereotypes that serve the purposes of profit-making, and we're left with no real insight into either the process of aging or what old women have to confront in the world every day of their lives.

Social agencies are one of the ways by which old women are defined for profit. They raise money by assuring the public of how capable service workers are and how needy and incapable the women they serve are. Of course they're not out to insist on changes in the economic and social system that is the source of their clients' problems.

So we have organizations like the United Way of Massachusetts raising funds with an ad that shows an old woman in a room alone, staring out the window. The caption reads: "One day you wake up old and all your friends are gone." The advertisement goes on to feed the idea that—naturally—as you grow old, your

See Barbara Macdonald's speech to NWSA in this issue of CALYX.

friends will all be old like yourself, and when they die—naturally—no younger women are going to be interested in you. The message is that an old woman shouldn't even expect friendship or companionship from a younger woman. Who says that's natural? It's insulting and it's a self-fulfilling prophesy. It's also self-serving—only United Way is willing to be friends with an old woman.

Just as bad is the stereotype developed by advertisers of consumer products. Because the numbers of old women are growing so rapidly, manufacturers see there are profits to be made off those old women who aren't yet divorced or widowed, and who still have access to some of their husband's money. These aren't most old women, but there's a market there. So advertising has begun to portray the old woman as the sensuous grandmother, as the woman who gets off the plane in her little tennis suit and puts on her Oil of Olay. She is a white woman, of course, and she is very comfortably off. Unlike most old women, she's not worried about whether to pay the gas bill or buy groceries—she just wants to bring out her beauty.

Another way old women—both Black and white—are stereotyped for exploitation is by always showing them as grandmothers. Here the message is that the only real joy or meaning in an old woman's life comes from being with children. So we have all sorts of programs like Foster Grandparents. It's another way of cashing in on more of women's unpaid work. The most blatant example of that is an agency in Orlando, Florida, called "Dial-a-Grandma, Hire-a-Grandpa." Most old women worked hard raising their own family of children, and didn't have many other choices. Now they're expected to go on and raise another generation. Why are old women supposed to be interested only in "future generations" and not in themselves or each other? Why is it that kids on the street call Barbara "Grandma"—as in "Move along, Grandma"? Who's making these definitions?

The central issue here is that it's only old women who can define what it means to be an old woman in America. Statistics tell us something, though, about the extent to which ageism is a woman's issue, not to be covered up by the term "elderly." Old women who are single or widowed or divorced—that is, women who are not at that moment by the warm side of a man—are four times as likely to live at poverty levels of income. And two-thirds of all old women aren't living with a husband. More than twice as many old women as men live in poverty.

Almost all the residents of public housing for the elderly are women. Over two-thirds of nursing home beds are occupied by women. So when we read about cutbacks in Social Security or shocking stories about nursing homes, we have to see that these are women's problems.

S: You've said that as soon as a woman ceases to be useful to a man in terms of bearing his children or taking care of him, she is no longer valuable. Also, my understanding of your essays in the book is that if she doesn't play the role of grandmother, she may be seen as a witch.

R: Historically, and as far as I can tell cross-culturally, men have been afraid of what they perceived as old women's power. There is this kind of mythic thing that men have done with women in their heads—a splitting-off of woman into the "good" woman and the "bad" woman. In many cultures, it's the old woman who has been the mythic image of what men most fear in women, which is the woman who claims her own self. And so we have the old woman, the terrible witch, who actually devours children, who is the opposite of the good woman, the good mother. All old women have to carry that.

The woman who no longer serves men is potentially powerful and potentially dangerous. In some cultures, she's bought off—they let her into the boy's club as a token woman. In this culture, in the United States of America of 1984, the way this fear is dealt with is by making the old woman invisible, and by pushing her back into family again—or if that doesn't work, then portraying her as crazy, incompetent, overexcitable, and childlike.

S: *What about women who really are that way? I think of my grandmother who died of one of the dementia diseases. My head tells me that one of the ways these stereotypes work is that they have some part that is true, and that the balance is off, but my heart knows what I saw. What do you think?*

R: I think we can't possibly know what the natural processes of aging are until we understand ageism—just as we can't know what is natural to womanhood without understanding sexism and patriarchy. We know that women of all ages seek therapy or are institutionalized much more often than men. But how do we interpret that statistic?

You need only look at the ads in our feminist publications to see that younger women are out of our minds. We have therapy to survive our incest and rape, therapy for our drinking and our parents' drinking, therapy for eating problems and therapy for non-eating problems, therapy for stress, therapy for handling victimization, therapy for ex-mental patients—the list is endless. If it takes that much therapy to get through our twenties and thirties and forties, and we have not included old women in this liberation process, what do you expect to find at the far end of a life of oppression? Actually, what you find is a lot of strong survivors. This isn't to deny that old women suffer from burn-out, breakdowns, and disorientation, as other women do.

We've never used our feminist political framework to look at what happens to old women. It's as if suddenly, after 60 or 65, everything that happens to a woman is just "natural." Right now a huge amount of attention and money is going toward Alzheimer's disease. I'm not saying that there's no such thing as Alzheimer's, no diseases that are specific to people over 50. But nowhere near as much attention has gone to the recent revelations that many, many old women have been diagnosed as having senile dementia who in fact have brain tumors, or, more often, are overdosed with drugs or—even more often—are severely depressed. Loss of memory, poor concentration, fatigue, apathy, are classic symptoms of depression in a 20 or an 80 year old. What does it mean to be depressed because people's attitudes towards you are so annihilating, and then to have your depression diagnosed as hopeless senility?

Younger women need to know the issues in old women's lives. Many of these issues connect directly with issues younger women face, so it is crazy that we are not facing them together.

For example, male violence. Old women are even less safe on the street than younger women—many old women won't leave the house after sundown, or only go out while school is in session. Enforced heterosexuality controls the lives of both lesbian and non-lesbian old women, since the "solution" to the issues for old women is always seen as a heterosexual-family solution.

It's really odd that infirmity is so much the stereotype of old age, and yet when we discuss questions of disability and access for younger women, issues for physically challenged old women are essentially never raised. The connections just aren't seen; it's as if these were two different worlds.

Women who take seriously the issue of women's unpaid work don't hesitate to use their mothers for babysitting. When the old woman is grandmother, her continuing labor of childcare without any kind of compensation is seen as just part of her nature.

The connections between ageism, sexism and racism become clear when we learn that 44 percent of old Black women—but only 7 percent of old white men—are poor.

And yet the women's movement has not seemed to feel that the issues facing women in the last thirty years of our lives are critical to an understanding of sexism. Even when we talk about women's poverty, we rarely mention old women— although worldwide, in both industrial and agricultural countries, old women are the poorest of the poor. I think we have to ask ourselves how this can be, since we are all headed in this direction.

S: I see that I have asked you about ageism in the women's movement and ageism in our social agencies, but I haven't asked you about what this experience is like for you.

R: It changes for me all the time. When I wrote the essays in the book, I still identified as a younger woman, and much less as a woman who would have to face ageism herself. At first, ageism was my problem only because I am Barbara's lover and attitudes in the outside world were bringing a lot of pain into our lives. Later I became increasingly aware of how the lives of other old women I knew were controlled by ageism. But I didn't really believe I'd ever be old myself—I'd had to face the possibility of death at 41, but I'd never had to take in my own aging in a deep, life-changing way. When I re-read the ending of [the essay] "The Women in the Tower," I can see that what I was really doing was pushing myself to take that next step. I knew it would be freeing, and it has been.

Now more and more I feel connected to the woman I'll be in my eighties or nineties if I'm lucky enough to live that long. I don't know her, but I know more about her, and I like her values. I feel much closer to her than I do to that woman I used to be in my twenties and thirties.

I didn't come out to myself as a lesbian until I was in my late thirties. I feel the same excitement about growing old that I've felt about being a lesbian—we can't believe what they tell us so we have to create it every step of the way, discover for ourselves what it means to be an old woman. It's a frontier.

JEAN SWALLOW

Jeannette Foster   *June Arnold*

REMEMBERING AS A WAY OF LIFE   *TEE CORINNE*

Recently I attended a Women in Print conference, the third national conference of its kind in the last ten years. June Arnold, author and publisher, was a prime mover in conceiving and creating the first conference in 1976. Now, in 1985, three years after her death, many women attending the third conference had never heard of June Arnold. Her books are out of print. Daughters, Inc., the publishing house she co-founded with her lover, Park Bowman, no longer exists. No one, to my knowledge, is working on a biography. This is common within our movement and it is a disaster.

When death comes into our lives, it is important not to become victims of our own grief, for in the passivity pain may induce we suffer not only personal losses but the loss of our own history, our culture. Somehow we must take the time, summon the energy to write obituaries, to insure the survival of work, to honor the dead in ways that will be visible and available to succeeding generations.

June Arnold's accomplishments include a novel without gender-specific pronouns, published anonymously (*The Cook and the Carpenter*) and a novel (*Sister Gin*) about older lesbians.

What is radical anyway? What expands our understanding of that which is possible? June Arnold certainly expanded the vision for many of us, lesbians and other women, who loved the written word, the published word, dreams in print.

Jeannette Foster, who died the year before June Arnold, fed a different range of lesbian dreams with her literate and witty *Sex Variant Women in Literature*, first published in 1956. Jeannette Foster finally self-published her 40 years of research because no established

Valerie Taylor   *Anita Cornwell*

publisher would touch it. Diana Press brought out an edition of this unique and extraordinary work in 1975. Naiad Press published an edition of it in 1985.

I took pictures of Jeannette because I need images of women like her to be part of my heritage as a lesbian. I need models of intelligent, determined women who survived, who made their ways in the world, who left an impression, a dent in whatever realities they passed through.

Jeannette Foster died in 1981 at the age of 85. She died quietly and with little notice taken in the women's press and none at all in the larger world. Many people remember her, but again, no biography is in progress. Who is going to write about Jeannette Foster's life, her dedication, her passion?

It seems important to me that we conserve and nourish our lesbian role models while they are still alive. Author Valerie Taylor, for example, is a veteran of the lesbian pulp fifties and sixties with paperback titles like *Whisper Their Love, Unlike Others, Stranger in Lesbos, The Girls in 3-B*. I met Valerie Taylor at her home in Albany, New York, where she fed me soup and filled my mind with stories of her travels, her struggles to make a living as a writer, life in Chicago, and the origins of that city's Lesbian Writers Conference. She currently lives and writes in Tucson where she gives talks as a Gay Grey Panther and keeps trying to find ways of helping a straying world to find saner paths toward world peace.

Another among the living lesbian elders is Anita Cornwell whose *Ladder* essays and other writings were published in 1983 as *Black Lesbian in White America*. I remember first seeing Anita on a panel with Audre Lorde, discussing butch/femme relationships and the women who fell outside of those parameters. Who's going to write about Anita's clarity, her honesty, her tenacity, her willingness still to take on community issues and write about

Sara Aldridge   Sonny Wainwright

them with eloquence?

And then there's Sarah Aldridge who began writing novels after retiring from a demanding professional career. With six or seven novels now to her credit, Sarah has a large and devoted following but remains a thoughtful, private person. How can we honor her in her lifetime? What kinds of attention are appropriate and not intrusive? Will anyone think to record her life while she's still living it?

At the 1985 Women in Print conference I learned that Sonny Wainwright had recently died of the cancer she wrote about so movingly in *Stage V: A Journal Through Illness.* Sonny Wainwright, so thoughtful and strong, so incredibly vibrant. Sonny spent years learning to live with and around her illness, empowered others with her insights and sharing. Who is going to write Sonny Wainwright's biography, keep her book in print, gather our memories of her life and work?

And where can we have city parks named for openly lesbian women? Parks with formal gardens framing statues of our foremothers, of our cultural heras? Where are the cast bronze plaques announcing the houses we've lived and died in, the public monuments and cemetery markers, the written guides with quaint encapsulated histories, noting where we are buried, what we did, how long we lived? Where is the evidence of our history?

TEE A. CORINNE

Photograph by Lyn Cowan

The Ladies Who Lunch, cast: front row (left to right), *Kay Hinz, Rose Scwarz, Lillian King;* back row, *Phyllis Jane Rose* (director), *Cecilia Larson, Geri Dodge, Dorothy Crabb*

THE LADIES WHO LUNCH is a comic play about older women that was produced by Minneapolis' Feminist Theatre, *At the Foot of the Mountain,* in September and October of 1985. The play, written by Marilyn Seven, was commissioned specifically for a cast of 64- to 84-year-old women who for the last year and a half participated in weekly acting workshops as part of a special program called *The Coming of Age Project.*

The play is the story of Daisy and her friends. Suffering from social security cutbacks, the rising costs of living, evictions of friends, and the loss of driver's licenses, they are finally fed up when they hear that their favorite restaurant hangout is closing. This moves them to action and they plot a strategy to bring the

The Ladies Who Lunch, performer Lillian King

Photograph by Lyn Cowan

misconceptions about the elderly to the public's attention while saving the restaurant. In the process they take on city hall, the police department, and the mayor's office in some hilarious shenanigans that defy the stereotypes of old women as powerless and unimaginative.

All performances during the run of the play were sold out and the audience of women over 55 increased from 1 percent to 40 percent. On October 17, 1985, the play was performed for Maggie Kuhn's 80th birthday party, which was celebrated by the Twin Cities Gray Panthers. In October and November the play toured the Midwest. *At the Foot of the Mountain* is planning a revival of the play with the original cast in April of 1986.

GIFTS OF AGE: THIRTY-TWO RE-MARKABLE WOMEN. *Charlotte Painter, photography by Pamela Valois,* Chronicle Books, San Francisco, October 1985, Cloth $25; Paper $14.95.

I wish this book were a catalogue, like old-time ads for pioneer brides. I'd like to know these women. Stella Patri apprenticed herself to an Italian bookbinder in her sixties, and trained volunteer restorers when Florence flooded. Frances Mary Albrier was a maid for the Pullman Company, a shipyard worker, and an active politician since the thirties. I would love to visit with these and others, to talk about photography and cooking, healing and organizing, dance and good works.

It might be better if the catalogue accompanied an exhibit of the photographs of these women. They were done by Valois, a younger woman who looked for active, interesting women over seventy for this project. She believed that their strength and joy in living would show in their faces. (I can't say if she succeeded; the review copy did not include the photos. I like pictures of the elderly. Something has been going on with them, and it shows.)

The women in this volume fascinated, even awed me. The precis of each life compresses education, travel, work, and marriage in tight prose. How can these women have been so many places and done so many things? The answer of course is that they have had a lifetime in which *to be,* and they have—all of them—a special talent for living.

Yet, as a book, *Gifts of Age* does not succeed, at least for me. It doesn't give me what I was seeking, nor does it satisfy the stated intentions of the author.

I'm past forty. My joints ache in wet weather. I can't remember names. I feel vulnerable. I want to know what old age is like for women who have lively curiosity, artistic sensibility, and the luck not to have worn out young, from work, the way the women in my family have. I'm especially interested in the way women see their work, whether they entered it late or spent a lifetime mastering it. I want to know how they face death. I didn't learn these things from this book, and I can say why very simply: I didn't hear these women's voices. The author stood between us, instead of bringing us together.

Valois says that she set out to build a collective portrait. She hoped her subjects' character *"might come through,"* and help overcome stereotypes of the old as sick and needy. She chose women who, with one exception, were in good health and in some cases astonishingly active. All the women live in northern California, though most have lived other places too in this country and abroad. The effect may be to make the book have only regional appeal—there are a lot of Berkeley graduates and Berkeley wives—but it isn't this that bothered me.

Painter seems to have been guided not only by Valois' goals, but by her own urgent desire to find old age a happy part of life's cycle. She writes that these women's lives *"are filled with rare imagery, some of it quite small in size, often shimmering with beauty."* She says that their lives are not *"linear"* and that they have a sense of faith, that *"their ground of being suggests a multicolored variety as rich as the Grand Canyon's layers."* The problem is I don't know what these descriptors mean. I'm doubly disappointed because Painter's earlier book *Revelations*, an anthology of women's diaries, is one of my favorite books.

I wonder about the women in this collection. In what way are they *"remarkable?"* They are presented as exemplars of character and achievement, and I do not question their worth as human beings. But in at least one instance we are asked to believe that a woman is remarkable for what seems no more than a zest for living. To me this smacks of stereotype—fragile old age, belied by this particular subject. In several cases the most remarkable factor appears to be marriage. Although it is treated tangentially, the quality of marriage alluded to in these biographies is extraordinarily appealing. These women have had good and interesting husbands. Julia Child married a diplomat whose station in France introduced her to French cooking. Inez Loudermilk worked with her husband in China after the first world war.

Some subjects intrigued me because I already knew of them, and their vignettes were among the most successful: Julia Child, the author M.F.K. Fisher, and the photographer Ruth Bernhard. I was interested in the few women who had made the greatest changes in circumstance and work, like Cecil Pierce, who was first a seamstress and then an actress very late in life. Overall, though, these are women who have enjoyed enormous privilege in their lives, some of it earned, surely, but much from sheer good fortune. As much as I admire them, as much as I'd like to know them, I wonder what the book says about class in this country.

Obviously, Painter admired her subjects, and that may be the fault of the book. She used a kind of oral history to gather information, asking the women to tell a story about life in later years; she also compiled their biographies (my favorite reading!). Rather than presenting the women's stories, she "translated" or "focused" them into vignettes that tried to capture each woman in a *"moment of being."* The result is a book of portraits of old women who have no bitterness, no faults, no regrets. The result is sentimental, cloying, and, I suspect, false. I want to know how the old absorb their losses, how they look back on lost opportunity and bear disappointments in their families and friends. I want to know how they live with their dark sides. There isn't even a real discussion of how it feels to be treated as an old person, except for the gardener who is shunted aside to a certain table at a luncheon (and whose professed dislike of other old women makes her unsympathetic); this is not enough in a book about growing old.

I longed for the women to speak. Even when the vignette was told first person, I heard Painter's voice. I sensed Painter's "load" about racism, aging, etc., and her eye for detail. I had hoped to see these women *doing something*; instead I read projected reflections of what each woman was thinking in a caught moment. As a result, a lot of the book is reverie, which becomes sentimental and fuzzy. The real theme of this book is Painter's admiration for these ladies, and that's not enough to hold it together.

Themes do emerge: dreams as vehicles for remembering and understanding the past, for example. (Do busy, happy old women spend all of their time looking back?) There is a love of growing things, and an accounting, still, of the imperatives of parents and grandparents. What the women think about these things is muffled by the author's own voice. Painter wrote, at the end of her introduction, that these women *"have learned to live in the moment, like true existentialists, released from the burden of the past and without fear of the future."*

I wish I'd seen that. I want to be old like that myself.

This book suggests alternative ways to meet its goal. I think of oral history, journals, biographies, and fiction. Let me suggest a few possibilities.

Oral histories work when there is a sharp focus for them, when they have a thread that runs through them and makes you know something collectively as well as singly. Studs Terkel is the master; though his subjects are widely various (crossing age, sex, color, and class) they share experience, too, and pass it on to us *in their own voices.* Another Chronicle book uses this approach, amended to "conversations," quite well. Gloria Frym's *Second Stories* (Chronicle Books, San Francisco, 1985, 225 pages, $7.95 paper) is about women who began artistic careers after thirty-five. Art is interpreted broadly, and the women speak for themselves. Intensely committed, candid, and articulate, they tell us things worth knowing. I especially like that the subjects are not famous; I am grateful to Frym for taking their *"ambition, obsession, and intention"* seriously. The book would probably mean most to other women artists.

Marilyn Yalom focuses on *Women Writers of the West Coast: Speaking of Their Lives and Careers* (Capra Press, 1983, 142 pages, $10.00 paper). Some are better known than others, but I especially enjoyed discovering Jessamyn West, whom I had dismissed as a writer of Quaker stories, and Janet Lewis, author of wonderful historical novels (medieval France), published by Swallow Press and virtually unknown. These older women speak of their work with pride and conviction, without bitterness that their best writing has been so poorly treated.

Journals offer us a much richer experience with an author. I know of no one rival to May Sarton, a prolific poet and novelist who has given us, in her journals, unrivaled intimacy with the spirit of the writer. Her new journal *At Seventy* (Norton, 1984, 344 pages, $15.95) is a book to relish, as Sarton relishes life. The journal lets us share the interweaving of Sarton's rich inner life and her carefully nurtured outer life of friends, work, and nature. She speaks of *now*, and she looks forward. She reveals her relief at having let go of past ties, of being free in old age to savor solitude and work. She has learned that *"a rich life is bought at a high price in energy,"* and she accepts it, but she has arranged her life to allow peace and space for her muse. She writes, *"This morning I am fully aware that the presence of a muse literally opens the inner space, just as November light opens the outer space . . . The clutter falls away. The nonessential things cease to trouble the mind. A miracle indeed."* I read Sarton slowly, and I re-read. Hers is a book for the patient reader; it is a little like having a dear friend with whom I enjoy the small talk of flowers, birds, the weather, but who sometimes speaks of her work and feeds my own. Sarton doesn't write about aging; she writes about living. But she says it is good to be old. *"Because,"* she says, *"I am more myself than I have ever been."*

A journal that surely merits "classic" status, and is specifically focused on reflections on aging, is Florida Scott-Maxwell's *The Measure of My Days* (Knopf, 1968, $7.95). Scott-Maxwell began training as an analytical psychologist (under Jung) at fifty. Her opening paragraph gives a good idea of this beautiful, small book:

We who are old know that age is more than a disability. It is an intense and varied experience, almost beyond our capacity at times, but something to be carried high. If it is a long defeat it is also a victory, meaningful for the initiates of time, if not for those who have come less far.

I also want to note two recent books of fiction, now in paper, that satisfy the best expectations of fiction, illuminating lives so that they become knowable and strange at the same time. They are also quite different.

M.F.K. Fisher's *Sister Age* (Random House, 1984, 243 pages, $5.95 paper) is, she tells us, the culmination of a lifetime of *"observing aging."* She says that she intended since she was very young to *"study the art of aging for several years, and then tell how to learn and practice it."* Her way of doing this is to dramatize *"human strength in the unavoidable encounter with the end of life . . . "* Fisher writes eloquently yet sparingly, with precision and insight, sympathy without sentimentality. There are fifteen "stories" which overlap the forms of essay, memoir, and journal; her book is catalogued: Old age—Philosophy. In "A Kitchen Allegory," we find Mrs. Quayle, *"an agreeable and reasonable woman, in her private estimation, at least,"* coming to terms with the loss (through marriage and moving) of her daughter. Mrs. Quayle's character is brilliantly exposed in the description of her peculiar dietary pattern, the exception she makes (unsuccessfully) for her daughter's visit, and her acceptance of her life as it is. In contrast to that deceptively simple tale, "The Second Time Around" involves us in the narrator's memories of the household, after World War II, of Mme. Duval, of Aix-en-Provence. In Mme. Duval's beautiful but impoverished household, boarders, family, and *"a parade of castoff maids"* (called slaveys!) show us the courage and foolishness of brave and beleaguered people, especially old women *"of a certain class."* That story, like others in the collection, demonstrates resilience of the old in a way only fiction can do. I had not read Fisher before (she often writes about food), but I now intend to read everything she has written. Her perceptions are sharp, original, and wonderfully written.

The other novelist, also an elderly woman, who must be read is Molly Keane. Her book *Time After Time* (Dutton, 1985, 249 pages, $8.95 paper) tells the story of a household turned crazy by the return of Leda, once dismissed to become *"as unreal as any old dancer in a forgotten ballet,"* to the household of April and May, Baby June and Jasper, so odd that we watch them at first with a kind of startled amusement. Keane's talent is such that we think we are amused (these are batty women) and safe (we watch as if at a zoo), but by novel's end we have been slyly brought into a comic, passionate, wicked encounter with life. What we learn about the old is how they survive. Here is a brief glimpse at poor widowed Leda, come back to stay, and *"blind as a bat."*

It was a performance, as she crossed the room and set herself down as confidently and provocatively as though she could see an audience. In these ways she repudiated her blindness, insisting that it should be forgotten. Her hands lay along the chair arms, her feet were crossed with elegance. She leaned a little forward, waiting for entertainment, or ready to give it. She was not a weighty or demanding guest. She could neither read nor sew nor play cards, but she could talk beguilingly and funnily. All the memories of their childhood and youth were easily within her recall. The absurdities and successes and lamentable moments came out like toys from a box, alerting them to young forgotten people: themselves.

SANDRA SCOFIELD

THE GIRL. Meridel Le Sueur, West End Press, Box 7232, Minneapolis, MN 55407, 1978, 148 pages, $4.95.

Born in 1900, Meridel Le Sueur has been writing for 60 years about people's struggles against injustice. She shows how American capitalism can deaden.

It separates us from life-affirming values and throws many into a stark battle to survive. Often focused on working-class women, her fiction argues for the nourishment and power of solidarity, the beauty and reward of natural cycles. Women's suffering and celebrations, their regenerative abilities, the continuity of their collective lives have preeminence for Le Sueur, making her work compelling.

Nowhere in Le Sueur are women's concerns and their need for sisterhood as important, as moving, as in *The Girl*. Much of the novel, based on actual accounts of women during the Depression, is a relentless drama of poverty, violence, prostitution, electric shock treatment, inadequate welfare, murder, and death. What provides hope is a group of women who, despite oppressive conditions, persist in supporting life.

Drafted in the '30s and printed originally as separate stories, the complete novel, published in 1978, is notable for its historical accuracy, its memorable characters (many whose names, mannerisms, and activities we easily recall), and its use of colorful street talk. But *The Girl* is most impressive for its narrator. Her story is a song of suffering.

The heroine's voice—consistent, vibrant, longing—and her sometimes passionate, often hazardous experiences are among the most individualized in documents of the period.

At the same time, she symbolizes Everywoman. Readers are unlikely to forget the particular circumstances that force her to cry, *"Sure. Yes. I want everything. Sure. I got hungers. I want the earth. I feel rich. I feel heavy. I want meat, bread, children. I am starving."* But we also appreciate the universality of this young woman's struggle and of the childbirth that makes her, at the novel's end, *"belong to the whole earth."*

Late in the book, the Girl—we never learn her name—sees the futility of her single voice. This realization ties together two topics that resonate in Le Sueur's work and that are themes of this novel: the importance of knowledge and of unity. The principal spokesperson for this duality is Amelia, a leader of the Workers' Alliance (and the only character in *The Girl* who is stiff, moralizing). Amelia lectures the young woman mourning for her lover: *"You can't cry just for yourself . . . . We must know that our suffering is together . . . the same enemy after us . . . the same mother over us."* And the narrator, who has had many awakenings in her young life, finally understands that when women combine information with solidarity, they are empowered.

The Girl's discoveries, which she eventually sees as binding her to all women, are initially self-centered. She is initially a frightened but capable farm girl who, seeking work in St. Paul, falls in with a desperate speakeasy crowd, discovers the fickle pleasures of loose living, and is coerced into prostitution and robbery. Her life explodes in tragedy.

Yet the Girl's ability to learn, her fortitude, and the help of supportive women continue to sustain her. Le Sueur uses cinematic speed and force — short episodic chapters span the months between the heroine's sexual initiation and the birth of her own girl — to compose a revealing portrait of the process of knowing.

In an afterword to the novel, Le Sueur argues that a writer should mirror a people's beauty, should encourage their expressions of creativity and of social opinion. For, as she says elsewhere, *"Memory in America suffers amnesia." The Girl*, then, is Le Sueur's memorial to the heroic women of the 1930s.

BARBARA HORN

NEW AS A WAVE, A RETROSPECTIVE: 1937-1983. Eve Triem, edited by Ethel Fortner, Dragon Gate, Inc., 914 East Miller St., Seattle, WA 98102, 134 pages, $16.00 cloth, $7.00 paper.

Although she has been writing for most of her life, recognition in terms of book publication came late to Eve Triem. Her first poetry collection, *Parade of Doves,* appeared when she was 44. Subsequent books came out at ages 63, 65, 74, 80 and, in her 82nd year, this book. In addition to poetry, she wrote a study of e. e. cummings for the University of Minnesota American Writers Series.

New as a Wave has been edited with sensitivity to Triem's music as it has continued throughout her career. The first half is made up of selections from previously published books and the second half of uncollected poems which, stylistically, span the entire career and range from a villanelle to several poems with the looseness of prose.

Triem's work is consistently graceful, balanced, and restrained. She has worked to make word and syntax serve her; each bears all the meaning it can but is not burdened with it. The poems are sinewy, compressed, but at the same time, open and full of light. The book is a delight to read for the lovely, liquid sound of it.

Many times the verbal beauty of poems is merely decorative, or it is nonsense. The following lines, the first pretty and the other two making no sense to me, come from "Midsummer Rites," one of the better poems:

Then a boy in a silvered wild-oat time, reading Keats

the dazzled sperm and ovum swimming close
in the milky ocean of his sounding stars.

That sort of thing was common in the '20s and '30s and later. Although Triem's poetry changed over the years, both formally and thematically, it never lost the stamp of its early influences. H. D. seems to have made a mark on it, and Housman as well. All three poets studied Greek, and all have a classical temper. (The poems in *Heliodora*, Triem's third book, are translations from Sappho and others.) I also hear the lushness and mysticism of Yeats in lines like these from the title poem:

It is not as a stranger he will rise
Upon his bones to enter his new days.

Everywhere are lines that please simply by being exquisite works of art, like this from "To Sing Again the Verses of Hesiod":

Mist is the music enchanting these bricks
To move like awakened lions in their walls,
Like the bronzes and gold on the Shield of Herakles -

Or this from "The End of an Exile":

. . . like a carving
Of seated women drowsing over jars of oil.

Think of the sureness of ear that produced a line like *"some are girls in long flowery dresses"* ("Bach Concert"), instead of "some are girls in long flowered dresses" or "some are girls wearing long flowered dresses." Such choices follow long study of sound values or intuition of them or both.

Of current interest is the autobiographical element in poetry, and Triem, after years of restraint, puts some of her emotional life, undisguised by abstractions, into her verse. The poems from *Dark to Glow*, a chapbook about her husband's death, are moving. After so much feminist writing on the small cruelties of parents, it is refreshing to read Triem's poem on that sub-

ject, "One Memory of Rose," written with compassion and humor, a poem as clean and cool as marble.

On the way to school
this group hesitating at the door
Kiss me, said the Maenad tearing at her head,
a fear and a disdain of earthly chances
glaring her sea-purple eyes,
you'll never see me again.
A daily ritual.
Always we kissed her.

"On the way to school/this group hesitating at the door" might be a fragment from a Greek frieze.

Surprises in the book are a poem ("Film Revival") for Marilyn Monroe and another explaining why travelers to Dubuque, Iowa, might mistake it for Bangor, Providence, or New Orleans.

It's a pleasure to meet the vibrant, discerning mind and the witty intelligence that have been shaping this book for forty-six years.

NONA NIMNICHT

A LEAK IN THE HEART. Faye Moskowitz, David R. Godine, Boston, 1985, 161 pages, $13.95 cloth.

"The Matriarchs grow old, my models, women who were women when I was a child," writes Faye Moskowitz, looking back, at 52, over the valley of childhood and ahead to the peaks of very old age. Somewhat elegiac, often humorous, always vividly written, this collection of 24 autobiographical essays transcends

class, race, and religion as it explores the common theme of growing old.

Raised in a struggling orthodox Jewish family surrounded by the Christian Midwest, daughter of a junk-dealer father and a courageous, spirited, immigrant mother (*"We're not poor, no one's poor as long as they have hope."*), Moskowitz recaptures for us some *rites de passage* of growing up in the thirties and forties.

She defies dietary laws on a Mars Bars binge with Sara, the rabbi's rebel daughter; has her first period in the eye doctor's chair, caught in a panic of sexual fantasies and fears of going blind; and tries to make herself over to fit first a Zionist and then a Socialist ethic without much success. She notes with regret the disappearance of the autograph album, that old fashioned graduation artifact with its sentimental, hortatory, and even racy inscriptions of which she offers this seventh-grade example of daring: *"The ocean is wide,/ the sea is level/ come to my arms/ you little devil!"*

Her mother died during her adolescence. At 18 she married a student and became part of another struggling family, that of the mother-in-law and her mother-in-law's mother, the strong-willed Bobbe Frieda who kept watch over everything, calling imperiously from her bed to the males of the household, *"Lift the seat."*

In one of the most touching and powerful essays in the book, Moskowitz describes how she and the Bobbe (Yiddish for grandmother) come to love and trust each other, in a glorious scene culminating in Bobbe's bed.

I can remember so clearly how gingerly I crawled into the tiny bed, struggling to keep myself at the edges so I would not have to touch the misshapen little bone bag that was her body. She pulled the blanket over to cover us both and said 'When you are old you never want to sleep because there are so many years to sleep soon anyway.'

She shows Moskowitz her marriage wig and a thick brown braid of real hair, smelling of naphthalene.

I had the strangest feeling touching the crumbling hair that if I stretched my fingers hard enough I could touch, too, the tender young woman bride who must have cried so bitterly when the women came to shear her heavy hair.

With the same stretch of the imagination, Moskowitz evokes for us in the book's final episode the gallantry-under-fire of the old. Readers who have assumed full-time care of elderly relatives will understand better than most the awful paradox of the child becoming the parent of the parent. The pain and confusion, anger and guilt of daughter-in-law and mother-in-law are poignantly depicted as Moskowitz tries to persuade her mother-in-law to enter a nursing home for a few days so she and her husband can take a much-needed vacation. Fighting down her fears of being abandoned as her own mother was, the mother-in-law agrees at last and recounts bravely to a grand-daughter *her* decision to go.

Wondering about her own capacity to endure, Moskowitz writes:

The women of whom I speak: their lives were tempered by pogroms, the blast from the gas ovens. They endured loss of land and language, answered to 'Greenhorn' before they knew what the word meant . . . I pray I never endure their crucible, but I covet the nature of their strength.

Along with recognition of that strength, Moskowitz understands fully how youth and age are linked in the ecosystem of life. In a brief portrait of her beautiful aunt Itke, now in a nursing home, she sums up the nourishing relationship that exists between old and young. *"Aunt Itke, as I am a child still in you, so are you a young woman yet in me."*

How much we need history, our own and that of others! Moskowitz' generation will be the last to be in touch with the women of the Depression and east European immigrations, and one of the pleasures of the book is the recording of the braiding of their lives. What the bonding will be like between the writer and her children's and grandchildren's generations no one can predict.

Admittedly, the book has flaws. Some of the pieces are slight. None are longer than 2500 words. Many of them, it appears, were written for newspapers, which accounts for a certain formulaic approach, a tendency to "wrap up" a subject that can be irritating. It is a tribute to Moskowitz' deft writing that she can convey so much in such a limited space. At the same time, because she is so good, the reader hungers for more. My sense is that Moskowitz is a writer who doesn't yet quite trust herself. I hope the success of this book will give her the encouragement she needs to go back and write at greater length about the lives of the women to whom she was and is connected.

A Leak In the Heart is not a book that has answers, nor even asks questions about society's role in the treatment of older women, yet I think of it as an *active* book, one that modestly, but with clarity, enhances our own efforts to come to terms with aging.

CELIA GILBERT

LIMBO. Carobeth Laird, Chandler & Sharp, Novato, California, 1979, 178 pages, $6.95.

This *"memoir about life in a nursing home by a survivor,"* as described by the publisher, throws into strong relief the limbo of a typical nursing home of the affluent times in which we live, a place from which the writer surfaced in 1974 to continue her writing and publishing career after her rescue and nurturing by a loving family, the Michelsons, to whom the book is dedicated. With great tenacity of body and spirit, she writes of the experience in this nursing home, which she was able to survive.

Carobeth Laird tries to keep a daily diary, but it is impossible given her surroundings and her fluctuating mental and physical conditions. This is why the length of her occupancy at Golden Mesa seems inexact, but it began in a September in the early '70s when she was transferred from the Indian Public Health Hospital at Parker, Arizona, to a nursing home in Phoenix.

Golden Mesa Nursing and Convalescent Home of Phoenix is a devised name; the institution apparently did little to earn the title "Convalescent." I realize from my own observations that this is as unbiased a portrait of the majority of nursing homes as I have read about or visited. It is written in well-considered language, lucidly recalling a period of nearly dumb despair and fear on Carobeth's part, layered together with positivity and a kind of wry humor that is typically the root of this woman's spirit.

We who have passed sixty will come to realize how intensely unfree such places will eventually render our human spirits; I frequently stopped in my reading to give thought to how such a future might affect my friends or myself, so very literal was this writing.

On Carobeth's entrance to Golden Mesa, she asks the social worker, Vi, whom she recognizes as an Indian, *"'For how long?'*

'Why, for the rest of your life if you want to stay,' Vi responded brightly, Carobeth tells us, adding, *"Somewhere in my mind an iron door clanged shut."*

Within the walls, as days progress, it comes to her that small indignities, built up daily, are more traumatic by far than broad events. She notices that overt cruelties are very rare. But she watches closely the overworked and weary aides, on whom descends the heaviest work, who actually keep the nursing home going. Carobeth thinks little of the food; it is of low, *"prison quality,"* she says. The patients' lives revolve around bodily functions.

She is the widow of a Chemuhuevi Indian and has for a lifetime been doggedly writing and studying. About her (recently published) book *Encounter with an Angry God*, the writer-critic Tom Wolfe remarked in Harpers Bookletter that he was convinced we now had an "exciting new literary talent bursting forth at the age of eighty."

She has done extensive scholarly work on the manners and mores of the Chemuhuevi Tribe, a small and little-known tribe in the semi-desert of California east of San Diego. This work, *The Chemuhuevis*, and *Encounter* were both published after her emergence from Golden Mesa. The bulk of both was written in the period after her husband's death, before her entry to the nursing home.

During the whole time she wrote *Limbo* she suffered incredible pain and multiple illnesses. This book is really a monumental achievement resulting from her intensity for life, her gifts for observation, her love of people, her awareness of the humbling of such a life for women aging, and her unquenchable desire and resolve to make their predicaments known.

Her brief descriptions are telling and give a sense of immediacy. Surely the publisher needed to edit very sparsely; I feel Carobeth kept the material so close in her memory banks that little was needed to bring life to the scenes.

Memories of earlier times with her family are evocative of our own condition. I stopped my reading many times to remind myself that this story represents another blotch on the history of our country. It came to me that in its way *this is excellent political writing.*

Now only a few of the events that moved me most. I shall not tell too much, though it is tempting.

After a gall bladder operation prior to entering the nursing home, Carobeth awakes in the dim light of a curtained intensive care unit. Beyond, a woman's voice says tiredly, *"Tengo hambre."* There is silence. No one understands Spanish. Somehow broth is brought, but the woman says *"No! Quero un hamburger!"* and Carobeth later learns the woman had great pain in her digestive tract and since surgery has taken it away, she can't see why they won't bring her a hamburger, her usual food. After Carobeth's catheters are all pulled she's also brought broth, and remembers, thinking that now she understood why the Spanish woman said such an emphatic No! *"The color and flavor of the broth were as appetizing as*

if a chicken had done his duty in the kitchen."

Leaving intensive care she is *"helpless. . . . No one to care for me, nowhere to go. . . . George had been dead 34 years and the children were scattered, and there was no little farm to go back to."* In those moments I shared a terribly moving recognition of the past, confronted with Carobeth's pictures of the seemingly endless parade of wheelchairs, the mummy-cased bodies lying under bright coverlets knitted by invisible donors who had been other, younger women. I gave myself up to Carobeth's longings for home, and have almost, in my spirit, endured those longings with her.

Then there were the accidents. She has no glasses to watch the color TV provided each bed in the hospital, so she turns up the sound in order to keep in touch with the news and with the outside world, which in her mind is fading far away. So her mind ticks on, with her a constant sense of lying idle, safe, warm in thunderstorms visible outside the windows; but the cold fact is her dread of *"imminent expulsion in all her helplessness into a world which has no place for her."* Then she is (finally, as she believes) sent to Golden Mesa. At that time, she fully believes there will be no way out.

At the nursing home, as in most medical facilities, there is some distinction in the status of the nurses vis-a-vis the aides. Carobeth writes that Jewell, one of the kindest of the aides, *"almost invariably handed each of us a warm washcloth, a nicety . . . ."* So small, these things that please patients so inordinately. But collectively—the bedpans, the drafts, the washrags, the bathing water too hot, too cold, the wheelchairs charging full-speed into each other, the peripatetic nightstands, the nurse's bell just out of reach, the missing little piece of jewelry, or the dress that *"was hanging there yesterday,"* the fretting over drawing or not drawing the drapes, the loud voices and shouting needed to enter someone's deafened world, the slowly indrawing silence and alienation, the sounds of approaching trays, cranking of beds, clanks of crockery and silver being arranged and spoken of in multiple tones—all this, the stuff of life brought to its nethermost ebb.

Two women who share her room provide endless thought, mental observation, and comment. She delineates them clearly: first an old dancer who upon being told by the doctor to point her leg to the ceiling does so in a swift, long-practised gesture of grace. Carobeth notices her toes are now for ever fixed into the point clump. Then the dancer returns to her monologic stuff-of-days with a shrug. The other sharer is fine and fragile as a white rose, and nearly as silent, except when her husband comes to visit, and Carobeth mourns that they *"were reduced to visit in a room with two other women!"*

And so the days follow each other, with the dull sameness of routine, the occasional high mirth, and the thought-provoking disappearances from time to time of a neighbor. Carobeth was becoming anxious that her mind might not be able to remain strong, yet her strong spirit did save her from sinking into the humdrum of the days. She wrote letters. She read. She thought out plot and character. Her retentive mind held them.

At last, after a long space of not knowing where Carobeth WAS, her friends Ralph and Micki Michelson locate her, come and see her, invite her home with them. *"It was like a dream . . . . To be offered a home, a refuge, was almost beyond comprehension,"* she said.

So Carobeth Laird's valiant spirit has brought her through and the *"iron door has clanged,"* this time to let her out.

This fine writing, done at such great cost by way of emotional and physical trauma, will help many women now in the process of aging to realize their need to prepare for the certainties and eventualities ahead; and hopefully to come upon the thought, as I have done, that it is possible for us together to start doing something constructive to better the situation of insufficient planning for the lives of the aging here in the United States of America.

Jonathan Sharp, one of *Limbo's* publishers, informed me that Carobeth died in another August two years ago, in 1983. She was at the hospital in

Poway and the old friends were near to her. Her unpublished works are being arranged for print, and taped and untranscribed material is being typed and readied for editing and publishing.

MARY TALLMOUNTAIN

LOOK ME IN THE EYE: OLD WOMEN, AGING AND AGEISM. Barbara Macdonald with Cynthia Rich, Spinsters Ink, San Francisco, 1983, 128 pages, $5.95 paper.

Look Me in the Eye is a book that will surely be difficult to pick up, difficult to read, but for those whose courage and need—or even curiosity—pull them past Barbara Macdonald's piercing eyes in the cover photograph, it will be difficult to put down.

In this series of essays—seven by Barbara Macdonald and four by her twenty-year-younger lover and friend, Cynthia Rich—these two writers define ageism and then relentlessly deal with the real problems: the "invisibility" of the older woman even within the left and/or women's communities, the paternalism and confusion, and the very important interrelationships between the oppressions suffered by women—working class women, woman-identified women and/or women whose sexual preference is for other women, women of color, and women who are old. I think the deep grasp of class,

race, gender, and age in this book is one of its most powerful contributions.

There are moments of discovery in this book, beautiful moments that take us and bodily lift us from the role cast for us and nurtured daily within the consumer society. Like this one, in which Macdonald tells us:

"I like growing old." I say it to myself with surprise. I had not thought that it could be like this. There are days of excitement when I feel almost a kind of high with the changes taking place in my body, even though I know the inevitable course my body is taking will lead to debilitation and death. I say to myself frequently and with wonder, "This is my body doing this thing." I cannot stop it, I don't even know what it is doing, I wouldn't know how to direct it. My own body is going through a process that only my body knows about. I never grew old before; never died before. I don't really know how it's done. I wouldn't know where to begin, and God knows, I certainly wouldn't know when to begin—for no time would be right. And then I realize, lesbian or straight, I belong to all the women who carried my cells for generations and my body remembers how for each generation this matter of ending is done.

There is also a consistent honesty. Neither Macdonald nor Rich pretends that this is an easy subject, nor that they have any total answers. Sometimes they simply ask the questions, but they always move as far as they can within those questions. We are simply *invited* to explore both our ways of looking at aging in others and the processes our own minds and bodies are going through.

For me, the book makes its most complex and important statements in Macdonald's last essay, "The Power of the Old Woman," when she explores this response to aging:

... the denial that says, "I'm not old, I'm just eccentric!" This kind of response to aging is not surprising as it has always been a common response of oppressed people. It is a forced response. The midget, the court jester, the Black funny man, the fat lady, the tramp—with his clothes that don't fit, smoking the thrown-away cigar, telling us that poverty and powerlessness are funny—all are responding to the oppressor who says entertain me, amuse me, deny in front of me, what I am doing to you daily. One has the moral choice to play to an audience who prefers the lie in the laugh, or to confront the oppressor with the truth that dwarfism is not funny, Black is not funny, fat is not funny, poverty and powerlessness are not funny, and old is not funny.

It is Barbara Macdonald's ability to make connections, to link these different but connected oppressions, that takes her insights beyond being simply a moving account of a personal experience and makes them a tool in understanding how our society uses us. In the same piece, she asks:

What is the power of the old woman? Some would suggest that it is her knowledge because she has lived longer. At 69, I can tell you that I don't know all that much, and when I try to tap this source of power in other old women I find that they don't know much either.... Though it is by no means necessarily so, years of experience can also be years of brainwashing ....

Societal distortion runs deep, and Macdonald asks the obvious question and answers it:

Does the power of the old woman have to come so late in life, often in our late eighties? Or can we draw on that power much sooner? The time I spend proving I am as young as I think I am is lost time.... On my best days I live deeply with the knowledge that my choices are narrowing but that all my life they were much more narrowed when I bought into society's denial of death. My wrinkled face now reminds me of what the terms were every day of my life and on my best days, I agree to that contract in a moral way.

Look Me in the Eye is an important contribution from Spinsters Ink, a small publisher that has brought out a promising list of titles. The publishers are to be thanked for their insightfulness and courage, as are the authors: for their lives, their talent in the telling, and their generosity in the sharing.

MARGARET RANDALL

SILVER LINING. *Photographs by Anne Noggle, Text by Janice Zita Grover, Foreword by Van Deren Coke*, University of New Mexico Press, Albuquerque, 1984, 194 pages, $45.00.

Silver Lining is a book of photographs by Anne Noggle. As you make your way through its pages, you'll see women—and some men—most of them directly engaged with the camera's eye, some of them engaged with one another or with a particular passion, many of the women visibly aging (for age and aging are specific concerns of Noggle's)—something from which we have been taught to turn away, but to which Noggle turns us back through her exploration and celebration of the event.

In this book you'll meet the women members of Noggle's family: her mother, her aunt, her sister; and you'll experience an arresting series of self-portraits in which the photographer pilots a plane (she is, among much else, Captain Anne Noggle), grins in glee "As a Guggenheim Fellow 1982," nestles her Dachshund Pepe against her full and naked breasts, undergoes a face-lift, sits resolutely against the stark space of her found Southwest, floats languidly on the water of Cochiti Lake, becomes "Stonehenge Decoded 1977," or almost, but not quite, loses herself in thought in the shadowed interior of an automobile.

Anne Noggle makes pictures of aging women, among them herself. Her self-portraits are not the emphatically and wonderfully playful images of a Cindy Sherman; even as they are absolutely photographic, I would venture a claim that her eye relates in some powerful way to painters Paula Becker and Alice Neel.

Janice Zita Grover, whose essay accompanying these images is in itself a work of art and of love, calls the series *"Anne Noggle's Saga of the Fallen Flesh."* She writes:

. . . we seldom see—we are not looking for—the gleam of carnality, the self-deprecating humor, the witty maliciousness, the sensuality, for these are qualities we have appropriated and redistributed exclusively among the young. Noggle sees these traits in age; she tricks them out of her subjects . . . .

Noggle was born in Illinois in 1922.

Grover, in her introductory essay, tells us:

She was raised among women: her mother supported her two daughters by managing a bookstore in Chicago's Loop, and the three of them lived together in a boarding house from which Anne, the younger and dreamier daughter, spun out fantasies of flying.

She became a pilot at an early age and at a time when that profession was all but off-limits to women, and she became a flight instructor as a Women's Air Force Service Pilot (WASP) during the second world war. Later she taught piloting, joined an aerial circus doing stunt flying, and crop dusted in the Southwest.

Crop dusting led, among other things, to an emphysema disability and a move to Albuquerque. In 1959, she entered the University of New Mexico as a 38-year-old freshman, majoring in art history. In a photography class, as she saw her first print emerging, she recalls: *"It was the first time since I'd been grounded that I felt the same excitement that flying always gave me. I was purely and completely happy. Now I knew what I was going to do for the rest of my life."* She was accepted as a graduate student in photography, is now an Adjunct Professor of Art with that department, and combines teaching with travelling and lecturing—and of course making pictures.

When seeking points of reference for Noggle's eye, Grover mentions painters Holbein, Bronzino, Watteau, Gainsborough, and Degas—among others—and photographers August Sander, Julia Margaret Cameron, and Diane Arbus. These are valuable clues, but Noggle's strength, I think, moves fundamentally in her departures. She is both interested in stripping her subjects of all artifice, and in creating artifice through which her subjects may be more perfectly seen.

Several of the images in this collection of unusually powerful images are particularly moving to me. One is "Southwest Passage 1982." Noggle's grossly oversized eye and head, in demanding profile, lead into a more normally proportioned arm and hand on the wheel of her car, and out through the windshield glass onto dry, desert land. There is a tension in this image only possible when she who made it gives up all vanity and even "normalcy" to explore the relationship of person to place, and time. The subject of this picture is not the Arbus freak or the Buñuel freak; she is the freak within us all, the consciousness of that outer limit, at the same time temporal, speaking of only part of the persona, a moment in her perception and our perception of her.

In "The Late Great Me 1983" (the last picture in the book), Anne appears with downcast eyes, shrouded in black with her face behind a sheer black veil. There is both pathos and humor in the image and its title. In this one, as in so many, Noggle is both subject and storyteller. Dead and alive. Moving within her own revealing process, and revealing that process in an act of intense (and intensely funny) generosity.

But nowhere in *Silver Lining* is a sense of process more apparent than in "Darkroom 1981." This is perhaps because we see the photographer in her darkroom, the place where the thing is made. In this image the photo plane is almost equally divided. The very close up right-hand side is Anne, the real terrain of her face and neck, eyes seriously down, lips strongly pursed, old, comfortable and indifferent cotton shirt with a small rip on its right shoulder sitting almost dead center in the picture. She is very close, very illuminated, yet very brooding. The left half of the image is in shadow. We can barely see a door, a hanging towel, objects that say "darkroom" only because the picture's title says it (and titles are important to Noggle).

It is the staying power, and growing power, that is part of Anne Noggle's photographic message. There is everything in a gesture, a positioning, a fact of relationship, or stance. Often these gestures, positionings, relationships or stances are worked out in the artist's mind long before the shutter is snapped. Preparation is important. Preparation that is thoughtful, detailed, but always allows for what the subject herself will bring to the moment.

Anne Noggle's work has extraordinary impact—a quiet, solid, staying impact. You open the book again, days or weeks later, and a whole new world joins the one that revealed itself to you the first time around. The first world is remembered, in its entirety; the new world surfaces, and there are many additional worlds there, waiting.

MARGARET RANDALL

AN ENDURING SPIRIT: THE ART OF GEORGIA O'KEEFE. Katherine Hoffman, The Scarecrow Press, Metuchen, NJ, 185 pages, $29.50.

> *I hung on the wall the work I had been doing for several months. Then I sat down and looked at it. I could see how each painting or drawing had been done according to one teacher or another, and I said to myself, "I have things in my head that are not like what anyone taught me — shapes and ideas so near to me — so natural to my way of being and thinking that it hasn't occurred to me to put them down." I decided to start anew — to strip away what I had been taught — to accept as true my own thinking. This was one of the best times of my life. There was no one around to look at what I was doing — no one interested — no one to say anything about it one way or another. I was alone and singularly free, working into my own, unknown — no one to satisfy but myself. I began with charcoal and paper and decided not to use any color until it was impossible to do what I wanted to do in black and white. I believe it was June before I needed blue.*

> — Georgia O'Keefe

With the exception of Georgia O'Keefe herself, very few people have written well about Georgia O'Keefe.

Art critics, in particular, manage to fail her in fundamental and harrowing ways. In this, they have been consistent for well over fifty years — for at this writing, O'Keefe is in her 97th year, largely oblivious to any but her own struggle. A stance which affords her, if not ᴜᴇ last laugh, at least the last chuckle.

Katherine Hoffman's *An Enduring Spirit: The Art of Georgia O'Keefe* attempts to approach the long flight pattern of O'Keefe's life through the historical context of the 20th Century — at heart, a good idea, since O'Keefe has lived every minute of it. And yet the result is a dry, uninspiring text held hostage by academic overtones and an inability to embrace O'Keefe in either body or spirit.

> *By the late thirties, the United States' economy seemed to be on the mend and O'Keefe's work was selling fairly well. In 1938 she was awarded an honorary degree from the College of William and Mary, the only degree she had except for her high school diploma. In 1938 the Nazis also annexed Austria and Czechoslovakia. Artistic discussion at An American Place and at O'Keefe's and Stieglitz's apartment was frequently interrupted to turn on the radio to hear the latest news from Europe. Stieglitz, with his European heritage, was again more concerned than Georgia about the oncoming war.*

This paragraph is typical of the way Hoffman drops O'Keefe down into quasi-newsreel history and then jerks her out again just as unceremoniously. *"Public despair concerning conditions in America was symbolized in 1932 by reaction to the kidnapping of Charles Lindbergh's child. Lindbergh had become a national hero* with his transatlantic flight in 1932." Or: "Many writers of the time probed into the middle-class environment and American self-deceptions. Sinclair Lewis' Main Street and Babbitt were published and Upton Sinclair wrote The Goose Step. F. Scott Fitzgerald's and Ernest Hemingway's work portrayed much of the atmosphere and feeling of the twenties." I found these references distracting rather than insightful—random samplings, not unlike musak, which fail to locate O'Keefe in her time. Hoffman writes historical reportage around O'Keefe as though the artist were making a series of guest appearances in the 20th Century. I read many passages, often wondering where in the world O'Keefe was, only to find her suddenly and inexplicably spliced in. I was left with an artist and a century that did not mesh and thus a pervading sense of loss with The Milieu, the first section of the book.

The second section is as disappointing as its heading: The Critics and Their Backgrounds. Dating back to 1916, Hoffman's list of critics offers critical opinion "representative of the body of critical literature dealing with a particular topic in relation to O'Keefe's work." This is where the book falls down upon frail and thesis-like knees, never to rise again. The subsequent chapters, "The Feminine Experience," "Symbolism," and "The World of Nature" may glow faintly on the horizon of promise, but upon arriving I could not find one zesty thought about a woman who is surely our most incisive and original artist. Even the great pursuit of discussing those sexual flowers has been nipped in the bud.

Some have described paintings such as . . . Gray Line with Black, Blue and Yellow of 1923, or Green-Gray Abstraction, 1931, in sexual terms, relating the paintings' shapes to the vaginal form. However, it seems unfair to describe the paintings and artist's intentions in such narrow (emphasis mine) terms. The works may have sexual overtones to some, but other ways of looking at the paintings are indeed possible. Part of the beauty of the work is in its ambiguity of interpretation for the viewer. Indeed, it is not necessary to speak of any specific subject matter.

That's all she wrote. Hoffman has collected a wide range of critical opinion on O'Keefe and this is, in fact, the heart of the book. A critical composite may or may not be your cup of O'Keefe—just be prepared for no new ground, no interior glimpses, no penetrating excursions, and no surprise when you discover the forty shocking black-and-white plates.

If you already know something about O'Keefe, An Enduring Spirit won't be much fun.

KIM VAETH

WOMEN AS ELDERS/NOS AÎNÉES: Resources for Feminist Research/Documentation Sur La Recherche Féministe. Edited by Emily M. Nett, Department of Sociology, Ontario Institute for Studies in Education, 252 Bloor St. W., Toronto, Ontario, Canada M5S 1V6, 1982, 87 pages, $20 individuals ($15 in Canada), $35 institutions ($30 in Canada).

The old woman – the hag, the crone – is *"a symbol conveying foolishness, wickedness, death and decay"* to others and to women themselves, especially in Western societies, according to Marilyn J. Bell, one of 25 contributors to *Women as Elders* published by RFR/DRF. Because growing old carries such negative connotations – societal as well as physical and psychological – we ignore what is inevitable: that if we do not die accidentally or because of illness in our youth or middle age, we will grow old. As a result, *"no one has much knowledge about women over the age of 65 years, if that is indeed the magic age at which we become 'old women,'"* guest editor Emily Nett writes in her introduction.

Though more than half of the contributors to this 1982 RFR/DFR issue are Canadians examining research on older women in Canada, the information is relevant to any woman in the North American hemisphere – a wealth of different opinions, studies, and useful information on growing old. The issue includes 13 articles and addresses in a variety of writing styles, one a personal account; nine book reviews; two bibliographies; four syllabi; and a 30-page annotated bibliography of 14 categories listing works about research in progress, widowhood, violence, minority elders, resources, and conferences. Titles range from a folder,

"World Population Aging Faster Than Ever," published by the United Nations, to "Struggle in the Frontiers of 'Caring': A Biography of Eunice Henrietta Dyke – 1883-1969," published at the Ontario Institute for Studies in Education, to "Bridges: For the Woman Alone," a quarterly newsletter published in New York for women living alone because of widowhood or divorce or choice.

Though a number of the 13 articles stress the fact that much is not known about aging, what is known is that life for many older women is – and will be – difficult. Research on aging is inadequate. And research on aging women is particularly inadequate, considering the fact that they must endure a double stigma of being both old – and female. And very likely alone. By the year 2000 there will be six females for every male over the age of 80 years in the more developed areas of the world. Statistics show that many older women also are occupying the bottom rungs of the economic ladder; they are less educated than men; they have a life history of limited participation; and they are regarded by politicians as *"dependent, harmless old ladies."*

In "Aging Women in Rural Society: Out of Sight, Out of Mind," Elizabeth Cape writes about the suggestion at a meeting of the men's service club in a village in an Ontario township she studied that the club sponsor a wheels-to-meals program. The members voted down this suggestion and discussed the means of raising funds to pave a parking lot.

And while they have been caretakers most of their lives, many women often end up isolated and lonely. As Arlene T. McLaren from the Department of Sociology and Anthropology at Simon Fraser University wrote, a great many elderly women are *"underemployed, underpaid, underfinanced, underhoused, undervalued, and underloved."*

Nett and the other women who contributed to this issue of RFR/DRF stress the fact that the job facing researchers, government and social agencies, as well as women themselves, in trying to change this negative picture of elderly women will not be an easy one. Nor will it be accomplished overnight. But *Women as Elders* does not leave one feeling overwhelmed. In fact, McLaren and others offer positive developments that have emerged with more research, personal accounts of women who have improved their lives, and information about what women can do for each other and for themselves. *"Researchers are increasingly discovering that elderly women are not merely isolated, 'roleless,' or dependent recipients of services from their children or the state,"* McLaren writes.

Women are taking a role in changing things, she and others claim. Diaries and journals show the wisdom and pride women have experienced as old women. The Ojibwe Cultural Foundation is a powerful local force in southern Ontario that seeks to revitalize the cultural transmission function of the elders in a modern society. Women elders are being involved in the counseling of girls who move from the reserve schools to the integrated high school, a critical and difficult stage of their lives, and in the revival of traditional crafts. And Helen Levine of the School of Social Work, Carleton University, writes about The Crones in Ottawa, a group of about eight women in their forties, fifties and early sixties who meet once a month for dinner, talk, sharing, and friendship. She and others talk about the importance of contact with older feminists and for the necessity of groups, networks, and education— whether we're young or already an elder. For one thing, we can start referring to ourselves as *"elders,"* a word Nett says applies to men as well as women, and is therefore non-sexist, and which carries a positive connotation. We can realize that in other societies a postmenopausal woman is viewed as *"a knowledgeable person who has had a life full of rich experience;"* they become the shaman or the medicine woman who can control spirits and diagnose and cure illness. We can help each other develop self confidence and an ability to speak out—among ourselves and in social and political circles.

In *"Women Aging,"* an address before the United Nations NGO Committee on Aging at the Secretariat, New York, 1982, Linda M. Rhodes agreed that the most important demographic fact for women is that the aging society is a female society. But she went further by saying, *"I would like to rephrase that quote and state that, 'The single most important demographic fact PERIOD is that the aging society is a female society.' This is not a problem for the women. They alone will not change the status quo."*

This issue of *RFR/DRF, Women as Elders*, is a good beginning, both for individuals and groups concerned about what we can do to help ourselves and to help change the status of elders in our society.

SUSAN LANDGRAF

ALL OF OUR LIVES. Directed by Helene Klodawsky. Produced by Laura Sky and Helene Klodawsky. Cinematography by Serge Giguere. Available from Filmakers Library, Inc., 133 E. 58th St., New York, NY 10022, (212) 355-6545. Available in 16mm ($500, $55 rental) and VHS ($450). 28 minutes, color.

This brief but resonant Canadian documentary interweaves imagery from history and the memories and lives of women today to create a compelling film about coming to grips with the disparity between the myths of our socialization as women and the harsh realities of our adult lives.

All of Our Lives describes the economic hardship and emotional isola-tion faced by many old/older women in today's society. Director Helene Klodawsky and co-producer Laura Sky also focus on gaining pension equality and compensation for years of domestic service.

PAULA E. LANGGUTH

THE HEARING TRUMPET. Leonora Carrington. Published by St. Martin's Press, New York, 1976; reprinted by Pocket Books, Simon & Schuster, 1977. Currently out of print.

In this surrealistic classic, Leonora Carrington presents heroines over ninety who are smart, resourceful, clever, witty, and feminist. Carrington integrates surrealism with a feminist awareness of religious history, weaving a fantastic epic that leaves one breathless with the sheer magic of its symbols. She provides a view of powerful older women in a surreal setting in which the edges of reality are as tilted as the ludicrous nature of the patriarchal history she portrays.

Marion Leatherby is 92 years old when her best friend Carmella gives her the gift of a hearing trumpet. As a result of finally being able to hear, she discovers that her son is going to put her into an old people's home called The Well of Light Brotherhood. This home is a very peculiar place on the grounds of an old castle somewhere in

Mexico. The administrators are a husband and wife with a rather sadistic bent who practice strange occult doctrines with religious overtones. As Marion contemplates her son's decision, she realizes:

I have a death grip on this haggard frame as if it were the limpid body of Venus herself. . . my body, the cats, the red hen . . . . A separation from these well-known and loved, yes loved, things were "death and Death indeed."

Carmella tries to help:

In case they lock you up in a tenth storey room . . . you could take a lot of those ropes you weave and escape. I could be waiting down below with a machine gun and an automobile you know. I don't suppose it would be too expensive for an hour or two.

Carmella's idea of the institution does not match its actual eccentricities as Marion is confronted with its peculiarities.

Marion discovers the Leering Abbess and unwittingly becomes the catalyst for a revolt among the institution's occupants. As the story progresses, it shifts into more and more fantastic territory. There is a death, is it a murder? Marion and another friend discover someone was not a woman after all but a man. Why would a man have disguised himself as a woman? Why live in this institution? What is the secret of the Leering Abbess? She finds an old book. What are these ancient writings about and what has the Holy Grail to do with this tale? Marion's world grows more and more fantastic.

In the end, with Carmella's help, the old women change the world:

This is how the Goddess reclaimed her Holy Cup with an army of bees, wolves, six old women, a postman, a Chinaman, a poet, an atom driven ark, and a werewoman. The strangest army, perhaps, ever seen on this planet.

This novel is a classic surrealist tale that should be enshrined on all feminist reading lists.

MARGARITA DONNELLY

HOPE AND DIGNITY: Older Black Women of the South. Text by Emily Herring Wilson, Photographs by Susan Mullally, preface by Maya Angelou, Temple University Press, Philadelphia, Pennsylvania 19122, 1983, 200 pages, $19.95, cloth.

Twenty-seven in-depth interviews/portraits and twenty shorter portraits in the epilogue form a book that documents older black women from North Carolina. The forty-seven women portrayed show remarkable achievements in a variety of roles and provide a revealing glimpse into a part of southern history that has been too long ignored. Each is remarkable for very different reasons, yet all reveal a strength of character that is a result of a deep sense of dignity and an overriding sense of hope. Each has at one or more points in her life overcome adversity.

Minnie Jones Evans is an artist whose work has been classified as surrealistic, mystic, and primitive. She was 91 when she was interviewed. For most of her life she worked selling fish, and as a housekeeper, and a gatekeeper. She was "discovered" in 1960. Now she is the subject of a PBS documentary and her work has been exhibited in the Whitney Museum, the Museum of Folk Art, Portal Gallery (London), and many others. When she looks at her work she talks about her dreams: *"I didn't sleep when I was a child. I couldn't sleep for dreams . . . . When I start a picture, I don't know no more what I'm going to do than you do."*

Nelle Coley taught English at Dudley High School in Greensboro. Two of the students she taught sat at the Woolworth's lunch counter on that historic day, February 1, 1960 (when the sit-ins that started the civil rights movement began). *"They weren't doing a thing but what we had taught them to do . . . we had taught them not to accept it."* As a retired educator she still voices her concern for what is happening to black students in the classrooms as a result of segregation.

By birth and marriage, Lyda Moore Merrick is a member of North Carolina's two most prominent families. Lyda and her sister attended Fisk University and Columbia University. In the 1950's Lyda Merrick began working for the blind and founded the Negro Braille Magazine, which is the only national publication for blind black people. In her interview she says: *"You just read what happens to us, discrimination, and those of our people in jails. Innocent,*

innocent . . . the unfairness of it . . . . The jails are crowded with innocent black people."

Viola Turner was the first black woman on Wall Street. When she retired in 1965 she had been there for more than thirty years and was the vice president of Mutual Life Insurance Company and a member of the board of directors. She reminisces about the ways the office developed to require white visitors to address the staff by their proper titles.

". . . they'd stop and say, 'Is Ed in?' or 'Is John in?' . . . Well, we had a standard act . . . . they got '[MISTER] Merrick' until they were ready to drop . . . . One, in particular . . . he says, 'Is the preacher in?' . . . we could work with that all day long! 'What preacher? Where a preacher?' . . . 'Merrick.' 'Oh? Did you mean [MISTER] Merrick . . . ?"

In the preface Maya Angelou points out, *". . .the women collected in this book appear to be speaking more to their ancestors and even to their unborn progeny than to Emily Wilson . . . since Wilson is white . . . . It is a compliment to Wilson to say that she was wise enough to pose her questions then stand aside. . . ."*

The book is beautifully produced on high quality paper with excellent photographic reproductions. My only quibble is that it is designed with double columns of type on the page as if it were intended to be a textbook, yet it lacks an index and the Table of Contents doesn't include the women's names, so it is a difficult book to use for reference. But that is a minor complaint. This is a wonderful treasurehouse providing readers a look into older black women's lives that defy stereotyping and present a richly textured accounting of strength, humor, wit, endurance, and bravery.

MARGARITA DONNELLY

 BIBLIOGRAPHY

WOMEN AND AGING BIBLIOGRAPHY

This bibliography is compiled from a wide range of sources. The compilers wish to extend special thanks to Susan Searing, University of Wisconsin System Women's Studies Librarian, for use of her bibliography on Women and Aging.

Portions of this bibliography are reprinted from *Older Women in 20th-Century America, A Selected Annotated Bibliography* by Audrey Borenstein (1982) with the permission of Garland Publishing, Inc.

LITERATURE: POETRY, PROSE, SHORT STORIES

Adams, Alice. *Listening to Billie.* Novel. NY: Alfred A. Knopf, Inc., 1978.

Aldridge, Sarah. *Misfortune's Friend.* Novel. Tallahassee: Naiad, 1985.

Aldridge, Sarah. *The Nesting Place.* Novel. Tallahassee: Naiad, 1982.

Aldridge, Sarah. *The Latecomer.* Novel. Tallahassee: Naiad, 1974.

Aldridge, Sarah. *All True Lovers.* Novel. Tallahassee: Naiad, 1979.

Aldridge, Sarah. *Madame Aurora.* Novel. Tallahassee: Naiad, 1983.

Aldridge, Sarah. *Cytherea's Breath.* Novel. Tallahassee: Naiad, 1976.

Aldridge, Sarah. *Tottie.* Novel. Tallahassee: Naiad, 1975.

Anderson, Barbara Tunnel. *Southbound.* Novel. NY: Farrar, Straus and Co., 1949.

Arnold, June. *Sister Gin.* Novel. Plainfield, VT: Daughters, Inc., 1975.

Atherton, Gertrude. *Black Oxen.* Novel. NY: Boni and Liveright, 1923.

Azpadu, Dodici. *Saturday Night in the Prime of Life.* Novel. Iowa City: Aunt Lute Book Co., 1983.

Bambara, Toni Cade. "My Man Bovanne." Short Story. In *Bitches and Sad Ladies: An Anthology of Fiction By and About Women.* Pat Rotter, Ed. NY: Dell, 1975.

Banning, Margaret Culkin. *The Will of Magda Townsend.* Novel. NY: Harper and Row, 1974.

Barrett, Mary Ellin. *American Beauty.* Novel. NY: E.P. Dutton and Co., Inc., 1980.

Beresford-Howe, Constance. *The Book of Eve.* Novel. Toronto: Macmillan of Canada, 1973.

Borenstein, Audrey. "On the Rites of Separation." Short Story. In *Womanblood: Portraits of Women in Poetry and Prose.* O'Brien, Rasmussen, Costello, eds. San Francisco: Continuing Saga Press.

Buck, Pearl S. *Pavilion of Women.* Novel. NY: The John Day Co., 1946.

Calisher, Hortense. *The Collected Stories of Hortense Calisher.* NY: Arbor House Publishing Co., Inc., 1975.

Carrington, Leonora. *The Hearing Trumpet.* Novel. New York: St. Martin's Press, 1976.

Carroll, Gladys Hasty. *Unless You Die Young.* Novel. NY: W.W. Norton and Co., Inc., 1977.

Cather, Willa. *A Lost Lady.* Novel. NY: Alfred A. Knopf, 1923.

Cather, Willa. *My Mortal Enemy.* Novel. NY: Vintage Books, 1926, 1954.

Cather, Willa. *The Old Beauty and Others.* Short Stories. NY: Alfred A. Knopf, Inc., 1948.

Cather, Willa. "Old Mrs. Harris." Short Story. In *Obscure Destinies and Literary Encounters.* Boston: Houghton Mifflin Co., 1938.

Chase, Mary Ellen. *The Plum Tree.* Novel. NY: The Macmillan Co., 1949.

Deming, Barbara. *We Are All Part of One Another: A Barbara Deming Reader.* Jane Meyerding, ed. Philadelphia: New Society, 1984.

Douglas, Ellen. *Apostles of Light.* Novel. Boston: Houghton Mifflin Co., 1973.

Ferber, Edna. *One Basket: Thirty-One Short Stories by Edna Ferber.* NY: Simon and Schuster, Inc., 1947.

Fisher, Dorothy Canfield. *A Harvest of Stories: From a Half Century of Writing by Dorothy Canfield.* NY: Harcourt, Brace and Co., Inc., 1956.

Fortner, Ethel, ed. *Eve Triem: New As a Wave, A Retrospective (1937-1983).* Poetry. Mercer Island, WA: Dragon Gate, Inc., 1984.

Fortner, Ethel. *Nervous on the Curves.* Poetry. Laurinburg, NC: St. Andrews Press, 1982.

Fortner, Ethel. *Clouds and Keepings.* Poetry. Cascade Press, 1973.

Fortner, Ethel. *A Sudden Clarity.* Poetry. Olivant, 1967.

Freeman, Mary E. Wilkins. *The Revolt of Mother.* Short Stories. Old Westbury, NY: Feminist Press, 1974.

Gale, Vi. *Odd Flowers and Short-Eared Owls.* Poetry. Portland, OR: Prescott Street Press, 1984.

Glasgow, Ellen. *Barren Ground.* Novel. NY: The Modern Library, 1936.

Glasgow, Ellen. *The Sheltered Life.* Novel. Garden City, NY: Doubleday, Doran and Co., Inc., 1932.

Glasgow, Ellen. *They Stooped to Folly, A Comedy of Morals.* Novel. Garden City, NY: Doubleday, Doran and Co., Inc., 1929.

Glasgow, Ellen. *Vein of Iron.* Novel. NY: Harcourt, Brace and Co., 1935.

Glaspell, Susan. *Brook Evans.* Novel. NY: Frederick A. Stokes Co., 1928.

Godwin, Gail. *The Odd Woman.* Novel. NY: Alfred A. Knopf, 1974.

Grumbach, Doris. *Chamber Music.* Novel. NY: E.P. Dutton and Co., Inc., 1979.

Hailey, Elizabeth Forsythe. *A Woman of Independent Means.* Novel. NY: Viking, 1978.

Hale, Nancy. "The Great-Grandmother." In *Short Stories from the New Yorker, 1925 to 1940.* NY: Simon and Schuster, Inc., 1940.

Hamalian, Linda and Leo Hamalian, eds. *Solo: Women on Woman Alone.* NY: Dell Publishing Co., Inc., 1977.

Hardwick, Elizabeth. *Sleepless Nights.* Novel. NY: Random House, Inc., 1979.

Howe, Helen. *The Fires of Autumn.* Novel. NY: Harper and Brothers, 1959.

Howland, Bette. *Blue in Chicago.* Short Stories. NY: Harper and Row, Inc., 1978.

Hunter, Kristin. *God Bless the Child.* Novel. NY: Charles Scribner's Sons, 1964.

Hurston, Zora Neale. *Seraph on the Suwanee.* Novel. NY: Charles Scribner's Sons, 1948.

Hurston, Zora Neale. *Their Eyes Were Watching God.* Novel. NY: Negro Universities Press, 1969; originally by The J.B. Lippincott Co., Philadelphia, 1937.

Irwin, Hadley. *The Lilith Summer.* Novel. Old Westbury, NY: The Feminist Press, 1979.

Jackson, Shirley. *Come Along with Me.* Short Stories. NY: The Viking Press, Inc., 1968.

Janeway, Elizabeth. *The Third Choice.* Novel. Garden City, NY: Doubleday and Co., Inc., 1959.

Jewett, Sarah Orne. *The Best Stories of Sarah Orne Jewett.* The Mayflower Edition. Gloucester, MA: Peter Smith, 1965.

Katzenbach, Maria. *The Grab.* Novel. NY: Pocket Books, 1977.

Keane, Molly. *Time After Time.* Novel. New York: Dutton, 1985.

Kensington Ladies Erotica Society. *Ladies Home Erotica.* Berkeley: Ten Speed Press, 1984.

Kumin, Maxine. *The Designated Heir.* Novel. NY: The Viking Press, Inc., 1974.

L'Engle, Madeline. *The Summer of the Great Grandmother.* Novel. New York: Seabury, 1974.

Lavin, Mary. "Senility." Short Story. In *The Shrine and Other Stories.* Boston: Houghton Mifflin Co., 1977.

Lawrence, Josephine. *Years Are So Long.* Novel. NY: Frederick A. Stokes Co., 1934.

L'Engle, Madeline. *The Summer of the Great Grandmother.* New York: Seabury, 1974.

Le Sueur, Meridel. *I Hear Men Talking and Other Stories.* Ed. by Linda Ray Pratt. West End Press, 1984.

Le Sueur, Meridel. *Harvest: Collected Stories.* Cambridge, MA: West End Press, 1977.

Le Sueur, Meridel. *Ripening: Selected Work 1927-1980.* Ed. by Elaine Hedges. Old Westbury, NY: Feminist Press, 1982.

Le Sueur, Meridel. *Harvest* and *Song for My Time.* Minneapolis: West End Press & MEP Publications, 1982.

Le Sueur, Meridel. *The Girl.* Novel. Minneapolis: West End Press, 1985.

Lyell, Ruth Granetz, ed. *Middle Age, Old Age: Short Stories, Poems, Plays, and Essays on Aging.* NY: Harcourt Brace Jovanovich, Inc., 1980.

Markus, Julia. "A Patron of the Arts." In *Two Novellas,* by Julia Markus and Barbara Reid. Cambridge, MA: Apple-wood Press, 1977.

Miner, Valerie. *Winter's Edge.* Novel. The Crossing Press, 1985.

Noble, Marguerite. *Filaree.* Novel. Albuquerque: University of New Mexico Press, 1985.

Olsen, Tillie. *Tell Me a Riddle.* Short Stories. NY: Dell Publishing Co., Inc., 1976.

Parker, Dorothy. *The Portable Dorothy Parker.* Short Stories. New York and Harmondsworth, Middlesex, England: Penguin Books Ltd., 1976.

Porter, Katherine Anne. *The Collected Stories of Katherine Anne Porter.* NY: New American Library, 1970.

Ray, Maryellen James. *A Pause for the Menopause.* Poetry. Los Angeles: Rising Publishing, 1984.

Rex, Barbara. *I Want To Be in Love Again.* Novel. NY: W.W. Norton and Co., Inc., 1977.

Sackville-West, Vita. *All Passion Spent.* NY: Doubleday, 1933.

Sarton, May. *The Magnificent Spinster.* Novel. New York: W.W. Norton and Co., 1985.

Sarton, May. *A Reckoning.* Novel. NY: Norton, 1978.

Sarton, May. *Crucial Conversations.* Novel. NY: W.W. Norton and Co., Inc., 1975.

Sarton, May. *Kinds of Love.* Novel. NY: W.W. Norton and Co., Inc., 1970.

Sarton, May. *Mrs. Stevens Hears the Mermaids Singing.* Novel. NY: W.W. Norton and Co., Inc., 1975.

Sarton, May. *The Small Room.* Novel. NY: W.W. Norton and Co., Inc., 1961.

Sarton, May. *As We Are Now.* Novel. NY: W.W. Norton and Co., 1983.

Schneider, Nina. *The Woman Who Lived in a Prologue.* Novel. Boston: Houghton Mifflin Co., 1980.

Smedley, Agnes. *Daughter of Earth.* Novel. Old Westbury, NY: The Feminist Press, 1973.

Stafford, Jean. *The Collected Stories of Jean Stafford.* NY: Farrar, Straus and Giroux, 1969.

Suckow, Ruth. *The Folks.* Novel. NY: The Literary Guild, 1934.

Suckow, Ruth. "Mrs. Vogel and Ollie." Short Story. In *Some Others and Myself: Seven Stories and a Memoir.* NY: Rinehart and Co., Inc., 1952.

Taylor, Valerie. *Prism.* Novel. Tallahassee: Naiad, 1981.

Thorne, Evelyn. *Of Bones and Stars.* Poetry. American Studies Press, 1981.

Walker, Alice. *In Love and Trouble: Stories of Black Women.* NY: Harcourt Brace Jovanovich, 1973.

Welty, Eudora. *A Curtain of Green.* Short Stories. NY: Doubleday, Doran and Co., Inc., 1943.

Welty, Eudora. *Losing Battles.* Novel. NY: Random House, Inc., 1970.

Welty, Eudora. *The Optimist's Daughter.* Novel. NY: Vintage Books, 1978.

Wharton, Edith. *Certain People.* Short Stories. NY: D. Appleton and Co., 1930.

Wharton, Edith. *The Collected Short Stories of Edith Wharton.* Vol. 1. NY: Charles Scribner's Sons, 1968.

Wharton, Edith. *The Mother's Recompense.* Novel. NY: D. Appleton and Co., 1925.

Wharton, Edith. *Old New York: The Old Maid (The 'Fifties).* Novel. NY: D. Appleton and Co., 1924.

Wharton, Edith. *Twilight Sleep*. Novel. NY: D. Appleton and Co., 1927.

Yezierska, Anzia. *The Open Cage: An Anzia Yezierska Collection*. Short Stories. NY: Persea Books, 1979.

NON-FICTION: BOOKS, REPORTS, BIOGRAPHIES, AUTOBIOGRAPHIES

Allyn, Mildred V. *About Aging: A Catalogue of Films*. Los Angeles: Andrus Gerontology Center, University of Southern California, 1981.

Almvig, Chris. *The Invisible Minority: Aging and Lesbianism*. Utica, NY: Utica College of Syracuse University, 1982.

Arts for Elders. *Drama in a Supportive Environment: It's More Than Just a Play*. 5450 S.W. Erickson Ave., Beaverton, OR 97005.

Arts for Elders. *Enriching An Older Person's Life Through Senior Adult Theatre*. 5450 S.W. Erickson Ave., Beaverton, OR 97005.

Arts for Elders. *A Guide to 49 New Plays for Senior Adult Theatre*. 5450 S.W. Erickson Ave., Beaverton, OR 97005.

Arts for Elders. *Stimu-Drama: An Eclectic Approach*. 5450 S.W. Erickson Ave., Beaverton, OR 97005.

Beauvoir, Simone de. *The Coming of Age*. New York: Warner Books, 1973.

Benary-Isbert, Margot. *These Vintage Years*. Personal Essays. NY: Abingdon Press, 1968.

Berdes, Celia. "Winter Tales: Fiction About Aging." *The Gerontologist* (April 1981) 21(2):121-5.

Blackman, Margaret B. *During My Time—Florence Edenshaw Davidson, a Haida Woman*. Biography. Seattle: University of Washington Press, 1982.

Block, Marilyn R., Janice L. Davidson, and Jean D. Grambs. *Women Over Forty: Visions and Realities*. New York: Springer, 1981.

Block, Marilyn R., Janice L. Davidson, and Kathryn E. Serock. *Uncharted Territory: Issues and Concerns of Women Over Forty*. College Park, MD: Center on Aging, University of Maryland, 1978.

Block, Marilyn R., ed. *The Direction of Federal Legislation Affecting Women Over Forty*. College Park, MD: National Policy Center on Women and Aging, University of Maryland, 1982.

Borenstein, Audrey. *Chimes of Change and Hours: Views of Older Women in Twentieth Century America*. Cranbury, NJ: Associated University Presses/Fairleigh Dickinson University Press, 1983.

Borenstein, Audrey. *Older Women in Twentieth-Century America: A Selected Annotated Bibliography*. New York: Garland, 1982.

Butler, Robert N. *Why Survive?* NY: Harper & Row, 1975.

Caine, Lynn. *Widow*. NY: William Morrow, 1974.

Callen, Anthea. *Women Artists of the Arts and Crafts Movement: 1870-1914*. NY: Pantheon Books, 1979.

Cather, Willa. *Not Under Forty*. NY: Alfred A. Knopf, 1936.

Clark, Martha. "The Poetry of Aging: Views of Old Age in Contemporary American Poetry." *The Gerontologist* (April 1980) 20(2):188-91.

Clay, Vidal S. *Women: Menopause and Middle Age*. Pittsburgh: KNOW, Inc., 1977.

Cohen, Leah. *Small Expectations: Society's Betrayal of Older Women*. Toronto: McClelland and Stewart, 1984.

Colgrove, Melba, Harold Bloomfield and

Peter McWilliams. *How to Survive the Loss of a Love.* New York: Bantam Books, 1976.

Cornwell, Anita. *Black Lesbian in White America.* Autobiography. Tallahassee: Naiad, 1983.

Dancy, Joseph Jr. *The Black Elderly: A Guide for Practitioners.* Detroit: University of Michigan-Wayne State University, 1977.

Davis, Lenwood G. and Elaine Brody. *The Black Aged in the United States: An Annotated Bibliography.* Westport, CT: Greenwood Press, 1980.

Davis, Linda J., and Elaine M. Brody. *Rape and Older Women: A Guide to Prevention and Protection.* Washington: U.S. Government Printing Office, 1979.

Derenski, Arlene, and Sally B. Landsburg. *The Age Taboo: Older Women-Younger Men Relationships.* Boston: Little, Brown, 1981.

Dissinger, Katherine. *Old, Poor, Alone, and Happy: How to Live Nicely on Nearly Nothing.* Chicago: Nelson-Hall, 1980.

Dulude, Louise. *Women and Aging: A Report on the Rest of Our Lives.* Ottawa: Canadian Advisory Council on the Status of Women, 1978.

Edelstein, Beth. *Age is Becoming: An Annotated Bibliography on Women and Aging.* Berkeley: Interface Bibliographers, 1977.

Eliason, Carol. *Neglected Women: The Educational Needs of Displaced Homemakers, Single Mothers, and Older Women: A Report.* Washington: National Advisory Council on Women's Educational Programs, 1978.

Fields, Mamie Garvin with Karen Fields. *Lemon Swamp and Other Places.* NY: Free Press, 1983.

Fine, Irene. *Midlife and its Rite of Passage Ceremony.* With a Midlife Celebration by Bonnie Feinman. San Diego: Women's Institute for Continuing Jewish Education, 1983.

Fisher, M.F.K. *Sister Age.* Essays. New York: Random House, 1968.

Frankel, Flo, and Sally Rathvon. *Whatever Happened to Cinderella? Middle-Aged Women Reveal Their True Stories.* New York: St. Martin's Press, 1980.

Franks, Helen. *Prime Time: The Mid-Life Woman in Focus.* London: Pan Books, 1981.

Frym, Gloria. *Second Stories: Conversations with Women Whose Artistic Careers Began After Thirty-Five.* San Francisco: Chronicle Books, 1979.

Fuchs, Estelle. *The Second Season: Life, Love, and Sex—Women in the Middle Years.* Garden City, NY: Doubleday, 1978.

Fuller, Marie Marschall, and Cora Ann Martin, eds. *The Older Woman: Lavender Rose or Gray Panther.* Springfield, IL: Charles C. Thomas, 1980.

Gelfand, Donald E. *The Aging Network: Programs and Services.* NY: Springer, 1984.

Giele, Janet Zollinger, ed. *Women in the Middle Years: Current Knowledge and Future Directions for Research and Policy.* New York: Wiley, 1982.

Gray, Madeline. *The Changing Years: The Menopause Without Fear.* 3rd ed. New York: New American Library, 1982.

Greenwood, Sadja. *Menopause Naturally: Preparing for the Second Half of Life.* San Francisco: Volcano Press, 1984.

Gross, Ronald, Beatrice Gross and Sylvia Seidman, eds. *The New Old: Struggling for Decent Aging.* Garden City, NY: Anchor Press/Doubleday, 1978.

Harris, Janet. *The Prime of Ms. America: The American Woman at Forty.* New York: New

American Library, 1976.

Hedges, Elaine, and Ingrid Wendt. *In Her Own Image: Women Working in the Arts.* Old Westbury, NY: The Feminist Press, 1980.

Hellman, Lillian. *Three.* Autobiography. Boston: Little, Brown and Company, Inc., 1979.

Hemmings, Susan, ed. *A Wealth of Experience: The Lives of Older Women.* London: Pandora Press, 1985.

Herring, Emily. *Hope and Dignity: Older Black Women of the South.* Philadelphia: Temple University Press, 1983.

Hing, Esther, and Beulah K. Cypress. *Use of Health Services by Women Sixty-Five Years of Age and Over: United States.* Washington: U.S. Government Printing Office, 1981.

Hollenshead, Carol, Carol Katz, and Berit Ingersoll. *Past Sixty: The Older Woman in Print and Film.* Bibliography. Ann Arbor: Institute of Gerontology, University of Michigan-Wayne State University, 1977.

Jackson, Jacquelyne Johnson. *Minorities and Aging.* Belmont, CA: Wadsworth, 1980.

Jacobs, Ruth Harriet. *Life After Youth: Female, Forty—What Next?* Boston: Beacon Press, 1979.

Kahne, Hilda. *Economic Security of Older Women: Too Little for Late in Life.* Wellesley, MA: Center for Research on Women, Wellesley College, 1981.

Kallir, Otto. *Grandma Moses.* NY: Harry N. Abrams, Inc., 1973.

King, Nancy, and Marjory G. Marvel. *Issues, Policies, and Programs for Midlife and Older Women.* Washington: Center for Women Policy Studies, 1982.

Kramer, Sydelle, and Jenny Mosur, eds. *Jewish Grandmothers.* Boston: Beacon, 1976.

Kubelka, Susanna. *Over Forty at Last: How to Avoid the "Mid-Life Crisis" and Make the Most of the Best Years of Your Life.* New York: Macmillan, 1982.

Kuhn, Maggie. *Maggie Kuhn on Aging: A Dialogue.* Ed. by Dieter Hessel. Philadelphia: Westminster Press, 1977.

Laird, Carobeth. *Limbo.* Memoir. Novato, CA: Chandler & Sharp, 1982.

Lake, Alice. *Our Own Years: What Women Over Thirty-Five Should Know About Themselves.* New York: Random House, 1979.

Laws, J.L. "Female Sexuality Through the Life Span." In: *Life-Span Development and Behavior,* vol. 3, ed. by P. B. Baltes and O. G. Brim, Jr. New York: Academic Press.

Le Sueur, Meridel. *Workers Writers.* Minneapolis: West End Press, 1982.

Le Sueur, Meridel. *Women on the Breadlines.* West End Press, 1982.

LeShan, Eda. *The Wonderful Crisis of Middle Age: Some Personal Reflections.* New York: David McKay, 1973.

Lesnoff-Caravaglia, Gari, ed. *The World of the Older Woman: Conflicts and Resolutions.* NY: Human Sciences Press, 1983.

Luce, Gay Gaer. *Your Second Life (Vitality and Growth in Middle and Later Years).* NY: Delacorte Press/Seymour Lawrence, 1979.

Macdonald, Barbara, and Cynthia Rich. *Look Me in the Eye: Old Women, Aging and Ageism.* San Francisco: Spinster's Ink, 1983.

Markson, Elizabeth W. *Older Women: Issues and Prospects.* Lexington, MA: Lexington Books, 1983.

Martin, Kathryn. *The Dorm and I: A Question of Age.* Memoir. Tompson & Rutter, Inc., 1984.

Matthews, Joseph L. *Sourcebook for Older*

Americans. Berkeley, CA: Nolo Press, 1983.

Matthews, Sarah H. *The Social World of Old Women: Management of Self-Identity.* Beverly Hills: Sage Publications, 1979.

Maxwell-Scott, Florida. *The Measure of My Days.* Journal. NY: Knopf, 1968.

McLeish, John A. B. *The Ulyssean Adult: Creativity in the Middle and Later Years.* Toronto: McGraw-Hill Ryerson Ltd., 1976.

Melamed, Elissa. *Mirror, Mirror: The Terror of Not Being Young.* New York: Linden Press/Simon and Schuster, 1983.

Miller, Luree. *Late Bloom: New Lives for Women.* NY: Paddington Press, 1979.

Mintz, Joan, et al. *An Older Woman's Health Guide.* New York: McGraw-Hill, 1984.

Monroe, Harriet. *A Poet's Life: Seventy Years in a Changing World.* NY: The Macmillan Co., 1938.

Monroe, Margaret Ellen, and Rhea Joyce Rubin. *The Challenge of Aging: A Bibliography.* Littleton, CO: Libraries Unlimited, 1983.

Moskowitz, Faye. *A Leak in the Heart: Tales from a Woman's Life.* Autobiography. Boston: David R. Godine, 1985.

Murguia, Edward, et al. *Ethnicity and Aging: A Bibliography.* San Antonio: Trinity University Press, 1984.

Musgrave, Beatrice, and Zoë Menell, eds. *Change and Choice: Women and Middle Age.* London: Owen, 1980.

Nevelson, Louise. *Dawn & Dusks—Taped Conversations with Diana MacKown.* NY: Charles Scribner's Sons, 1976.

Nudel, Adele. *For the Woman Over Fifty.* New York: Taplinger, 1978.

Older Women's League. *Growing Numbers, Growing Force: A Report from the White House Mini-Conference on Older Women.* Oakland: Older Women's League Educational Fund; San Francisco: Western Gerontological Society, 1981.

Olsen, Tillie. *Silences.* Essays. NY: Delacorte Press/Seymour Lawrence, 1978.

Olson, Laura Katz. *The Political Economy of Aging: The State, Private Power, and Social Welfare.* NY: Columbia University Press, 1982.

Page, Linda Garland and Eliot Wigginton, eds. *Aunt Arie: A Foxfire Portrait.* NY: Dutton, 1983.

Painter, Charlotte. *Gifts of Age—Thirty-two Remarkable Women.* Photography by Pamela Valois. SF: Chronicle Books: 1985.

Parton, Mary Field, ed. *The Autobiography of Mother Jones.* Chicago: Charles H. Kerr Publishing Co., 1977.

Paull, Irene. *Everybody's Studying Us: The Ironies of Aging in the Pepsi Generation.* SF: Volcano Press, 1976.

Person, E. S. "Sexuality as the Mainstay of Identity: Psychoanalytic Perspectives." *Signs: Journal of Women in Culture and Society.* vol. 5, pp. 605-630.

Place, Linna Funk, Linda Parker, and Forrest J. Berghorn. *Aging and the Aged: An Annotated Bibliography and Library Research Guide.* Boulder: Westview Press, 1981.

Porcino, Jane. *Growing Older, Getting Better: A Handbook for Women in the Second Half of Life.* Reading, MA: Addison-Wesley, 1983.

Rich-McCoy, Lois. *Late Bloomer: Profiles of Women Who Found Their True Calling.* New York: Harper and Row, 1980.

Rix, Sara E. *Older Women: The Economics of Aging.* Women's Research and Education

Institute of the Congressional Caucus for Women's Issues, 204 Fourth St. SE, Washington, DC 20003.

Rubin, Lillian B. *Women of a Certain Age: The Midlife Search for Self.* New York: Harper and Row, 1979.

Salber, Eva J. *Don't Send Me Flowers When I'm Dead.* Durham, NC: Duke Press, 1983.

Sarton, May. *At Seventy.* Journal. NY: W.W. Norton, 1984.

Sarton, May. *The House By the Sea: A Journal.* NY: W.W. Norton and Co., Inc., 1977.

Sarton, May. *I Knew a Phoenix: Sketches for an Autobiography.* NY: W.W. Norton and Co., Inc., 1959.

Sarton, May. *Journal of a Solitude.* NY: W.W. Norton and Co., Inc., 1977.

Sarton, May. *Plant Dreaming Deep.* Journal. NY: W.W. Norton and Co., Inc., 1968.

Sarton, May. *Recovering.* Journal. NY: W.W. Norton and Co., Inc., 1980.

Segalla, Rosemary Anastasio. *Departure from Traditional Roles: Mid-Life Women Break the Daisy Chains.* Ann Arbor: UMI Research Press, 1982.

Seskin, Jane. *Alone—Not Lonely: Independent Living for Women Over Fifty.* Washington: American Association of Retired Persons; Glenview, IL: Scott, Foresman, 1985.

Seskin, Jane. *More than Mere Survival: Conversations with Women Over Sixty-Five.* New York: Newsweek Books, 1980.

Seskin, Jane, and Bette Ziegler. *Older Women/Younger Men.* Garden City, NY: Doubleday, 1979.

Shields, Laurie. *Displaced Homemakers: Organizing for a New Life.* New York: McGraw-Hill, 1981.

Stevenson, Janet. *Woman Aboard.* Novato, CA: Chandler & Sharp, 1981.

Stewart, Dana, ed. *A Fine Age: Creativity as a Key to Successful Aging.* Little Rock, AR: August House, 1984.

Storey, James R. *Older Americans in the Reagan Era.* Washington, DC: Urban Institute Press, 1983.

Strugnell, Cécile. *Adjustment to Widowhood and Some Related Problems: A Selective and Annotated Bibliography.* New York: Health Sciences Publishing Corp., 1974.

Sunderland, J. T., N. J. Taylor and P. Smith, eds. *Arts and the Aging: An Agenda for Action.* Washington, D.C.: The National Council on the Aging, Inc., 1977.

Szinovacz, Maximiliane, ed. *Women's Retirement: Policy Implications of Recent Research.* Beverly Hills: Sage Publications, 1982.

Thomas, Sherry. *We Didn't Have Much, But We Sure Had Plenty.* NY: Doubleday/Anchor Books, 1981.

Tomb, David A. *Growing Old: A Handbook for You and Your Aging Parents.* NY: Viking, 1984.

Troll, Lillian E., Joan Israel, and Kenneth Israel, eds. *Looking Ahead: A Woman's Guide to the Problems and Joys of Growing Older.* Englewood Cliffs, NJ: Prentice-Hall, 1977.

U.S. Government Printing Office. *The Older Woman: Continuities and Discontinuities.* Report of the National Institute on Aging and the National Institute of Mental Health Workshop, Sept. 14-16, 1978. Washington: U.S. Government Printing Office, 1979.

Vesperi, Maria D. *City of Green Benches.* NY: Cornell University Press, 1985.

Vickery, Florence E. *Old and Growing: Conversations, Letters, Observations, and Reflections on Growing Old.* Springfield, IL: Charles C. Thomas, 1978.

Vining, Elizabeth Gray. *Being Seventy: The Measure of a Year.* NY: The Viking Press, 1978.

Walker, Alice. *In Search of Our Mothers' Gardens.* Essays. NY: Harcourt, Brace, 1984.

Walker, Barbara G. *The Crone: Woman of Age, Wisdom, and Power.* San Francisco: Harper and Row, 1985.

Wax, Judith. *Starting in the Middle.* New York: Holt, Rinehart, and Winston, 1979.

Westoff, Leslie Aldridge. *Breaking Out of the Middle-Age Trap.* New York: New American Library, 1980.

Wilson, Emily Herring. *Hope and Dignity: Older Black Women of the South.* Philadelphia: Temple University Press, 1983.

Yates, Martha. *Coping: A Survival Manual for Women Alone.* Engelwood Cliffs, NJ: Prentice-Hall, 1976.

Yglesias, Helen. *Starting: Early, Anew, Over, and Late.* NY: Rawson, Wade, 1979.

No Longer Young: The Older Woman in America: Proceedings of the 26th Annual Conference on Aging. Ann Arbor: Institute of Gerontology, University of Michigan-Wayne State University, 1975.

Older Women in the City. Sponsored by the Department for the Aging, City of New York. New York: Arno Press, 1979.

Women in Midlife—Security and Fulfillment: A Compendium of Papers. Submitted to the Select Committee on Aging and the Subcommittee on Retirement Income and Employment, U.S. House of Representatives, 95th Congress, Second Session. Washington: U.S. Government Printing Office, 1978.

PERIODICALS/SPECIAL ISSUES

"Aging." *Canadian Woman Studies,* vol. 5, no. 3 (Spring 1984).

"Growing Up...And Up...And Up." *MS.* vol. 10, no. 7 (January 1982).

"Midlife and Older Women: Taking Responsibility for Our Own Health." *Network News, The Newsletter of the National Women's Health Network,* vol. 9, no. 2 (March/April 1984).

"Older Wiser Stronger—Southern Elders." *Southern Exposure,* vol. 13, no. 2-3 (May-June 1985).

"On Being Old and Age." *Sinister Wisdom,* no. 10 (Summer 1979).

"Time Lines: The Years of Our Lives." *Sojourner: The New England Women's Journal of News, Opinions, and the Arts,* vol. 7, no. 1 (September 1981).

"Women and Aging." *Generations,* vol. 4, no. 4 (August 1980).

"Women as Elders." *Resources for Feminist Research/Documentation sur la Recherche Féministe,* vol. 11, no. 2 (July 1982).

Aging. Administration on Aging publication. $13/year. Address: Superintendent of Documents, Government Printing Office, Washington, DC 20402

Broomstick: A Periodical By, For, and About Women Over Forty. Bimonthly. $10/individuals, $20/institutions. Address: 3543 18th Street, San Francisco, CA 94110

Courageous Crones: A Web of Crones Newsletter. Quarterly. $6/year. Address: P.O. Box 6, Hornby Island, B.C., Canada VOR 12O Address: 207 Coastal Highway, St. Augustine, FL 32084

Fifty Upwards Network: A Newsletter for Single Women in Midlife. $2/sample copy. Address: Box 4714, Cleveland, OH 44126

Hot Flash: A Newsletter for Midlife and Older Women. Quarterly. Published by the National Action Forum for Older Women. $10. Address: School of Allied Health

Professionals, State University of New York at Stony Brook, Stony Brook, NY 11794.

Starshadows: An Older Women's Newsletter. $10 individual membership (more if you can, less if you can't) Address: 1105 N. Ontare Road, Santa Barbara, CA 93105

The Grey Panthers. Newsletter. $12/year. Address: 3700 Chestnut Street, Philadelphia, PA 19104

The OWL Observer. Monthly. Published by the Older Women's League. $5 (membership in OWL). Address: 1325 G Street N.W., Lower Level B, Washington, DC 20005

ORGANIZATIONS

Arts for Elders. Theatre Group. 5450 S.W. Erickson Ave., Beaverton, OR 97005 (503) 626-4897.

Associacion Nacional Por Personas Mayores (National Association for Spanish Speaking Elderly). 3875 Wilshire Blvd., Suite 1401, Los Angeles, CA 90010. (213) 487-1922.

American Association of Retired Persons (AARP). 1909 K St., NW, Washington, DC 20049. (202) 872-4700

Gray Panthers. 3700 Chestnut St., Philadelphia, PA 19104. (215) 382-3300.

National Caucus on the Black Aged. 1424 K St., NW, Suite 500, Washington, DC 20005. (202) 479-1200.

National Citizens Coalition for Nursing Home Reform (NCCNHR). 1825 Connecticut Ave. NW, Suite 417B, Washington, DC 20009. (202) 797-0657.

National Council on the Aging (NCOA). 600 Maryland Ave. SW, West Wing 100, Washington, DC 20074. (202) 479-1200.

National Council of Senior Citizens. 925

15th St. NW, Washington, DC 20005. (202) 347-8800.

National Indian Council on Aging. PO Box 2088, Albuquerque, NM 87103. (506) 766-2276.

Older Women's League (OWL). 1325 6 St. NW, Lower Level B, Washington, DC 20005. (202) 783-6686.

Senior PAC. 1302 18th St. NW, Washington, DC 20036. (202) 328-8105.

ART

Cunningham, Imogen. *After Ninety.* Photography. Seattle: University of Washington Press, 1980.

Freehand, Julianna. *Elizabeth's Dream.* Photography. Croton-on-Hudson: Menses, 1984.

Hoffman, Katherine. *An Enduring Spirit: The Art of Georgia O'Keefe.* Metuchen, NJ: The Scarecrow Press, 1984.

Layton, Elizabeth. *Through the Looking Glass: Drawings.* Kansas City: Mid-America Arts Alliance, 1984.

Noggle, Anne. *Silver Lining.* Photography. Albuquerque: University of New Mexico Press, 1984.

SILVER LINING

Photographs by Anne Noggle

Text by Janice Zita Grover   Foreword by Van Deren Coke

"I have something that I want to show and it concerns the way it is to *be*, and the way it is to see yourself and those around you as you have become. . . .

"I hope that all of my images have or hold in some sense the heroics of confronting life—I hope I speak more of immortality, of humanness and that our limited spans on this planet are notable. I'm trying to humanize the middle-aged and older, to find a new perspective that does more than simply deny older persons . . ."

—Anne Noggle, from the Text

203 pages, 80 duotone plates, 7 figures   Cloth: $45.00

Yolanda 1978

Menopause, Naturally

PREPARING FOR THE SECOND HALF OF LIFE

Sadja Greenwood, M.D.
Illustrations by Marcia Quackenbush

"An excellent book . . . I would recommend it for all women."

Journal American Medical Women's Association

". . . shows how it's possible to greet the natural changes of the menopause years as potential sources of pleasure, strength, and increased well-being . . . in a clear, measured way that combines comfort, respect, perspective and gentle humor."

Medical Self-Care Magazine

"Especially good on sexuality and nutrition."

Library Journal

". . . balances the natural with the medicinal, the cultural influences with the physical facts—and comes out with a unique, common sense guide for everywoman who will experience this rite of passage."

Gloria Steinem

Winner of a 1985 *Medical Self-Care Magazine* Book Award

$10.00 paper, 210p., illustrations

VOLCANO PRESS, INC.
330 Ellis Street, Dept. CYX
San Francisco, CA 94102

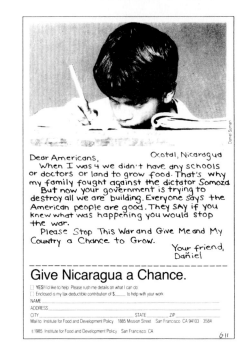

On Poetry

Anne Sexton
No Evil Star
**Selected Essays, Interviews,
and Prose**
Edited by Steven E. Colburn
August, 1985   paper $8.95

In this very special selection of her prose, Sexton speaks of her vocation as a poet and explores those themes that compelled her: family relationships, mental illness, death, and the "awful rowing toward God."

**Diane Wood Middlebrook and
Marilyn Yalom, Editors**
Coming to Light
**American Women Poets in the
Twentieth Century**
                    cloth $25.00/paper 12.95

This collection of sixteen essays on women poets, including Sylvia Plath, H.D., Gertrude Stein, Louise Bogan, Adrienne Rich, and Anne Sexton, discusses the relationship of women poets to the American literary tradition.

Lynda K. Bundtzen
Plath's Incarnations
Woman and the Creative Process
                    cloth $25.00

. . . a major contribution to honoring [Plath's] work permanently."
                    — *Los Angeles Times Book Review*

Jane Roberta Cooper, Editor
Reading Adrienne Rich
Reviews and Re-Visions, 1951-81
                    cloth $16.00/paper 8.95

"Rich is an outspoken and sometimes outrageous feminist. . . . Suffice it to say these essays will leave your ears ringing."
                    — *Santa Fe Reporter*

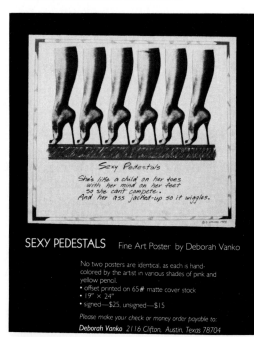

CALYX BOOKS

THE RIVERHOUSE STORIES

How Pubah S. Queen and
Lazy LaRue Save the World
by Andrea Carlisle

Glamorous Pubah

Pubah is an electrician, Lazy, a writer. The two may seem unlikely candidates to save the world but anything is possible as Pubah ponders solar powered inventions and Lazy dreams of ballooning over Ursula LeGuin's house. . . THE RIVERHOUSE STORIES are wacky, whimsical recountings of two women's lives on the river: lives that include ducks, spiders and muskrats; friends, neighbors, godchildren; work, dreams and love for each other.

Order Now for Spring 1986! (150pp, illus, paper, $7.95)

WOMEN & AGING: AN ANTHOLOGY

The largest proportion of the aging population is composed of women who have been ignored not only by society and the media but by feminists as well. This anthology provides insights into the problems, concerns, and images of women's aging. ISBN: 0-934971-00-5. $12.00.

BEARING WITNESS SOBREVIVIENDO

A special anthology of writings and art by Native American and Chicana/Latina women. The first anthology of its kind, it is out of print in the journal edition and is being reissued in a book edition. 128 pp., paper, 22 pp. art. $7.50. ISBN: 0-934971-02-1. Available spring 1986.

THE WHITE JUNK OF LOVE, AGAIN Sibyl James

Translitics of 16th C. French poet Louise Labe's sonnets in James' contemporary voice. Labe's work surfaces with new life in its obsessive struggle with passion and eroticism by this Northwest poet. Poetry. 75 pp., paper. $6.95. ISBN: 0-934971-03-x.

CALYX BOOKS
P.O. Box B Dept Q. Corvallis, OR 97339

CONTRIBUTORS' NOTES

MARJORIE AGOSIN, a native of Chile, is now a member of the Spanish Department faculty of Wellesley College. She has written five books: three of poetry and two of criticism. Her most recent book of poetry is *Brujas y algo más/Witches and Other Things*, issued in a bilingual edition by the Latin American Literary Review Press, Pittsburgh. Her most recent book of criticism, a study of Neruda, is scheduled for release early next year.

KATHLEEN J. ALCALÁ received an M.A. in English from the University of Washington, where she was a Milliman scholar. She has published short stories in *Ohio Renaissance Review, Seattle Arts,* and *The Written Arts.* "Amalia" is one of a collection of stories she hopes to publish in both English and Spanish. She is currently an associate editor of *The Seattle Review* for a special issue on science fiction and fantasy.

ELIZABETH ALEXANDER: "I have survived my mid-life crisis and am nearing fifty feeling better than ever about teaching, writing, and living in rural New Hampshire. I am an out-and-out lesbian feminist, and to this I owe most of my joy and purpose in life."

MARJORIE RAEDER ALTENBURG was born in Canada in 1906, studied at the Pratt Institute, then with Kuniyoshi at the Art Students League and with Hans Hoffman in New York City. Her exhibitions include the Monroe Gallery, Chicago; Provincetown Art Museum, Massachusetts; National Academy Galleries, Society of Independent Artists, and American Watercolor Society, New York City. She says of herself, "Art is the only thing that interested me. . . . I guess first of all I painted for me."

AUDREY BORENSTEIN has devoted many years of her life to research and writing on women and aging. In 1978, she was awarded a Rockefeller Foundation Humanities Fellowship in support of her research project, "the older woman as seen in social science and literature," which culminated in two books: *Chimes of Change and Hours: Views of Older Women in 20th-Century America* and *Older Women in 20th-Century America: A Selected Annotated Bibliography.* A Fellow of the National Endowment for the Arts, she has published 24 short stories in literary journals and collections.

BETTY COON has taught writing at Stanford University, Gettysburg College, and Diablo Valley College, and is currently teaching at Dominican College in San Rafael, California. Her poems have been published in a number of small magazines, including *CALYX, Southern Poetry Review, Buckle, The Berkeley Monthly, New Jersey Poetry,* and *East Bay Review.* Her poetry collection, *Seaward,* was published by the Berkeley Poets Cooperative in 1978.

BABA COPPER is a 66-year-old Crone Futurist who lives in Northern California. She is writing a book on Lesbian Mothers of Lesbian Daughters and would like to hear from others who share this experience.

TEE CORINNE moved west in 1972, settling in Oregon in 1981. Her art work is found in the *Cunt Coloring Book* (A.K.A. *Labiaflowers*), *Yantras of Woman Love, Women Who Loved Women,* and *Sapphistry.* She is best known for her *Sinister Wisdom* poster and is currently working on a group of portraits called "In Search of a Lavender Muse."

IMOGEN CUNNINGHAM was born in Oregon in 1883 and went to high school in Seattle where she saw Gertrude Kasebier's photographs and was so enchanted by her work that she decided to become a photographer. She majored in chemistry at the University of Washington, studied in Germany, worked for Edward S. Curtis, then married and moved with her husband and family to the San Francisco Bay Area. She founded a photographic movement with Edward Weston that changed the direction of West Coast photography. She taught on the faculty of the San Francisco Art Institute. Recognition for her work came late in life. She died at the age of 93 (in 1976) still actively working as a photographer and on the publication of her last book, *After Ninety* (University of Washington Press).

ANN DOMITROVICH: "I've always lived in West Virginia and can't imagine living anywhere else. I have only a high school education, but at age 35 I began taking all the art classes I could and fell in love with painting and anything related to it. Mostly, I express myself in a visual way but every now and then I enjoy writing little bits and pieces here and there. I loved writing my thoughts on aging because I feel so strongly about it."

MARGARITA DONNELLY is a founding editor of *CALYX*. Now that her daughter is out of the nest she finds herself single for the first time since she was 23 except for a flock of purebred sheep whose lambs add excitement and conflict every spring. In 1985 she was the recipient of a CCLM grant for her work at *CALYX*.

LIBBY DURBIN: "Born in 1929, I come from a blue-collar, small-town West Virginia background. By the time I was 20, I had a B.A. in journalism and a husband. Besides raising five children in the 50's and 60's, I was a social activist working against McCarthyism, racism, poverty, war, and oppressive institutions. Although permanently crippled by rheumatoid arthritis, I regained my health in the 70's, divorced, got an M.S. in psychology and established a counseling practice with specialties in dream work and sexuality. I live in the oldest stand of timber in Tigard with two of my daughters, Rachel and Moira, two dogs, and a hammered dulcimer."

SUE SANIEL ELKIND was born in 1913 and began writing poetry at age 64. Since then she has had more than 200 poems published in more than 75 magazines, and her first book, *No Longer Afraid*, was published by Lintel this year. She lives in Pittsburgh, where she organized and runs a poetry workshop sponsored by the Carnegie Library.

ETHEL N. FORTNER edited poetry for *Human Voice*, a Florida literary journal, for seven years. She grew up in the Rocky Mountains, taught in rural and city schools in Colorado, and came to Oregon in 1931 to teach in the Oregon State School for the Blind. More than 200 of her poems have appeared in small-press magazines, including *Song, Gryphon, Encore,* and *St. Andrews Review*, and in several anthologies. Her published collections include *A Sudden Clarity, Clouds and Keepings,* and *Nervous on the Curves.*

COLA FRANZEN translates the work of Marjorie Agosin and poets Juan Cameron and Saúl Yurkievich. Her work has appeared or is soon to appear in a number of literary journals, including *Boundary 2, The Chicago Review, Mundus Artium, Sulfur, Spectacular Diseases* (England), and *Temblor.* She is an editor of O.ARS publications.

PESHA GERTLER has retired (somewhat) from the single parenting of five children. Currently she devotes her time to her own writing and to teaching creative writing workshops through Adult Education at the University of Washington and North Seattle Community College. She is the co-founder of *Women's Voices and Visions*, a series of ongoing workshops, support groups, etc., for women in the visual and written arts. Her work has appeared in many publications, including *Poetry Northwest, Sinister Wisdom,* and *Backbone 11.* Her full-length manuscript, *The Mermaids and the Seated Women,* is currently seeking a publisher.

CELIA GILBERT is the author of two books of poetry, *Bonfire* and *Queen of Darkness.* She won a Pushcart IX Prize in 1984 for her poem "Lot's Wife" from *Bonfire.*

CAROL GORDON lives in Olympia, Washington, and works in Tacoma as a counselor in a mental health clinic. She hopes to explore feminist theology and reflect this in her poetry. Her work has appeared in *CALYX, Crab Creek Review, Bellingham Review, Jeopardy, Snapdragon,* and *Poetry Seattle.*

BETTY DONLEY HARRIS: "I grew up in a small rural town in western Pennsylvania . . . . Graduating from high school during the Great Depression meant turning down a college scholarship, borrowing money from my grandfather, attending business college, and working as a secretary in a bank to help my family. It was just something one did. . . . Now in my widowed sixties I am trying to write and I know this is something I have always wanted to do. My mother never realized her dream but into my life she poured books, music, wind in the pine trees, purple violets, sunsets, the new crop of dried lima beans—all the joys of small things—and her love: enough fuel for writing all the rest of my days. I am grateful for that and know that she would have been pleased that I am free for the both of us."

SHEVY HEALEY is a 63-year-old feminist who has just begun her own examination of aging and ageism. She is a clinical psychologist who recently partially retired. Her major clinical work as a feminist psychotherapist has been with women, both heterosexual and lesbian, and with disabled people. She is also a teacher and supervisor of M.S. Peer Counselors and is currently co-authoring a manual to train peer counselors.

JORJANA HOLDEN has exhibited her work widely, with one-, two-, and three-person shows at the Crocker Art Museum and Matrix Gallery in Sacramento, Pence Gallery in Davis, and the Redding Art Museum, among others. She is a founding member of Matrix, a workshop of women artists that maintains a gallery and classroom and serves as a support group for women.

RAYNA MERIDEL HOLTZ: "My parents named me Rayna Meridel Smith. Among my most vivid and earliest childhood memories was seeing Meridel [Le Sueur] enter our living room in Minneapolis, glowing from within with a mysterious power and energy, and accompanied by a dog that I and my sisters believed was half wolf. Years later, as I sorted pottery shards at an archaeological dig by the Dead Sea, a middle-aged woman sitting with me recognized my name and said she had known Meridel and my parents in the '30s and '40s. She and her husband had emigrated to Israel as political exiles, victims of McCarthyism. Everywhere she goes, Meridel hears these stories as she meets the grown children of her old friends and comrades. She says 'it's worth growing old for,' and that 'it really makes you feel the psychic continuity.'" Co-owner and co-editor of Laughing Dog Press, Holtz lives on an island in Washington's Puget Sound.

BARBARA HORN teaches writing and literature at a branch of the State University of New York and at the New School for Social Research in Manhattan. She has published reviews and personal narrative essays and is currently working on a collection of meditative pieces about her girlhood in rural Missouri and her womanhood in New York City. She was an assistant editor of *Victorian Studies Bulletin.*

SIBYL JAMES is currently teaching English in Shanghai, China. Her work is widely published, including: *CALYX, Ironwood,* and *Room of One's Own.* Her book of poetry, *The White Junk of Love, Again (Translitics from Louise Labé),* is forthcoming from CALYX Books in 1986.

TERRI L. JEWELL is a 30-year-old Black lesbian writer whose work has been accepted by more than 100 "little" magazines, including *Conditions, Woman's Journal Advocate, Sing! Heavenly Muse, Kalliope, Woman of Power, Hurricane Alice,* and *Broadsheet.* She coordinates a neighborhood "meals on wheels" program for elders (99 percent Black women) and says of this work: "I have been *stunned* by what I see out here—women sick and aged and alone and FULL OF LOVE & COURAGE & STRENGTH. A lot of my work is filled by them and their spirits."

ARLENE SWIFT JONES: "I was born in Iowa 1/3/28, graduated from Cornell College and Columbia University in the years 1949 and 1950. I married a Foreign Service Officer and lived abroad . . . for 20 years, raising three daughters and . . . employed as teacher or head of school. Now I live in Connecticut where I devote much of my time to writing poetry and fiction."

DEBORAH KLIBANOFF received her bachelor's degree in media arts from the University of Southern California. After working professionally for several years, she has spent the past eight years personally investigating many forms of Buddhism and Hinduism. Three years ago she took vows as a Tibetan Buddhist nun and is presently living in Seattle in the Tibetan Buddhist Monastery.

SUSAN LANDGRAF is a poet, freelance writer, and photographer, who has been published in a variety of magazines and newspapers. Formerly a newspaper reporter, she recently earned her B.A. and has been accepted for graduate school in the Creative Writing Program at the University of Washington where she has a teaching assistantship.

PAULA E. LANGGUTH is a Midwestern transplant currently freelancing in New York City. Her non-fiction writing, which includes feature articles and film reviews, appears regularly in *WomaNews.*

ELIZABETH LAYTON discovered in the fall of 1977 that by drawing pictures of herself she could cure the depression she'd had for more than 30 years. At the age of 68, she enrolled in her first art class. By drawing large pictures of herself while looking into her hand mirror, she expressed on paper all the rage, fear, love, and understanding she had not been able to express in any other way. Her drawings of herself, exaggerating her wrinkles, sags, and age spots, became not simply personal but universal. A one-person exhibition of her work, sponsored by the Mid-America Arts Alliance in Kansas City, is now touring the country. Two major upcoming exhibits are at the Chicago Public Library Cultural Center (November 16, 1985 through January 18, 1986) and the Phoenix Art Museum (December 31, 1985 through February 28, 1986).

REVA LEEMAN teaches English at Portland Community College in Oregon, where she lives with her housemate and two sons. She has published poetry in the *Portland Review*.

URSULA K. LE GUIN, born in California and living in Oregon, is a novelist and poet whose books include *Hard Words and Other Poems*, *The City of Illusions*, *The Adventures of Cobbler's Rune*, and many others. Her latest book, *Always Coming Home*, was published by Harper & Row in September 1985.

MERIDEL LESUEUR was born in Iowa in 1900. For more than 60 years she has been writing work that illustrates the struggles of working-class people. She states: "The artist's duty now is to recreate a new image of the world, to return to the people their need and vision ... of a new birth of abundance and equality." She is the author of a large volume of work, including: *Salute to Spring, Northstar Country, The Girl* (West End Press), *Song for My Time* (West End Press), *I Hear Men Talking* (West End Press), and *Woman on the Breadlines* (West End Press). In 1980 she was the recipient of an NEA memorial grant. She is currently working on three novels.

LUCY LIPPARD, whose most recent book is *Get the Message? A Decade of Art for Social Change* (Dutton), writes on art and politics monthly for *In These Times*. She is an editor of *Heresies* and received a 1985 CCLM Editors Grant.

BARBARA MACDONALD is a radical feminist and author with Cynthia Rich of *Look Me in the Eye: Old Women, Aging and Ageism* (Spinsters Ink). She lives with Cynthia Rich on the Anza Borrego desert, where both of them continue to write on ageism and its politic.

ELLIE MAMBER has poems in the current issues of *Connecticut River* and *New Voices*, and another in *Lyrical Forms*, an anthology forthcoming from Quixsilver Press. Of herself she says, "I'm 58, divorced, have been a partner in a couple of small businesses ... and have for the last year been taking university courses in writing and literature. This fall I'll be exploring whether or not I want to make the commitment required in an M.F.A. program in creative writing."

MARCELINA MARTIN is a freelance photographer in San Francisco. Her prints have been published in *Women See Woman, Southern Ethic, Womanspirit: A Guide to Women's Wisdom,* and *Elsa: I Come With My Songs,* among others. Her work has also been exhibited in the United States, Australia, and Germany.

LOUISE MATTLAGE is an artist-poet-dancer who performs to her own poetry, speaking the words as she dances with music created for her choreographies by her accompanists. She most recently presented her "Peace Poems" at the opening of the New Peace Museum in Chicago. For many years she has been the director and choreographer of The Dancers of Faith, a non-sectarian dance group that appears in churches, synagogues, and temples to present their upbeat perspective of life. She taught modern dance and has twice circumnavigated the world performing for peace. Among her five published books are *Dances of Faith* and *Big Dragon and Other Poems from a Chinese Journey.*

ANN MEREDITH studied art at the California College of Arts and Crafts, California State University at Hayward, University of California at Berkeley, and University of California at Santa Barbara. She curated a recent multi-media exhibit in Berkeley titled "With Age— Images of our Elders" and "Don't Call Me Honey ..." Her own photography has been shown widely in galleries and institutions, including the Vida Gallery in San Francisco, the Monterey Peninsula Museum of Art, and the Camaraderie Gallery in Berkeley.

LOUISE MONFREDO is 75, grew up on a Kansas farm, walked to a one-room school, rode horseback or drove a buggy to a rural high school. She has two B.S. degrees and a master's degree and taught school for 40 years. She has received grants from the Worcester, Massachusetts, Cultural Commission for workshops with young students and senior citizens. Her first book of poetry, *Thin Ice*, was published by Wampeter Press in 1981. Other poems have been published in *Dark Horse* and *Kansas Quarterly*, among others.

SHARON MOONEY lives in a rural area near San Francisco where she is a partner in a small cleaning business to allow time and money to write. She has edited and published *Fallow Deer*, a journal of local writers and visual artists and has written a play in poetry form to be produced in 1986. A California Arts Council grant recipient, she is most concerned in her writing about being a womon and what that means in relationship to history, personal power, relationships, and the oppression of womyn and men by society.

BARBARA MOREHEAD has been a professor emeritus of a small college in northwestern Pennsylvania for eight years. She is "going strong . . . [and] trying with some small success to write good poetry."

ANNE NOGGLE: "I learned to fly at age seventeen and was a Woman Air Force Service Pilot (WASP) in World War II. Then, in turn, I was a flight instructor, stunt pilot and crop duster. Active duty USAF during the Korean War as an Intercept Controller. Retired for disability as a captain in 1959. Studied photography with Van Deren Coke at the University of New Mexico where I am now an Adjunct Professor of Art. For seven years Curator of Photography at the Fine Arts Museum of New Mexico. Guest curator for the exhibition *Women of Photography: An Historical Survey* at the San Francisco Museum of Modern Art in 1975. Awarded two National Endowment for the Arts Grants in Photography in 1975 and 1978, and a John Simon Guggenheim Fellowship grant in 1982. A book of my photographs titled *Silver Lining* was published in 1982."

NONA NIMNICHT was a 1984/85 recipient of a National Endowment for the Arts fellowship. Her work has appeared in *CALYX, Berkeley Poets Cooperative, Colorado State Review,* and *Iris*.

ALICIA OSTRIKER is a poet and critic, whose most recent books are *A Woman Under the Surface* (poetry) and *Writing Like a Woman* (essays). She has just finished a book on the women's poetry movement, *Stealing the Language*, which will be published by Beacon Press in 1986. Her next book of poetry will be *The Imaginary Lover*. She is a professor of English at Rutgers University.

MARGE PIERCY is a poet and novelist whose latest volume of poetry, *My Mother's Body*, was published by Knopf. Her novel, *Fly Away Home*, recently came out in paperback. She is currently at work on a novel set during World War II.

KATHIAN POULTON has worked on a research project concerning children and their attitudes about self-aging. Her publications include education-related articles and an occasional poem or book review. She designs and exhibits original needlework and teaches kindergarten in Columbus, Ohio.

MARGARET RANDALL spent the past 23 years living in Mexico, Cuba and Nicaragua, but is currently living in New Mexico. She has published some 40 books, several of which the Immigration and Naturalization Service recently deemed too political for Margaret to be allowed to stay in the United States. Her books include: *Inside the Nicaraguan Revolution, Cuban Women Now, Sandino's Daughters,* and *Risking a Somersault in the Air.*

LAUREL RUST worked for four years as a nurses' aide in nursing homes. Her poetry has appeared in *Common Lives/Lesbian Lives* and *CALYX* and is forthcoming in *Fine Madness.*

MAY SARTON has published 43 books, the last a novel, *The Magnificent Spinster,* Norton, October 1985. Her last book of poems was *Letters From Maine,* Norton, 1984. She is 73 years old, has twelve honorary doctorates and is a Fellow of the American Academy of Arts and Sciences. Her journal, *At Seventy,* is a best seller.

DEIDRE SCHERER, a resident of Williamsville, Vermont, was selected as an Artist-in-Residence by the Vermont Council on the Arts after receiving her BFA from the Rhode Island School of Design. Her solo and collaborative exhibitions include the Brattleboro Museum and Arts Center in Brattleboro, Vermont; The Schoharie County Arts Council in Cobleskill, New York; Gallery 2 in Woodstock, Vermont; and Areta in Boston.

SANDRA SCOFIELD worked for many years as an educator but has been writing full time for the past two years. She has published stories and poems in numerous small magazines, including *Ploughshares, Moving Out, Plainswoman, The Missouri Review,* and *13th Moon.* Her two novels, currently being considered for publication, are *Natural Allies* and *Real Collisions.* She recently won a Katherine Anne Porter Fiction Prize, and her story "Trespass" is included in a Pushcart Press anthology.

SUSAN E. SEARING has worked as a reference librarian at Yale and, since 1982, as Women's Studies Librarian for the University of Wisconsin system of 26 campuses. She is the author of *Introduction to Library Research in Women's Studies* (Westview Press, 1985), co-editor of Feminist Collections: A Quarterly of Women's Studies Resources, and publisher of *Feminist Periodicals: A Current Listing of Contents.*

JUDITH SORNBERGER lives in Littleton, Colorado, and is the recipient of a Presidential Fellowship from the University of Nebraska. She has poems forthcoming in *Kalliope* and a portfolio of poems in *Prairie Schooner.*

M. ANN SPIERS' poems have appeared in *CALYX, Seattle Review, Dark Waters, Backbone,* and others. Her plays *Startup, Water System,* and *Chainsaws* have been performed in Seattle and Off Off Broadway. "The Last Fringie" is one piece from a series focusing on women working through their day.

ELAINE STARKMAN's "Hold the Blessing" is part of a larger manuscript for which she is currently seeking a publisher. Other sections have appeared in *Broomstick, Across the Generations,* and *Ariadne's Thread.* Editor of a forthcoming anthology, *State of Peace,* she has also completed a play about Beate Klarsfeld, a German-born Nazi hunter. Her work has also appeared in *The Things that Divide Us, Between Ourselves,* and *The Woman Who Lost Her Names.* She teaches English at Diablo Valley College in San Francisco's east bay.

PAULINE STIRISS, born in New York City in 1907, studied at the Corcoran School of Art and Pratt Institute and currently lives in Longmeadow, Massachusetts. Her one-woman exhibitions include the G.W.V. Smith Museum of Art in Springfield, Mass., and the Edward J. Brown Gallery in New York. Her work has also appeared in New York's Museum of Modern Art, the Lincoln Center, and the Larcada Gallery.

JEAN SWALLOW is a freelance journalist, writer, and editor. She edited the anthology *Out from Under: Sober Dykes and Our Friends* and has been widely published in the lesbian, feminist, and gay presses. Currently she is at work on a novel, *Oakland Lights*.

MARY TALLMOUNTAIN: "In June I was at a Spirit Camp for children in the wilderness of the Chilcoot; and I know this was the land of my roots, this mystical, magical Alaska. Though I've spent most of my life in San Francisco, part of me has been in that unspoiled, clean place. I think we all have a retreat for our spirits, somewhere."

GAIL TREMBLAY is Onondaga/Mic Mac and teaches at The Evergreen State College. She has published two collections of poetry, *Night Gives Woman the Word* and *Talking to the Grandfathers* which is in the Annex 21 #3 American Poetry Series. She has published in numerous periodicals and anthologies such as *A Nation Within* and *Other Geographies*. She has had five poems accepted for the Harper and Row *Anthology of 20th Century Native American Poetry,* and is included in *CALYX's* special anthology, *Bearing Witness/Sobreviviendo*. She is also an artist who exhibits her fiber/mixed media work internationally. Of herself she says, "I'm never bored."

KIM VAETH lives in Provincetown, Mass., where she produces *Bookwaves*, a weekly program for WOMR public radio. Her reviews have appeared in *The San Francisco Review of Books* and *13th Moon*. Currently she is translating selected work of the late Swedish poet, Karin Boye.

ELIZABETH WEBER lives in New Mexico. Her translations of Qarah Kirsch have appeared in *Kalliope*. She has also been published in *CALYX*.

FLORENCE WEINBERGER has always written in spurts but has been taking it more seriously for the last five or six years. Her poetry has appeared in *Poetry/LA, Fedora, Blue Unicorn, Nimrod,* and *Four Quarters*. More is forthcoming in *Touchstone* and *Blood to Remember: Anthology of American Poets on the Holocaust*.